DIONYSIUS THE AREOPAGITE

DIONYSIUS
THE AREOPAGITE

THE DIVINE NAMES
and
THE MYSTICAL
THEOLOGY

TRANSLATED BY
C. E. ROLT

SPCK

First published in the series
Translations of Christian Literature, *1920*

New Edition 1940
Eleventh Impression 1986

SPCK
Holy Trinity Church
Marylebone Road
London NW1 4DU

Printed in Great Britain by
Whitstable Litho Ltd,
Whitstable, Kent

ISBN 0 281 01255 5

PREFACE

THE translations of which the present volume consists are the work of a scholar who died at the age of thirty-seven. It has been felt that since the translator did not live to write a preface his work should be introduced by a few prefatory words. My excuse for accepting that office is that I probably knew the lamented writer as well as any one living. He was deprived of both his parents while very young, left almost friendless, and entrusted to my care from the age of fourteen. He had already shown promise of unusual ability. I sent him to King's College School, where in the opinion of its distinguished Head, the Rev. Dr. Bourne, he could have done anything if only he had been given the health. At Oxford he was awarded the Liddon Studentship.

Nothing can show more clearly what was thought of him by competent judges in Oxford than the following letter written by the Professor of Latin, A. C. Clark :

"He was one of the best scholars who passed through my hands at Queen's College, and I know no one who made greater progress after coming into residence. In those early days he had wonderful powers of work. I was seldom so delighted as when he earned the great distinction of being 'mentioned' for the Hertford University Scholarship in Latin. At the time everything seemed to be within his grasp. But most unfortunately his health failed shortly afterwards, and he was never able to do himself justice. Still, of recent years he wrote a remarkable book, full of fine thought, brilliantly expressed, which was much admired by good judges. I well remember, too, his Latin sermon preached at St. Mary's not long ago. It was delivered with feeling and fire, and seemed to me an admirable performance. I am sure that he would have gained distinction in the Church, if he had lived.

"He seemed to me a fine and noble character, free from all mortal taint."

He was a singularly refined and religious character, combining the acuteness of a philosophic mind with the fervour of a mystic. He therefore possessed undoubted qualifications for a study of Dionysius, with whose neo-Platonic ideas and mystical tendencies he was in the warmest sympathy.

The Introduction, containing a masterly exposition of Dionysian principles, is entirely the translator's work, and, within the limits which he set himself, may be called complete. Rolt's fervid and enthusiastic disposition led him to expound Dionysius with increasing admiration as his studies continued. He laid his original introduction aside, because to his maturer judgment it seemed insufficiently appreciative.

In its final form the Introduction is beyond all question a very able and remarkable piece of work. There are, however, several instances where the writer's enthusiasm and personal opinions have led him to unguarded language, or disabled him from realizing the dangers to which the Areopagite's teaching tends. He does indeed distinctly admit that Dionysius has his dangers, and says in one place definitely that the study of him is for the few: but the bearing of the whole theory of the Supra-Personal Deity on the Person of Christ and the Christian doctrine of the Atonement requires to be more thoroughly defined than is done in the exceedingly able pages of Rolt's Introduction. It is not the business of an editor to express his own views, but yet it seems only reasonable that he should call the reader's attention to questionable expositions, or to dogmatic statements which seem erroneous. In four or five places the editor has ventured to do this: with what effect the reader must decide. The Introduction of course appears exactly as the Author left it. The few additional remarks are bracketed as notes by themselves.

It is only right to add that the translator laboured under certain disadvantages. The original text of Dionysius is perplexing and confused, and no modern critical edition has as yet been produced. Rolt was frequently in doubt what the Author had really written.

But, beside the drawback incidental to any student of Dionysius, there was the fact of the translator's solitary position at Watermillock, a village rectory among the Lakes, shut off from access to libraries, and from acquaintance with former writers on his subject. This is a defect of which the translator was well aware, and of which he pathetically complained. Friends endeavoured to some extent to supply him with the necessary books, but the lack of reference to the literature of the subject will not escape the reader of these pages. He was always an independent thinker rather than a person of historical investigation.

Hence it is that one branch of his subject was almost omitted; namely, the influence of Dionysius on the history of Christian thought. This aspect is far too important to be left out. Indeed Dionysius cannot be critically valued without it. An attempt therefore has been made to supply this omission in a separate Essay, in order to place the reader in possession of the principal facts, both concerning the Areopagite's disciples and critics.

W. J. S.-S.

CONTENTS

                                                                    PAGE
PREFACE V
     By W. J. SPARROW-SIMPSON, D.D.

INTRODUCTION—

    1. THE AUTHOR 1

    2. HIS LEADING IDEAS: THE NATURE OF THE
       GODHEAD IN ITSELF. 4

    3. ITS RELATION TO CREATION 6

    4. THE PROBLEM OF EVIL 20

    5. CONTEMPLATION 25

    6. DIONYSIUS AND MODERN PHILOSOPHY . . 30

    7. THE PSYCHOLOGY OF CONTEMPLATION . . 33

    8. THE SCRIPTURAL BASIS OF DIONYSIUS'S
       DOCTRINES 40

    9. CONCLUSION 44

    10. BIBLIOGRAPHY 47

THE DIVINE NAMES 50

THE MYSTICAL THEOLOGY 191

    THE INFLUENCE OF DIONYSIUS IN RELIGIOUS
    HISTORY (BY W. J. SPARROW-SIMPSON, D.D.) 202

INDEX 221–223

DIONYSIUS THE AREOPAGITE

INTRODUCTION

I.—THE AUTHOR AND HIS INFLUENCE IN THE LATER CHURCH

THE writings here translated are among the extant works of a theologian who professes to be St. Paul's Athenian convert Dionysius, and points his claim with a background of historical setting. But the claim collapses beneath a considerable weight of anachronisms, by far the chief of which is the later neo-Platonism in almost every paragraph. In fact, these writings appear to reflect, and even to quote, the doctrines of the Pagan philosopher Proclus, who began lecturing at Athens in A.D. 430. Moreover, it is probable that the Hierotheus, who figures so largely in them, is the Syrian mystic Stephen bar Sudaili: a later contemporary of the same thinker. The Dionysian writings may therefore be placed near the very end of the fifth century.

The true name of their author is entirely unknown. He was probably a monk, possibly a bishop, certainly an ecclesiastic of some sort. His home is believed to have been Syria, where speculative theology was daring and untrammelled, and his works are the chief among the very few surviving specimens of an important school. The pious fraud by which he fathered them upon the Areopagite need not be branded with the harsh name of "forgery," for such a practice was

I

in his day permitted and even considered laudable.
Nor does it rob them of their value, any more than
certain parts of the prophecies ascribed to Isaiah are
worthless because they are by another hand. If the
Dionysian writings were historical documents the
matter would be otherwise, just as the Gospel Nar-
rative would lose nearly all its value if it were a later
fabrication. But they are not historical documents.
Their scope is with the workings of man's mind and
spirit in a region that does not change, and their
findings are equally valid or invalid whatever be their
date. And yet even historically they have an interest
which does not depend on their authorship. For, in
any case, they spring from a certain reputable school
within the Christian Church, and they were accepted
by the Church at large. And thus their bold path
of contemplation and philosophy is at least permissible to Christians. This path is not for all men, but
some are impelled to seek it; and if it is denied
them within the Christian pale, they will go and
look for it elsewhere. Nietzsche is but one of those
who have thus disastrously wandered afar in search
of that which is actually to be found within the fold.
Had he but studied the Dionysian writings he might
have remained a Christian. At the present time
these works have an added interest in the fact that,
since neo-Platonism has strong affinities with the
ancient philosophies of India, and may even owe
something directly to that source through the sojourn
of Plotinus in the Punjab, such writings as these
may help the Church to meet with discriminating
sympathy certain Indian teachings which are now
becoming too familiar in the West to be altogether
ignored. The bearings of this matter on the mis-
sionary problem are obvious.

The first mention of "Dionysius" (to give him by
courtesy the name he takes upon himself) is in the

year 533, when, at a council held in Constantinople, Severus, Patriarch of Antioch, appealed to these writings in support of Monophysite teaching. In spite of this unpromising beginning they soon acquired a great reputation; indeed, they presumably possessed some authority already when this first recorded appeal to them was made. They were widely read in the Eastern Church, being elucidated by the Commentary of St. Maximus in the seventh century and the Paraphrase of the learned Greek scholar, Pachymeres, in the thirteenth or fourteenth. Through Erigena's Latin translation in the ninth century they penetrated to the Western Church, and were so eagerly welcomed in this country that (in the words of the old chronicler), "The Mystical Divinity ran across England like deer." They are often quoted with reverence by St. Thomas Aquinas, and were, indeed, the chief of the literary forces moulding the mystical theology of Christendom. Ruysbroeck slaked his thirst at their deep well, and so they provided a far greater than their author with stimulus and an articulate philosophy. Were this their only service they would have the highest claims on our gratitude.

But they have an intrinsic value of their own in spite of their obvious defects. And if their influence has too often led to certain spiritual excesses, yet this influence would not have been felt at all had they not met a deep spiritual want. It arose not merely on account of their reputed authorship but also because the hungering heart of man found here some hidden manna. This manna, garnished though it be in all these writings with strange and often untranslatable terms from the Pagan Mysteries and from later neo-Platonism, is yet in itself a plain and nourishing spiritual meat. Let us now try to discover its quality from the two treatises before us.

II.—His Leading Ideas: The Nature of the Godhead in Itself

The basis of their teaching is the doctrine of the Super-Essential Godhead (ὑπερούσιος θεαρχία). We must, therefore, at the very outset fix the meaning of this term. Now the word " Essence" or " Being" (οὐσία) means almost invariably an individual existence, more especially a person, since such is the highest type that individual existence can in this world assume. And, in fact, like the English word "Being," it may without qualification be used to mean an angel. Since, then, the highest connotation of the term " Essence" or " Being" is a person, it follows that by " Super-Essence" is intended " Supra-Personality." And hence the doctrine of the Super-Essential Godhead simply means that God is, in His ultimate Nature, Supra-Personal.

Now an individual person is one who distinguishes himself from the rest of the world. I am a person because I can say: "I am I and I am not you." Personality thus consists in the faculty of knowing oneself to be one individual among others. And thus, by its very nature, Personality is (on one side of its being, at least) a finite thing. The very essence of my personal state lies in the fact that I am not the whole universe but a member thereof.

God, on the other hand, is Supra-Personal because He is infinite. He is not one Being among others, but in His ultimate nature dwells on a plane where there is nothing whatever beside Himself. The only kind of consciousness we may attribute to Him is what can but be described as an Universal Consciousness. He does not distinguish Himself from us ; for were we caught up on to that level we should be wholly transformed into Him. And yet we distinguish between ourselves and Him because from our lower plane of finite Being we look up and see that ultimate level beyond us.

The Super-Essential Godhead is, in fact, precisely that which modern philosophy describes as the Absolute. Behind the diversities of this world there must be an Ultimate Unity. And this Ultimate Unity must contain in an undifferentiated condition all the riches of consciousness, life, and existence which are dispersed in broken fragments throughout the world. Yet It is not a particular Consciousness or a particular Existence. It is certainly not Unconscious, Dead or, in the ordinary sense, non-Existent, for all these terms imply something below instead of above the states to which they are opposed.

Nevertheless It is not, in Its Ultimate Nature, conscious (as we understand the term) for consciousness implies a state in which the thinking Subject is aware of himself and so becomes an Object of his own perception. And this is impossible in the ultimate Nature of the Undifferentiated Godhead where there is no distinction between thinking Subject and Object of thought, simply because there is at that level no distinction of any kind whatever. Similarly the Godhead does not, in the ordinary sense, live (for life is a process and hence implies distinctions) nor does It even (in our sense) exist, for Existence is contrasted with non-Existence and thus implies relationship and distinctions. Consciousness, Life, and Existence, as we know them, are finite states, and the Infinite Godhead is beyond them. We cannot even, strictly speaking, attribute to It Unity, for Unity is distinguished from Plurality. We must instead describe It as a Super-Unity which is neither One nor Many and yet contains in an undifferentiated state that Numerical Principle which we can only grasp in its partial forms as Unity and Plurality.

III.—THE RELATION OF THE GODHEAD TO CREATION

This principle of Plurality which is thus transcendently contained in Its Undifferentiated Nature compels It to an eternal act of Creation. For all things pre-exist in It fused and yet distinct, as (shall we say?) in a single sensation of hunger there are indivisibly felt the several needs for the different elements of food which are wanted respectively to nourish the various kinds of bodily tissues, or as a single emotion contains beforehand the different separate words which issue forth to express it. Even so the Ultimate Godhead, brimful with Its Super-Unity, must overflow into multiplicity, must pass from Indifference into Differentiation and must issue out of its Super-Essential state to fashion a world of Being.

Now since the Godhead thus pours Itself out on to the plane of Being (which plane itself exists through nothing but this outpouring), it follows that the Godhead comes into relation with this plane: or rather (inasmuch as the act is timeless) stands in some relation to it. If the Godhead acts creatively, then It is related to the world and sphere of creation: eternally to the sphere of creation (which otherwise could not exist), and thus potentially to the world even before the world was made. Hence the Godhead, while in Its ultimate Nature It is beyond all differentiations and relationships, and dwells in a region where there is nothing outside of Itself, yet on another side of Its Nature (so to speak) touches and embraces a region of differentiations and relationships, is therefore Itself related to that region, and so in a sense belongs to it. Ultimately the Godhead is undifferentiated and unrelated, but in Its eternal created activity It is manifested under the form of Differentiation and Relationship. It belongs concurrently to two worlds : that of Ultimate Reality and that of Manifested Appearance. Hence, therefore, the possibility not only of Creation but also Revelation (ἔκφανσις). Just as the Godhead creates all things by virtue of that Aspect of Its Nature which is (as it were) turned towards them, so It is revealed to us by virtue of the same Aspect turned towards our minds which form part of the creation. Hence all the Scriptural Names of God, and this very Name "God" itself, though they apply to the whole Nature of the Godhead and not merely to some particular element or function thereof, yet cannot express that Nature in Its Ultimate Super-essence but only as manifested in Its relative activity. Dionysius, in fact, definitely teaches that doctrine which, when revived independently of recent years by Dr. Bradley was regarded as a startling blasphemy : that God is but an Appearance[1] of the Absolute. And this is, after all, merely a bold way of stating the orthodox truism that the Ultimate Godhead is incomprehensible : a truism which Theology accepts as an axiom and then is prone to ignore. The various Names of God are thus mere inadequate symbols of That Which transcends all thought and existence. But they are undifferentiated titles because they are symbols which seek (though unsuccessfully) to express the undifferentiated Super-Essence. Though the terms "God," "King," "Good," "Existent," etc., have all different connotations, yet they all denote the same undifferentiated Deity. There are, however, some Names which denote not the undifferentiated Godhead, but certain eternally differentiated Elements in Its Manifestation. These are the Names of the Three Persons in the Blessed Trinity. Whereas the terms "God," "King," "Good," "Existent," etc.,

---

[1] *Appearance and Reality* (2nd ed.), pp. 445 ff.

denote (though they cannot express it) the same
Reality : the term " Father " denotes something
different from that of " Son," and both of these
from that of " Holy Ghost." The whole Manifested
Godhead is " God," " King," " Creator," " Saviour,"
" Lord," " Eternal," " Living," etc., but only One
Persona of the Godhead is Father, or Son, or Holy
Ghost. The undifferentiated titles differ from each
other merely through our feeble grasp of the Manifestation, and coalesce as our apprehension of it
grows ; the differentiated titles (διακεκριμένα or
διακρίσεις) represent actual distinctions in the eternal
Manifestation Itself. Thus the Absolute Godhead
is the Super-Essence ; the eternally Manifested Godhead is the Trinity. As to the reasons of this
Dionysius deprecates all inquiry. He does not, for
instance, suggest that Relationship in this its simplest
form cannot but exist within that side of the Godhead which embraces and enters into this relative
world. Here, as elsewhere, his purpose in spite of
his philosophical language, is in the deepest sense
purely practical, and mere speculations are left on
one side. He accepts the Eternal Distinctions of the
Trinity because They have been revealed ; on the
other hand, he sees that they must belong to
the sphere of Manifestation or They could not be
revealed.

It was said above that the Ultimate Godhead is
Supra-Personal, and that it is Supra-Personal because personality consists in the faculty of knowing
oneself to be one individual among others. Are
the *Personæ* of the Trinity then, personal, since They
are distinguished One from Another? No, They are
not personal, because, being the infinite Manifestation of the Godhead, They are Super-Essential, and
Dionysius describes Them by that title. And if it
be urged that in one place he joins the same title

to our Lord's individual Human Name and speaks of "the Super-Essential Jesus," this is because the Personality of our Lord (and our own personality also through our union with Him) passes up into a region transcending personality, and hence while the Humanity of Jesus is Personal His Godhead is Supra-Personal. This is implied in a passage from Hierotheus (quoted with approval by Dionysius himself) which teaches that the Deity of Jesus is of an universal character belonging through Him to all redeemed mankind.

The teaching of Dionysius on the Trinity is, so far as it goes, substantially the same as that of St. Augustine or St. Thomas Aquinas; only it is expressed in more exact, if at first sight somewhat fantastic, terms. St. Augustine,[1] for instance, teaches that the inner Differentiations of the Trinity belong

---

[1] [Augustine says indeed that the Father and the Son exist, *non secundum substantiam, sed secundum relativum* (*De Trin.* v. 6). But Augustine's argument is, that while no attribute of God is accidental, yet all attributes are not said with reference to His substance. Certain attributes of God are neither accidental nor substantial, but relative. This applies to Divine Fatherhood and Sonship. For the Father is what He is in relation to the Son, and similarly the Son to the Father. But these are relations of " Beings," and are relations which are "eternal and unchangeable." Augustine does not affirm a supra-personal reality of God behind the Trinity of manifestation. For Augustine the Father and the Son are ultimate realities. " But if the Father, in that He is called the Father, were so called in relation to Himself, not to the Son ; and the Son, in that He is called the Son, were so called in relation to Himself, not to the Father ; then both the one would be called Father, and the other Son, according to substance. But because the Father is not called the Father except in that He has a Son, and the Son is not called Son except in that He has a Father, these things are not said according to substance ; because each of them is not so called in relation to Himself, but the terms are used reciprocally and in relation each to the other ; nor yet according to accident, because both the being called the Father, and the being called the Son, is eternal and unchangeable to them. Wherefore, although to be the Father and to be the Son is different, yet their substance is not different ; because they are so called, not according to substance, but according to relation, which relation, however, is not accident, because it is not changeable."—Aug., *De Trin.* v. 6.—ED.]

solely to the realm of eternal Manifestation when he says that They exist *secundum Relativum* and not *secundum Substantiam*.[1]   Also he teaches the Supra-Personality of the Trinity when he says that neither the undivided Trinity nor any of Its Three Persons is a particular individuality ;[2] and St. Thomas teaches the same thing when he says that the Human Soul of Jesus does not comprehend or contain the Word since the Human Soul is finite (*i. e.* a particular individuality) while the Word is Infinite.[3]

Thus while in the Undifferentiated Godhead the "Persons" of the Trinity ultimately transcend Themselves and point (as it were) to a region where They are merged, yet in that side of Its Nature which looks towards the universe They shine eternally forth and are the effulgence of those "Supernal Rays" through Which all light is given us, and whence all energy streams into the act of creation.   For by Their interaction They circulate that Super-Essence Which Each of Them perfectly possesses, and so It passes forth from Them into a universe of Being.

Now the Godhead, while It is beyond all particular Being, yet contains and is the ultimate Reality of all particular Being ; for It contains beforehand all the particular creatures after a manner in which they are ultimately identical with It, as seems to be implied by the phrase that all things exist in It fused and yet distinct.   Thus although It is not *a* particular being, It in a transcendent manner contains and *is* Particularity.   Again It is beyond all universal Being, for universals are apprehended by the intellect,

---

[1] *De Trin.* v. 6.
[2] See *De Trin.* viii. 4.   "Not this and that Good, but the very Good . . .   Not a good Personality (*animus*) but good Goodness"; and vii. 11, where he condemns those who say the word *persona* is employed "in the sense of a particular man such as Abraham, Isaac, or Jacob, or anybody else who can be pointed out as being present."
[3] *Summa*, Pars III. Q. x. Art. i.

whereas the Godhead is incomprehensible and therefore is described as "formless." Nevertheless It contains and is the Ultimate Reality of all universals,
for, even before the world was made, It eternally
embraced and embraces all things and all the universal. laws of their existence. Thus after a transcendent manner It contains and is Universality.
And hence in Its transcendent Nature Universality
and Particularity are contained as one and the same
undifferentiated Fact.

But in this world of Being the particular and the
universal aspect of things must be mutually distinguished. Otherwise there could, on the one hand, be
no things, and on the other, no bond of unity between
them. Hence, when the Super-Essence overflows in
the act of creation, It runs, as it were, into the two
main streams of Universal and Particular Being.
Neither of these two streams has any independent or
concrete existence. Taken separately, they are mere
potentialities : two separate aspects, as it were, of the
creative impulse, implying an eternal possibility of
creation and an eternal tendency towards it, and yet
not in themselves creative because not in themselves,
strictly speaking, existent. Nevertheless these two
streams differ each from each, and one of them has a
degree of reality which does not belong to the other.
Mere universal Being, says Dionysius, does not
possess full or concrete existence ; at the same time,
since it *is* Being or Existence, he does not call it
non-existent. Mere Particularity; on the other hand,
he practically identifies with Non-entity, for the
obvious reason that non-existence itself is a universal
category (as applying to all existent things), and,
therefore, cannot belong to that which has no
universal element at all. Thus the universal stream
is an abstract ideal and possesses an abstract existence, the particular stream is an abortive impulse and

possesses no actual existence whatever. The one is the formal law of the existence universe, the other its rough material.

Thus these two emanating streams of potentiality have, from before all time, eternally welled forth and passed away, the universal into emptiness and the particular into nothingness, or rather, through nothingness back at once into the Super-Essence in a ceaseless revolution which, until the appointed moment arrives for Time and the temporal world to begin, leaves no trace outside Its Super-Essential Source and Dwelling and Goal. It is possible (though one cannot say more), that Dionysius is thinking especially of the difference between these two streams when he describes the various motions of the Godhead. The Particular stream of Emanation may be in his mind when he speaks of the circular movement, since the particular existences remain within the Super-Essence, until the moment of their temporal creation : the Universal stream may be that of which he is thinking when he speaks of the direct and spiral movements, since both of these indicate an advance and would therefore be appropriate to express the out-raying tendency of that emanating Influence which, even before the particular creatures were made, had a kind of existence for thought as the other stream had not.

This Universal stream consists of currents or Emanations, Very Being, Very Life, etc. ($a\dot{v}\tau o\varepsilon\tilde{\iota}\nu a\iota$, $a\dot{v}\tau o\zeta\omega\acute{\eta}$, $\varkappa.\tau.\lambda.$), and of these currents some are more universal than others ; Very Being is, obviously, the most universal of all. And since the Super-Essence transcends and so absorbs all Universality, it follows that the more universal the Emanations are the higher is their nature. This stream, in fact, runs, as it were, in the channel which our thought naturally traces ; for thought cannot but seek for universals,

and the abstract and bloodless tendency of mere
Philosophy comes from an undue exaltation of
thought over life. From this defect, however, Dionysius is free. For, while he holds that the highest
Emanation is the most universal, he also holds (as
was seen) that the Emanations are in themselves the
mere background of existence and are not fully
existent. And he expressly says that while the
Emanations become more and more universal the
higher we ascend towards their Source, the creatures
become more and more individual and particular the
higher they rise in the scale. The reason is, of course,
that the Super-Essence transcends and absorbs all
Particularity as well as all Universality ; and hence
it is that particular things become particularized by
partaking of It, just as universals become universalized
by a similar process. But of this more anon.

This Universal stream of Emanations thus eternally
possesses a kind of existence, but it is an empty
existence, like the emptiness of mere light if there
were no objects to fill it and be made visible. The
light in such a case would still be streaming forth
from the sun and could not do otherwise, and therefore it would not be an utter void ; but it would be
untenanted by any particular colour or shape.
Suppose, however, that the light could be blotted out.
There would now remain the utter void of absolute
darkness. Such darkness cannot exist while the sun
is shining in the cloudless heavens ; nevertheless the
very notion of light cannot but be contrasted in our
minds with that of darkness which is its absence ; and
so we conceive the light to be a positive thing which
fills the darkness even as water fills a void. When
the bowl is full of water, the void does not exist ; and
yet, since it would exist if the bowl could be wholly
emptied, we can regard this non-existent void as the
receptacle of the water.

Even so the Emanations of Very Being, etc., fill, as it were, a void which does not and cannot exist, since it is, and must be, saturated with them, and yet it is, by the very laws of our thinking, contrasted with them and would, in a manner, exist if the Emanations could cease to flow from the Super-Essence. They, streaming eternally (as they must) from that overflowing Source, permeate the whole boundless region of the world that is to be; a region beyond Time and Space. That region is thus their receptacle. The receptacle, if emptied of them (though this is impossible), would contain nothing, and be nothing whatsoever. Hence, it is called Not-Being, or the Non-Existent (τὸ μὴ ὄν).

So the two Streams flow timelessly without beginning and without end, and cross, but do not mingle : the Universal Stream perpetually advancing and the Particular Stream circling round and slipping through it, as it were, into the void of Nothingness (as a thing by its very nature invisible, would be in darkness even while surrounded by the light) and so returning into the Super-Essence without leaving a trace behind it. This activity, though it must be expressed thus in terms of Time, is really timeless and therefore simultaneous. For the Streams are not something other than the Super-Essence. They are simply distant aspects of It. They are the Super-Essence in Its creative activity. As the river flowing out of a lake consists of the water which belongs to the lake, or as the light and heat flowing from the sun are the same light and heat that are in the sun, so the emanating Streams are the same Power that exists in the Super-Essence, though now acting (or striving to act) at a distance. Or perhaps we may compare the Super-Essence to a mountain of rich ore, the inward depths of which are hidden beyond sight and touch. The outer surface, however, is touched and

seen, and this corresponds to the Persons of the
Trinity ; while the same mountain viewed at a
distance is the Stream of Universal Emanation.
And though the view becomes dimmer and dimmer
the farther away you go, yet it is always the same
mountain itself that is being viewed. The Particular
Stream, on the other hand, is like the same mountain
when invisible at night, for the mountain still sends
forth its vibrations, but these are lost in the darkness.

Or we may compare the Super-Essence to a
magnet and the Persons of the Trinity to its tangible
surface, and the two emanating Streams to the positive
and negative magnetism which are simply the essence
of the magnet present (so to speak) at a distance.
Even so (but in a manner which is truer because
non-spatial) the Super-Essence is in the emanating
streams outside the Super-Essential plane and thus
interpenetrates regions which are remote from Itself.
It is both immanent in the world as its Principle
of Being and outside it as transcending all categories
of Being. This contradiction is implied in the very
word "Emanation" (πρόοδος) which means an act by
which the Super-Essence goes forth from Itself.
And, in fact, Dionysius more than once definitely
says that the Super-Essence actually passes outside
of Itself even while It remains all the time wholly
within itself. This he expresses in one place by saying that the act of Creation is an ecstasy of Divine
Love. This thought is vital to his doctrine, and must
be remembered whenever in the present attempt to
expound him, the Super-Essence is spoken of as
"outside" the creatures. The Super-Essence is not,
strictly speaking, external to anything. But It is
"outside" the creatures because (as existing simul-
taneously on two planes) It is "outside" Itself. And
therefore, although the entire plane of creation is
interpenetrated by It, yet in Its ultimate Nature It is

beyond that plane and so "outside" it. Finite creatures though filled (according to their measure) with Its Presence, yet must, in so far as they are finite, look up to It as That which is Other than themselves. And, in this sense of being Other than they are, It must be described as "outside" them, even though (as their Principle of Being) It is within them.

Thus the two emanating streams, though they pass outside of the Super-Essence, yet actually are the Super-Essence Itself. And, in fact, the very term Emanation (πρόοδος) like the collateral term Differentiation (διάκρισις) may even be applied not only to the two Streams but also to the Persons of the Trinity ; not only to the Magnets radiating Energy, so to speak, but also to its actual Surface.

This matter needs a few words of explanation.

There is in the undifferentiated (ὑπερηνωμένη) Super-Essence a Differentiation between the Three Divine "Persons," which Dionysius compares to the distinction between different flames in the same indivisible brightness. And Each "Person" is an Emanation because Each is a Principle of outgoing creative Energy. There is also a Differentiation between the various qualities and forces of the creative Energy, rather as (if we may further work out the simile of Dionysius) the light seen afar through certain atmospheric conditions is differentiated into various colours. And each quality or force is an Emanation, for it is an outgoing current of creative Energy. Or, by a slightly different use of language, the entire creative process in which they flow forth may be called not merely a collection of emanations but simply "the Emanation." Thus an Emanation may mean, (1) a Person of the Trinity ; (2) a current of the Universal Stream (e.g., Very Being, or Very Life, etc.); (3) a current of the Particular Stream (i.e.

a particular force); (4) the entire process whereby the two Streams flow forth. This sounds confusing, but the difficulty vanishes if we classify these various meanings under two heads, viz. : (1) an Emanating Principle (*i. e.* a "Person" of the Trinity), and (2) an Emanating Act (whether regarded as a whole or in detail). This classification covers all its uses.

These two heads, in fact, correspond exactly to the two main uses of the word "Differentiation" as applying respectively to the Super-Essential sphere and to the sphere of Being. And here Dionysius certainly does cause needless difficulty by employing the same word "Differentiation" with these two distinct meanings in the same passage. The Persons of the Trinity are differentiated, but the Energy streaming from them is undifferentiated in the sense that it comes indivisibly from them all. In another sense, however, it is differentiated because it splits up into separate currents and forces. Each of these currents comes from the Undivided Trinity, and yet each current is distinct from the others. Dionysius expresses this truth by saying that the Godhead enters Undividedly into Differentiation, or becomes differentiated without loss of Undifference (ἡνωμένως διακρίνεται).

Let us follow this creative process and see whither it leads. The Super-Essence, as It transcends both Non-Existence and Existence, also transcends both Time and Eternity. But from afar It is seen or felt as Existence and as Eternity. That is to say Existence and Eternity are two emanating modes or qualities of the Universal Stream. The Particular Stream, on the other hand, is Time-non-existent as yet and struggling to come to the birth but unable to do so until it gain permanence through mingling with Eternity. At a certain point, however (preordained in the Super-Essence wherein Time slumbered), the two streams not only cross but actually mingle, and thus Time and the temporal world begin. The Particular stream no longer sinks wholly through the Universal, but is in part supported by it. Hence the world of things arises like a substance hitherto invisible but now becoming visible, and so, by this change, springing out of darkness into light.

Now, when the Particular stream begins to mingle with the Universal, it naturally mingles first with that current of it which, being most universal, ranks the highest and so is nearest the Source. It is only along that current that it can advance to the others which are further away. And that current is Being (αὐτο-εῖναι). Thus the world-process begins (as Dionysius had learnt from Genesis and from the teaching of Plato) as the level of dead solid matter, to which he gives the name of "merely existent "(οὐσιωδής). Thence, by participating more and more in the Universal stream, it advances to the production of plant and animal and man, being by the process enriched with more and more qualities as Life (αὐτοζωή), Wisdom (αὐτοσοφία), and the other currents of the Universal stream begin to permeate it one by one.

Thus the separate individuals, according to the various laws (λόγοι) of their genera and species, are created in this world of Time. And each thing, while it exists in the world, has two sides to its exist-ence : one, outside its created being (according to the sense of the word "outside" explained above), in the Super-Essence wherein all things are One Thing (as all points meet at infinity or as according to the neo-Platonic simile used by Dionysius, the radii of a circle meet at the centre), and the other within its own created being on this lower plane where all things are separate from each other (as all points in space are separate or as the radii of the circle are separate at the circumference). This paradox is of the very utmost importance.

The various kinds of existences being now created in this world of time, we can regard them as ranged in an ascending scale between Nothingness and the Super-Essence, each rank of being subsuming the qualities of those that lie below it. Thus we get the following system in ascending order: Existence, Life, Sensation, Reason, Spirit. And it is to this scale that Dionysius alludes when he speaks of the extremities and the intermediate parts of the creation, meaning by the extremities the highest and the lowest orders, and by the intermediate parts the remainder.

The diminution of Being which we find in glancing down the ladder is, Dionysius tells us, no defect in the system of creation. It is right that a stone should be but a stone and a tree no more than a tree. Each thing, being itself however lowly, is fulfilling the laws of its kind which pre-exist (after a transcendent manner) in the undifferentiated Super-Essence. If, however, there is a diminution of Being where such diminution has no place, then trouble begins to arise. This is, in fact, the origin and nature of evil. For as we ascend the scale of Being, fresh laws at each stage counteract the laws of the stage below, the law of life by which the blood circulates and living things grow upwards counteracting the mere law of inert gravitation, and again, the laws of morality counteracting the animal passions. And where this counter-action fails, disaster follows. A hindered circulation means ill-health, and a hindered self-control means sin. Whereas a stone is merely lifeless, a corpse is not only lifeless but dead ; and whereas a brute is un-moral, a brutal man is wicked, or immoral. What in the one case is the absence from a thing of that which has no proper place in it, is in the other case the failure of the thing's proper virtues.

IV.—THE PROBLEM OF EVIL

At wearisome length Dionysius discusses the problem of evil and shows that nothing is inherently bad. For existence is in itself good (as coming ultimately from the Super-Essence), and all things are therefore good in so far as they exist. Since evil is ultimately non-existent, a totally evil thing would be simply non-existent, and thus the evil in the world, wherever it becomes complete, annihilates itself and that wherein it lodges. We may illustrate this thought by the nature of zero in mathematics, which is non-entity (since, added to numbers, it makes no difference) and yet has an annihilating force (since it reduces to zero all numbers that are multiplied by it). Even so evil is nothing and yet manifests itself in the annihilation of the things it qualifies. That which we call evil in the world is merely a tendency of things towards nothingness. Thus sickness is a tendency towards death, and death is simply the cessation of physical vitality. And sin is a tendency towards spiritual death, which is the cessation of spiritual vitality. But, since the ground of the soul is indestructible, a complete cessation of its being is impossible; and hence even the devils are not inherently bad. Were they such they would cease *ipso facto* to exist.

Dionysius here touches incidentally on a mystical doctrine which, as developed by later writers, afterwards attained the greatest importance. This doctrine of a timeless self is the postulate, perhaps, of all Christian mysticism. The boldest expression of it is to be found in Eckhart and his disciple Tauler, who both say that even the lost souls in hell retain unaltered the ultimate nobility of their being. And lest this doctrine should be thought to trifle with grave matters, be it remembered that the sinfulness and gravity of sin are simply due to this indestructible nobility of our being. Man cannot become non-moral, and hence his capacity for wickedness. The soul is potentially divine, and therefore may be actually satanic. The very devils in hell cannot destroy the image of the Godhead within them, and it is this image that sin defiles.

It follows from the ultimate non-entity of evil that, in so far as it exists, it can only do so through being mingled with some element of good. To take an illustration given by Dionysius himself, where there is disease there is vitality, for when life ceases the sickness disappears in death. The ugliness of evil lies precisely in the fact that it always, somehow or other, consists in the corruption of something inherently good.

It is, however, this ugliness of things that Dionysius fails to emphasize, and herein lies the great weakness of his teaching. Not only does he, with the misguided zeal of an apologist, gloze deliberately over certain particular cruelties of the Creation and accept them as finite forms of good, but also he tends to explain away the very nature of evil in itself. He tends to be misled by his own true theories. For it is true that evil is ultimately non-existent. St. Augustine taught this when he said : " Sin is nought " ;[1] so did Julian of Norwich, who " saw not *sin*," because she believes " it hath no manner of substance nor any part of being."[2] The fault of Dionysius is the natural failure of his mental type to grasp the mere facts of the actual world as mere facts. He is so dazzled with his vision of ultimate Reality that he does not feel with any intensity the partial realities of this finite universe. Hence, though his theory of evil is, in the

[1] *Com. on St. John* i. 13. Cf. *Conf.* vii. 18 ; xii. 11.
[2] *Revelations of Divine Love*, xxvii.

main, true, he does not quite grasp the true application of his theory to this world of actual facts.

For this world is by its very nature finite. And hence, if the evil in it is (as Dionysius rightly says) but partial, it must also be remembered (as he for a moment forgets) that its very existence is but partial. And, therefore, though evil is ultimately non-existent, yet the bad qualities of things may, so far as this present world is concerned, have as much reality, or at least as much actuality, as their good qualities. And when we say that evil is ultimately non-existent we merely mean that evil *ought* to have no actuality here, not that it *has* none. Dionysius calls evil a lapse and failure of the creature's proper virtues. But a lapse or failure has in it something positive, as he in the same breath both admits by using the word and also tries to explain away. It is as positive as the virtues from which it lapses. The absence of light from the centre of a wooden block is nothing, for the light has no proper place there, but the absence of light from the air, where light should be, is darkness and is a visible shadow. St. Augustine has crystallized this truth in his famous epigram, quoted above in part, which runs in full as follows: "Sin is naught, and men are naughtes when they sin." The void left by the want of a good thing has a content consisting in the want. Probably had Dionysius seen more of the world's misery and sin he would have had a stronger sense of this fact. And in that case he would have given more prominence than he gives, in his extant writings at least, to the Cross of Christ.

Two things should, however, be borne in mind. In the first place he is writing for intellectual Christians in whom he can take for granted both an understanding of metaphysics and a horror of sin. To such readers the non-existence of evil could not have the same meaning as it would to the world outside. For the same reason he (like other Christian teachers after him) speaks of God's transcendent Non-Existence without fearing lest his words should be interpreted as atheism. In fact, to guard against misinterpretation he utters the express warning that mysteries can only be taught to the Initiated.[1]

In the second place throughout his whole treatment of evil, he is no doubt writing with an eye on the dualistic heresy of the Manichees, which was prevalent in his day. Hence the occasional indiscretion of the zeal with which he seeks to block every loop-hole looking towards dualism. The result is a one-sided emphasis in his teaching rather than positive error. He rightly denies a dualism of ultimate realities ; but he tends to ignore, rather than to deny, the obvious dualism of actual facts.

Before proceeding to the Method of Contemplation which crowns and vitalizes the entire speculative system of Dionysius, it will be well to bring together in one paragraph the various meanings he gives to Non-Existence.

(1) The Super-Essence transcends the distinction between the Aristotelian " Matter " and " Form " ; but in this world the two are distinct from each other. And whereas, in this world, Form without " Matter " has an abstract existence for thought, " Matter " without Form has none. Thus mere " Matter " is non-existent. And hence things both before their creation and after their destruction are non-existent, for their " Matter " has then no " form." (2) Similarly Good without evil exists as the highest Manifestation or " Form " of the Godhead, but evil without Good is formless and therefore non-existent. (This does not mean that " Matter " or the world-stuff is evil, but that neither it nor evil is anything at all.) And since

---

[1] *Div. Nom.* i. 8, *ad fin.* ; *Myst. Theol.* i. 2.

evil is ultimately altogether non-existent, all things
are non-existent in so far as they are evil. (3) Finally,
the Super-Essence is, in a transcendent manner, Non-
Existent as being *beyond* Existence. And hence the
paradox that the destructive force of evil and the
higher impulse towards the Godhead both have
the same negative principle of a discontent with the
existent world—the dangerous, yet true, doctrine
(taught, among others, by St. Augustine [1] and Dante [2])
that evil is a mistaken quest for Good.

The principle of this classification is quite simple.
It lies in the fact that *Being* is the most universal of
the Emanations or Forms, and that all things therefore exist only in so far as they possess Form. Hence
the want of all " form " is non-entity and makes
things which are without any form to be non-existent ;
that want of proper " form " which we call evil is a
tendency to non-entity and makes evil things to be
so far non-existent ; the want of complete substantial
or spiritual " form " makes merely existent things (*i. e.*
lifeless things) to be " un-existent " ; and the transcendence of all " Form " makes the Super-Essence to
be in a special sense " Non-Existent."

The theory of evil, as given above, is worked out in
a manner sufficiently startling.

We naturally divide existent things into good and
bad and do not think of non-existent things as being
things at all. Dionysius, with apparent perversity,
says all things are good, and then proceeds to divide
them into "Existent" and "Non-Existent"! The
reason is this : All things have two sides to their
being : the one in the Super-Essence and the other
in themselves. In the Super-Essence they are eternally good, even before their creation. But in themselves (*i. e.* in their created essence) they were wholly
non-existent before their temporal creation, and after

---

[1] *Conf.* ii. 6, 12–14.   *Parad.* v. 10–12.

it are partially non-existent in so far as they are tainted with evil.

V.—CONTEMPLATION

So far this doctrine of a dual state belonging to all things may seem an unprofitable speculation. We now come to the point where its true value will be seen. For it underlies a profound theory of Personality and a rich method of Contemplation. This part of the subject is difficult, and will need close attention.

The process of Creation advances from the simple to the complex as Life is added to mere Being, and Consciousness to Life, and Rationality to Consciousness. But from this point there begins a new phase in the process. Man, having as it were floated into the world down the Universal stream of Emanation, now enters into his spirit, and so plunges beneath the stream, and there below its surface finds an undercurrent which begins to sweep him in a contrary direction towards the Source. By the downward movement his personality has been produced, by this upward movement it will be transformed.

So man presses on towards God, and the method of his journey is a concentration of all his spiritual powers. By this method he gathers himself together away from outward things into the centre of his being. And thus he gradually becomes unified and simplified, like the Angels whose creation Dionysius was able to place at the very commencement of the developing temporal order precisely because their nature is of this utterly simple and concentrated kind. And, because the process of advance is one of spiritual concentration, and moves more and more from external things into the hidden depths of the soul, therefore man must cast away the separate forms of those elements which he thus draws from the circumference into the centre of his personal spirit. Having sucked the nourishment from the various fruits growing severally in their different proper zones by the margin of the stream up which he presses, he assimilates those vitalizing elements into his own tissues (finding each food suited in turn to his advancing strength) and casts the rind away as a thing no longer needed. And this rejection of the husk in which the nourishing fruit had grown is the process described by Dionysius as the *Via Negativa*.

Let us consider this matter more in detail.

The first stage of Religion is anthropomorphic. God is conceived of as a magnified Man with an outward form. This notion contains some low degree of truth, but it must be spiritualized. And in casting away the materialistic details of the conception we begin to enter on a *Via Negativa*. All educated Christians enter on this path, though very few are given the task of pursuing it to the end. So first the notion of an outward material form is cast away and then the notion of change. God is now regarded as a changeless and immaterial Being, possessing all the qualities of Personality and all the capacities of Sensation and Perception in an eternal and spiritual manner. This is a conception of God built up, largely, by the Discursive Reason and appealing to that side of our nature. But the Intuitive Reason seeks to pierce beyond this shimmering cloud into the hidden Light which shines through it. For the mind demands an Absolute Unity beyond this variety of Attributes. And such a Unity, being an axiom or postulate, lies in a region behind the deductions of the Discursive Reason. For all deduction depends upon axioms, and axioms themselves cannot be deduced.

Thus the human spirit has travelled far, but still

it is unsatisfied. From the simple unity of its own being it gazes up at the Simple Unity of the Uncreated Light which still shines above it and beyond it. The Light is One Thing and the human spirit is another. All elements of difference in the human spirit and in the Uncreated Light have disappeared, but there still remains the primary distinction between Contemplating Subject and Contemplated Object. The human self and the Uncreated Light stand in the mutual relationships of " Me " and " Thee." That which says " Me " is not the Being Which is addressed as " Thee "; and the Being addressed as " Thee " is not that which says " Me." The two stand over against one another.

This relationship must now be transcended by a process leading to ecstasy. The human spirit must seek to go forth out of itself (*i.e.* out of its created being) into the Uncreated Object of its contemplation and so to be utterly merged. So it ceases to desire even its own being in itself. Casting selfhood away, it strives to gain its true being and selfhood by losing them in the Super-Essence. Laying its intellectual activity to rest it obtains, by a higher spiritual activity, a momentary glimpse into the depths of the Super-Essence, and perceives that There the distinction between " Me " and " Thee " is not. It sees into the hidden recesses of an unplumbed Mystery in which its own individual being and all things are ultimately transcended, engulphed and transformed into one indivisible Light. It stands just within the borders of this Mystery and feels the process of transformation already beginning within itself. And, though the movements of the process are only just commenced, yet it feels by a hidden instinct the ultimate Goal whither they must lead. For, as Ruysbroeck says : " To such men it is revealed that they *are* That which they contemplate."

This transcendent spiritual activity is called Un-knowing, For when we know a thing we can trace out the lines of difference which separate it from other things, or which separate one part of it from another. All knowledge, in fact, consists in, or at least includes, the power of separating "This" from "That." But in the Super-Essence there are no lines of difference to trace, and there is no "This" or "That." Or rather, to put it differently, "This" and "That," being now transcended, are simply one and the same thing. While the human spirit is yet im-perfect, it looks up and sees the Super-Essence far beyond it. At this stage it still feels itself as "this" and still perceives the Super-Essence as "That." But when it begins to enter on the stage of spiritual Reflection (to use the technical term borrowed by Dionysius from the Mysteries) it penetrates the Super-Essence and darkly perceives that There the distinction ultimately vanishes. It sees a point where "this" is transfigured into "That," and "That" is wholly "this." And, indeed, already "That" begins to pour Itself totally into "this" through the act whereby "this" has plunged itself into "That."

Thus the ultimate goal of the "ego" now seen afar by Unknowing and attainable, perhaps, hereafter, is to be merged. And yet it will never be lost. Even the last dizzy leap into Absorption will be performed in a true sense by the soul itself and within the soul itself. The statement of Dionysius that in the Super-Essence all things are "fused and yet distinct," when combined with the doctrine of human immortality, means nothing else. For it means that the immortality of the human soul is of an individual kind; and so the self, in one sense, persists even while, in another sense, it is merged. This is the most astounding paradox of all! And Dionysius states the apparent contradiction without seeking to explain it simply because, here as elsewhere, he is not much concerned with theory but is merely struggling to express in words an overwhelming spiritual experience. The explanation, however (if such it may be called) can easily be deduced from his theory of existence and of personality.

All things have two sides to their existence: one in the Super-Essence, the other in themselves. Thus a human personality is (in William Law's words) an " outbirth " from the Godhead. And having at last made its journey Home, it must still possess these two sides to its existence. And hence, whereas on the one side it is merged, on the other it is not. Its very being consists of this almost incredible paradox. And personality is a paradox because the whole world is a paradox, and the whole world is fulfilled in personality.

For this principle of a twofold existence underlies all things, and is a reflection of the Super-Essential Nature. As the Super-Essence has an eternal tendency to pass out of Itself by emanation, so the creatures have a tendency to pass out of themselves by spiritual activity. As the Super-Essence creates the world and our human souls by a species of Divine " ecstasy," so the human soul must return by an answering " ecstasy " to the Super-Essence. On both sides there is the same principle of Self-Transcendence. The very nature of Reality is such that it must have its being outside itself.

And this principle of self-transcendence or ecstasy underlies not only the solitary quest of the individual soul for God, but also the mutual relations of the various individuals with each other. In all their social activities of loving fellowship the creatures seek and find themselves in one another and so outside of themselves. It is the very essence of Reality that it is not self-sufficing or self-contained.

Not only do the creatures in which the Super-Essence overflows possess, by an answering mystery, their true being in the Super-Essence, but, as a result of this, they possess their true being in each other; for in the Super-Essence each has its place as an element in One single and indivisible Reality. We have here, in fact, the great antinomy of the One and the Many, or the Universal and the Particulars, not solved indeed, but pronounced to be insoluble and therefore ultimate. It penetrates into a region beyond the intellect, and that is why the intellect is finally baffled by it.

The Dionysian theory that one side of our being is outside ourselves in the Super-Essence will be found incidentally to reconcile Pragmatism and Idealism together. For Dionysius teaches that on one side of our being we actually develop in Time. And, if this is so, we do as the Pragmatists assert literally *make* Reality. But the other side of our being is timeless and eternally perfect outside ourselves. And if this is so, then Reality, as Idealists tell us, is something utterly beyond all change. Perhaps this paradox is intended in Wordsworth's noble line :—

So build we up the being that we *are*.[1]

VI.—DIONYSIUS AND MODERN PHILOSOPHY

Let us now consider the bearings of the Dionysian theory on certain other currents of modern philosophy.

According to Dr. McTaggart each human soul possesses, behind its temporal nature, a timeless self and each one of these timeless selves is an eternal

[1] *Excursion,* iv., about 70 lines from the end. With "the being that we are," cf. *Prelude,* xiv. 113–115 :—
"The highest bliss
That flesh can know is theirs—the consciousness
Of whom they are."

differentiation of the Absolute.[1] Now if these timeless selves are finite, then none embraces the whole
system. And, if that is so, in what does the Spiritual
Unity of the whole consist? If, on the other hand,
they are infinite, then each one must embrace the
whole System ; and, if so, how can they remain distinct? Having the same context, they must coalesce
even as (according to Orthodox Theology) the "Persons" of the Trinity coalesce in the Unity behind
the plane of Manifestation.[2] Dr. McTaggart's philosophical scheme is noble, but it seems open to this
metaphysical attack, and psychologically it appears
to be defective as it leaves no room for worship,
which is a prime need of the human soul. The
Dionysian theory seems to meet the difficulty ; for
since our ultimate being is outside ourselves in the
Super-Essence, one side of our Being is supra-personal. Our finite selves are, on that side, merged
together in One Infinite "Self" (if It may be thus
inadequately described) ; and this Infinite Self (so to
call It) embraces, and is the Spiritual Unity of the
whole System. And this Infinite Self, seen from
afar, is and must be the Object of all worship until
at last worship shall be swallowed up in the completeness of Unknowing.

The paradox that our true existence is (in a sense)
outside ourselves is the paradox of all life. We live
by breath and food, and so our life is in these things
outside our individual bodies. Our life is in the air
and in our nourishment before we assimilate it as
our own. More astonishing still, Bergson has shown
that our perceptions are outside us in the things we
perceive.[3] When I perceive an object a living current passes from the object through my eyes by the

---

[1] *Studies in Hegelian Cosmology*, especially in chaps. ii. and iii.
[2] St. Thomas Aquinas, *Summa*, Pars I. Q. XL. Art. iii.
[3] *Matière et Mémoire*, chap. i.

afferent nerves to the brain, and thence by the efferent nerves once more to the object from which it started, causing a mere sensation in me (*i. e.* in my body) but causing me also by that sensation to have a perception outside me (*i. e.* outside my body) in the thing I look at. And all who gaze upon the same object have their perceptions outside themselves in that same object which yet is indivisibly one. Even so are we to find at last that we all have our true selfhoods in the One Super-Essence outside us, and yet each shall all the time have a feeling in himself of his own particular being without which the Super-Essence could not be his.

The doctrine of Unknowing must not be confounded with Herbert Spencer's doctrine of the Unknowable. The actual terms may be similar : the meanings are at opposite poles. For Herbert Spencer could conceive only of an intellectual apprehension, which being gone, nothing remained : Dionysius was familiar with a spiritual apprehension which soars beyond the intellect. Hence Herbert Spencer preaches ignorance concerning ultimate things ; Dionysius (like Bergson in modern times)[1] a transcendence of knowledge. The one means a state below the understanding and the other a state above it. The one teaches that Ultimate Reality is, and must always be, beyond our reach ; the other that the Ultimate Reality at last becomes so near as utterly to sweep away (in a sense) the distinction which separates us from It. That this is the meaning of Unknowing is plain from the whole trend of the Dionysian teaching, and is definitely stated, for instance, in the passage about the statue or in others which say that the Divine Darkness is dark through excess of light. It is even possible that the word "Unknowing" was (with this positive meaning) a

[1] See *Évolution Créatrice*, towards the end.

technical term of the Mysteries or of later Greek Philosophy, and that this is the real explanation and interpretation of the inscription on the Athenian altar: " To the Unknown God." [1]

VII.—THE PSYCHOLOGY OF CONTEMPLATION

Be this as it may, Dionysius is unquestionably speaking of a psychological state to which he himself has been occasionally led. It must, however, be carefully distinguished from another psychological state, apparently the same and yet really quite different, of which there is also evidence in other writers.

Amiel speaks of a mental condition in which the self lies dormant, dissolved, as it were, and absorbed into an undifferentiated state of being; and it is well known that a man's individuality may become merged in the impersonal existence of a crowd. The contrast between such a state and Unknowing consists wholly in the difference of spiritual values and spiritual intensity. Amiel felt the psychic experience mentioned above to be enervating. And the danger is fairly obvious. For this psychic state comes not through spiritual effort but through spiritual indolence. And the repose of spiritual attainment must be a strenuous repose.

The same psychic material may take either of two opposite forms, for the highest experiences and the lowest are both made of the same spiritual stuff. That is why great sinners make great saints and why our Lord preferred disreputable people to the respectable righteous. A storm of passion may produce a *Sonata* of Beethoven or it may produce an act of murder. All depends on the quality and direction of the storm. So in the present instance. There is a higher merging of the self and a lower

---

[1] Acts xvii. 23. Cf. Norden's *Agnostos Theos.*

merging of it. The one is above the level of personality, the other beneath it; the one is religious the other hedonistic; the one results from spiritual concentration and the other from spiritual dissipation.

Apparently our souls are crystallizations, as it were, out of an undifferentiated psychic ocean. So our personalities are formed, which we must keep inviolate. To melt back, though but for a time, into that ocean would be to surrender our heritage and to incur great loss. This is the objection to mere psychic trances. But some have been called on to advance by the intensification of their spiritual powers until they have for a moment reached a very different Ocean, which, with its fervent heat, has burst the hard outer case of their finite selfhood, and so they have been merged in that Vast Sea of Uncreated Light which has brought them no loss but only gain.

Just as in early days some had special gifts of prophecy through the power of the Holy Ghost, but some through the power of Satan, and the test lay in the manifested results,[1] so in the present instance. We cannot doubt that the experience is true and valid when we see its glory shining forth in the humble Saints of God.

To illustrate this experience fully from the writings of the Saints would need a volume to itself. Let us take a very few examples from one or two writers of unquestioned orthodoxy.

And first, for the theory of personality implied in it we may turn to Pascal, whose teaching amounts to very much the same thing as that of Dionysius. "*Le moi,*" he says, "*est haissable. . . . En un mot, le Moi a deux qualités: il est injuste en soi, en ce qu'il se fait centre du tout; il est incommode aux autres, en ce qu'il les veut asservir: car chaque Moi est l'ennemi*

---

[1] 1 Cor. xii. 1-3; 1 John iv. 1-3.

et voudrait être le tyran de tous les autres." [1]   Thus
a self-centred *Moi*, or Personality, is wrong inherently
and not only in its results.   And it is inherently
wrong because a personality has no right to be the
centre of things.   From this we may conclude
(1) that God, as being the rightful Centre of all
things, is not a *Moi*, or Personality ; and (2) that the
transcendence of our *Moi*, or Personality, is our highest
duty.   What, then, is the goal to which this transcendence will lead us ?   Pascal has a clear-cut
answer : " *Il n'y a que l'Être universel qui soit tel. . . .
Le Bien Universel est en nous, est nous mêmes et n'est
pas nous."* [2]   This is exactly the Dionysian doctrine.
Each must enter into himself and so must find Something that is his true Self and yet is not his particular
self.   His true being is deep within his soul and yet
in Something Other than his individuality which is
within his soul and yet outside of him.   We may
compare St. Augustine's words : " I entered into the
recesses of my being . . . and saw . . . above my
mind an Unchanging Light.[3]   Where, then, did I
find Thee except in Thyself above myself?" [4]

Now for the actual experience of Unknowing and
of the Negative Path that leads to it.   The finest
description of this, or at least of the aspiration after
it, is to be found in the following passage from the
Confessions of St. Augustine : [5]

"Could one silence the clamorous appetites of the
body ; silence his perceptions of the earth, the water,
and the air ; could he silence the sky, and could his
very soul be silent unto itself and, by ceasing to think
of itself, transcend self-consciousness ; could he
silence all dreams and all revelations which the mind
can image ; yea, could he entirely silence all language and all symbols and every transitory thing—

---

[1] *Pensées*, vi. 20 (ed. Havet).   [3] *Ib.* 26, xxiv. 39.
[3] *Conf.* vii. 16.   [4] *Ib.* x. 37.   [5] *Ib.* ix. 25

—inasmuch as these all say to the hearer : ' We made not ourselves but were made by the Eternal '—if, after such words, they were forthwith to hold their peace, having drawn the mind's ear towards their Maker, and He were now to speak alone, not through them but by Himself, so that we might hear His word, not through human language, nor through the voice of an angel, nor through any utterance out of a cloud, nor through any misleading appearance, but might instead hear, without these things, the very Being Himself, Whose presence in them we love—might hear Him with our Spirit even as now we strain our intellect and reach, with the swift movement of thought, to an eternal Wisdom that remains unmoved beyond all things—if this movement were continued, and all other visions (being utterly unequal to the task) were to be done away, and this one vision were to seize the beholder, and were to swallow him up and plunge him in the abyss of its inward delights, so that his life for ever should be like that fleeting moment of consciousness for which we have been yearning, would not such a condition as this be an 'ENTER THOU INTO THE JOY OF THY LORD'?"

This passage describes the *Via Negativa* in terms of aspiration drawn (we cannot doubt) from experience. The soul must cast all things away : sense, perception, thought, and the very consciousness of self ; and yet the process and its final result are of the most intense and positive kind. We are reminded of Wordsworth's—

"Thought was not ; in enjoyment it expired."[1]

Perhaps more striking is the testimony of St Thomas à Kempis, since, having no taste for speculation, he is not likely to be misled by theories. In

[1] *Excursion*, Book I.

the *Imitation of Christ* [1] occurs the following passage :
" When shall I at full gather myself in Thee, that for
Thy love I feel not myself, but Thee only, above all
feeling and all manner, in a *manner not known to
all ?* "

Thus he speaks longingly of a state in which the
individual human spirit is altogether merged and has
no self-consciousness whatever, except the mere consciousness of its merging. It is conscious of God
alone because, as an object of thought, it has gone
out of its particular being and is merged and lost in
Him. And the way in which St. Thomas describes
this state and speaks of it as not known to all
suggests that it was known to himself by personal
experience.

The clearest and profoundest analysis of the state,
based also on the most vivid personal experience of
it, is given by Ruysbroeck. The two following
passages are examples.

" The spirit for ever continues to burn in itself, for
its love is eternal ; and it feels itself ever more and
more to be burnt up in love, for it is drawn and transformed into the Unity of God, where the spirit burns
in love. If it observes itself, it finds a distinction and
an otherness between itself and God ; but where it is
burnt up it is undifferentiated and without distinction,
and therefore it feels nothing but unity ; for the flame
of the Love of God consumes and devours all that it
can enfold in its Self." [2]

" And, after this, there follows the third way of
feeling ; namely, that we feel ourselves to be one *with*
God ; for, through the transformation in God, we feel
ourselves to be swallowed up in the fathomless abyss
of our eternal blessedness, wherein we can nevermore
find any distinction between ourselves and God.
And this is our highest feeling, which we cannot

[1] Book III., chap. xxiii.   [2] *The Sparkling Stone*, chap. iii.

experience in any other way than in the immersion in love. And therefore, so soon as we are uplifted and drawn into our highest feeling, all our powers stand idle in an essential fruition ; but our powers do not pass away into nothingness, for then we should lose our created being. And as long as we stand idle, with an inclined spirit and with open eyes, but without reflection, so long we can contemplate and have fruition. But, at the very moment in which we seek to prove and to comprehend what it is that we feel, we fall back into reason, and there we find a distinction and an otherness between ourselves and God, and find God outside ourselves in incomprehensibility." [1]

Nothing could be more lucid. The *moi* is merged in the Godhead and yet the *ego* still retains its individuality un-merged, and the existence of the perfected spirit embraces these two opposite poles of fusion and distinction.

The same doctrine is taught, though with less masterly clearness, by St. Bernard in the *De Diligendo Deo*. There is, he says, a point of rapture where the human spirit " forgets itself . . . and passes wholly into God." Such a process is " to lose yourself, as it were, like one who has no existence, and to have no self-consciousness whatever, and to be emptied of yourself and almost annihilated." " As a little drop of water," he continues, " blended with a large quantity of wine, seems utterly to pass away from itself and assumes the flavour and colour of wine, and as iron when glowing with fire loses its original or proper form and becomes just like the fire ; and as the air, drenched in the light of the sun, is so changed into the same shining brightness that it seems to be not so much the recipient of the brightness as the actual brightness itself : so all human sensibility in

[1] *The Sparkling Stone*, chap. x.

the saints must then, in some ineffable manner, melt and pass out of itself, and be lent into the will of God. . . . The substance (*i. e.* personality) will remain but in another form." [1]

Of this transcendent experience St. Bernard bluntly says : " To experience this state is to be deified," and " Deification " is a technical term in the Mystical Theology of both the Eastern and the Western Church. Though the word θέωσις was perhaps a Mystery term, yet it occurs, for instance, in the writings of St. Macarius, and there is therefore nothing strange or novel in the fact that Dionysius uses it. But he carefully distinguishes between this and cognate words ; and his fantastic and uncouth diction is (here as so often) due to a straining after rigid accuracy. The Super-Essence he calls the Originating Godhead, or rather, perhaps, the Origin of Godhead (Θεαρχία), just as he calls it also "the Origin of Existence" (οὐσιαρχία). From this Origin there issues eternally, in the Universal stream of Emanation, that which he calls Deity or Very Deity (θεότης or αὐτοθεότης). This Deity, like Being, Life, etc., is an effluence radiating from the Super-Essential Godhead, and is a distant View of It as the dim visibility of a landscape is the landscape seen from afar, or as the effluent heat belongs to a fire. Purified souls, being raised up to the heights of contemplation, participate in this Effluence and so are deified (θεοῦνται) and become in a derivative sense, divine (θεωδεῖς, θεῖοι), or may even be called Gods (θεοί), just as by participating in the Effluence or Emanation of Being all created things become in a derivative sense existent (οὐσιωδῆ, ὄντα). The Super-Essential Godhead (θεαρχία) is beyond Deity as It is beyond Existence ; but the names " Deity " (Θεότης) or " Existent " (ὤν) may be symbolically or

[1] *De Dil. Deo*, chap. x.

inadequately applied to It, as a fire may be termed "warm" from its results though its actual temperature is of an intenser kind than this would imply. And the name of "Godhead," which belongs to It more properly, is given It (says Dionysius) merely because it is the Source of our deification. Thus instead of arguing from God's Divinity to man's potential divinity, Dionysius argues from the acquisition of actual divinity by certain men to God's Supra-Divinity. This is only another way of saying that God is but the highest Appearance or Manifestation of the Absolute. And this (as was seen above) is only another way of stating the orthodox and obvious doctrine that all our notions of Ultimate Reality are inadequate.

VIII.—THE SCRIPTURAL BASIS OF DIONYSIUS'S DOCTRINES

In the treatise "Concerning the Divine Names," Dionysius seeks to reconcile his daring conceptions with Scripture. Nor can he be said to fail. His argument, briefly, is that in Scripture we have a Revealed Religion and that things which are Revealed belong necessarily to the plane of Manifestation. Thus Revealed Religion interprets to us in terms of human thought things which, being Incomprehensible, are ultimately beyond thought. This is merely what St. Augustine teaches when he says [1] that the Prologue of St. John's Gospel reveals the mysteries of

---

[1] *Com. on St. John*, Tr. I. 1: "For who can declare the Truth as it actually is? I venture to say, my brothers, perhaps John himself has not declared it as it actually is, but, even he, only according to his powers. For he was a man speaking about God—one inspired, indeed, by God but still a man. Because he was inspired he has declared something of the Truth—had he not been inspired he could not have declared anything of it—but because he was a man (though an inspired one) he has not declared the whole Truth, but only what was possible for a man."

Eternity not as they actually are but as human thought can grasp them.[1] The neo-Platonism of Dionysius does not invalidate Scripture any more than that of Plotinus invalidates the writings of Plato. Dionysius merely says that there is an unplumbed Mystery behind the words of Scripture and streaming through them, just as Plotinus and other neo-Platonists hold that there is an unplumbed Mystery streaming through from behind Plato's categories of thought. And if it be urged that at least our Lord's teaching on the Fatherhood of God cannot be reconciled with the doctrine of a Supra-Personal Godhead, the answer is near at hand.[2] For the Pagan Plotinus, whose doctrine is similar to that of Dionysius, gives this very name of "Father" to his Supra-Personal Absolute—or rather to that Aspect of It which comes into touch with the human soul.[3] Moreover in the most rigidly orthodox Christian theology God the

[1] [What Augustine says is that St. John, because he was only human, has not declared the whole Truth concerning Deity. But this is very different from saying that what St. John has declared does not correspond with the eternal Reality. While Augustine holds that the Johannine Revelation is not complete, he certainly held that it was correct as far as it goes. Augustine had no conception of a Deity whom the qualities of self-consciousness and personality did not essentially represent. It is more than questionable whether Augustine would have accepted the statement that the Prologue of St. John's Gospel does not record the mysteries of Eternity "*as they actually are.*" Augustine had a profound belief that God as He is in Himself corresponds with God as He is revealed.—ED.]

[2] [The writer argues that Christ and Plotinus both employ the same expression, Father, to the Deity. But the use of the same expression will not prove much unless it is employed in the same meaning. No one can seriously contend that the Pagan Plotinus meant what Jesus Christ meant of the Fatherhood of God. Surely it is unquestionable that the Fatherhood of God meant for Jesus Christ what constituted God's supreme reality. It was employed in a sense which ·is entirely foreign to the metaphysical doctrine of a Supra-Personal Deity. The Semitic conception of the Godhead was not that of a neo-Platonist metaphysician.—ED.]

[3] e.g. *Enn.* I. 6, 8 : "We have a country whence we came, and we have a Father there."

Father is not a Personality. St. Augustine, for instance,[1] teaches that the " Persons " of the Trinity are Elements whose true nature is unknown to us.[2] They correspond however, he says, to certain elements in our individual personalities, and hence the human

[1] [What Augustine says is that we do not speak of three essences and three Gods, but of one essence and one God. Why then do we speak of three Persons and not of one Person ?

" Why, therefore, do we not call these three together one Person, or one Essence and one God ; we say three Persons, while we do not say three Gods or three Essences ; unless it be because we wish some one word to serve for that meaning whereby the Trinity is understood, that we might not be altogether silent when asked, what three, while we confessed that they are three ? "

1. Augustine's distinction is between the genus and the species. Thus Abraham Isaac and Jacob are three specimens of one genus. What he contends is that this is not the case in the Deity. 2. The essence of the Deity is unfolded in these Three. And "there is nothing else of that Essence beside the Trinity." " In no way can any other person whatever exist out of the same essence " whereas in mankind there can be more than three. 3. Moreover the three specimens of the genus man, Abraham Isaac and Jacob, are more, collectively, than any one of them by himself. " But in God it is not so ; for the Father, the Son and the Holy Spirit together is not a greater essence than the Father alone or the Son alone." What he means is that the Trinity is not to be explained by spacial metaphors (*De Trin.* vii. 11).

Augustine then is not teaching that the Persons of the Trinity are Elements whose true nature is unknown to us. He certainly does teach that Personality in the Godhead must exist otherwise than what we find under human limitations. But Augustine's conception of Deity is not the Supra-Personal Absolute. To him the Trinity was not confined to the plane of Manifestation. We have only to remember how he regards Sabellianism to prove this. Moreover, who can doubt that Augustine's psychological conception of God as the Lover, the Beloved and the Love which in itself is personal, represented to his mind the innermost reality and ultimate essence of the Deity? God is not for Augustine a supra-personal something in which both unity and trinity are transcended. The Trinity of Manifestation is for Augustine that which corresponds with and is identical with the very essential being of Deity. God is not merely Three as known to us but Three as He is in Himself apart from all self-revelation.—ED.]

[2] *De Trin.* vii. 11 : " Why . . . do we speak of Three ' Persons ' . . . except because we need some one term to explain the meaning of the word ' Trinity,' so as not to be entirely without an answer to the question : ' Three What ? ' when we confess God to be Three."

soul is created (he tells us) not in the image of one
Person in the Godhead but in the image of the whole
Trinity.[1] Thus he by implication denies that God
the Father is, in the ordinary sense of the word, a
Personality. And the teaching of St. Thomas
Aquinas is very similar.[2] It may, perhaps, even be
said that the germ of the most startling doctrines
which Dionysius expounds may be actually found in
Scripture. A state, for instance, which is not knowledge and yet is not ignorance, is described by St.
Paul when he says that Christians "know God or
rather are known of Him."[3] This is the mental
attitude of Unknowing. For the mind is quiescent
and emptied of its own powers and so receives a
knowledge the scope and activity of which is outside
itself in God. And in speaking of an ecstatic experience which he himself had once attained St. Paul
seems to suggest that he was, on that occasion, outside
of himself in such a manner as hardly, in the ordinary
sense, to retain his own identity.[4] Moreover he
suggests that the redeemed and perfected creation is
at last to be actually merged in God ($\ell\nu a$ $\tilde{\eta}$ δ $\Theta\epsilon\delta\varsigma$ $\tau\grave{a}$
$\pi\acute{a}\nu\tau a$ $\grave{\epsilon}\nu$ $\pi\tilde{a}\sigma\iota\nu$[5]). And the doctrine of Deification is
certainly, in the germ, Scriptural. For as Christ is
the Son of God so are we to be Sons of God,[6] and
Christ is reported actually to have based His own
claims to Deity on the potential Divinity of the
human soul.[7] Moreover we are to reign with Him[8]
and are, in a manner passing our present apprehension, to be made like Him when we see Him as
He is.[9]

Now all the boldest statements of Dionysius about

[1] *De Trin.* vii. 12.
[2] *Summa*, Pars I. Q. XLV. Art. vii.
[3] Gal. iv. 9.
[4] 2 Cor. xii. 2–5.
[5] 1 Cor. xv. 28.
[6] New Testament, *passim*.
[7] John x. 34–36.
[8] 2 Tim. ii. 12 ; Rev. i. 6; v. 10; xx. 6.
[9] 1 John iii. 2.

the ultimate glory for which the human soul is destined are obviously true of Christ, and as applied to Him, they would be a mere commentary on the words " I and the Father are One." [1]   Therefore if Christ came to impart His Life to us so that the things which are His by Nature should be ours by Grace, it follows that the teaching of Dionysius is in harmony with Scripture so long as it is made to rest on the Person and Work of Christ.   And, though Dionysius does not emphasize the Cross as much as could be wished, yet he certainly holds that Christ is the Channel through which the power of attainment is communicated to us.   It must not be forgotten that he is writing as a Christian to Christians, and so assumes the Work of Christ as a revealed and experienced Fact.   And since he holds that every individual person and thing has its pre-existent limits ordained in the Super-Essence, therefore he holds that the Human Soul of Christ has Its pre-existent place there as the Head of the whole creation.   That is what he means by the phrase " Super-Essential Jesus," and that is what is taught in the quotation from Hierotheus already alluded to.   No doubt the lost works of Dionysius dealt more fully with this subject, as indeed he hints himself. And if, through this scanty sense of the incredible evil which darkens and pollutes the world, he does not in the present treatise lay much emphasis upon the Saviour's Cross, yet he gives us definite teaching on the kindred Mystery of the Incarnation.

IX.—CONCLUSION

A few words on this matter and the present sketch is almost done.   The Trinity (as was said) is Super-

[1] John x. 30.

Essential or Supra-Personal. It is that Side of the Godhead which is turned towards the plane of Creation. Each " Person " possesses the whole Super-Essence and yet Each in a different manner. For the Father is originative and the other Two " Persons" derivative. The entire Super-Essence timelessly wells up in the Father and so passes on (as it were), timeless and entire, to the Son and Spirit. Thus the Second " Person " of the Trinity possesses eternally (like the other Two " Persons " in the Godhead) nothing but this Formless Radiance. But when the Second " Person " becomes Incarnate this Formless and Simple Radiance focuses Itself (shall we say ?) in the complex lens of a Human Individuality. Or perhaps Christ's Humanity should rather be compared to a prism which breaks that single white radiance into the iridescent colours of manifold human virtues. Thence there streams forth a glory which seeks to kindle in our hearts an answering fire whereby being wholly consumed we may pass up out of our finite being to find within the Super-Essence our pre-determined Home.

Such is, in outline, the teaching of this difficult writer who, though he tortured language to express the truth which struggled within him for utterance, yet has often been rashly condemned through being misunderstood. The charge of Pantheism that has been laid at his door is refuted by the very extravagance of the terms in which he asserts the Transcendence of the Godhead. For the title " Super-Essence " itself implies a Mystery which is indeed the ultimate Goal of the creatures but is not at present their actual plane of being. It implies a Height which, though it be their own, they yet can reach through nothing else than a complete self-renunciation. With greater show of reason Dionysius has been accused of hostility to civilization and external things. Yet here again unjustly. For, if in his solitary hermitage he lived far from the haunts of men, yet he wrote an entire treatise on the institutional side of Religion ; and he describes with impassioned enthusiasm the visible beauties of Nature. And, in fact, in his treatment of evil, he goes out of his way to assert that the whole material world is good. Outward things are assumed as the starting-point from which the human spirit must rise to another region of experience. Dionysius does not mean that they are all worthless ; he simply means that they are not ultimate. In the passage concerning the three movements of the soul he implies that the human faculties are valuable though they must finally be transcended. Even so Macarius tells us that " Revelation " is a mental state beyond " Perception " and beyond " Enlightened Vision." [1] All our natural activities must first silt together the particles which form the block of marble before we can by the *Via Negativa* carve the image out of it. And if this process of rejection destroys the block's original shape, yet it needs the block to work upon, and it does not seek to grind the whole material into powder. All life, when rightly understood, is a kind of *Via Negativa*, and we must struggle after certain things and then deliberately cast them aside, as a musician must first master the laws of Counterpoint and then sometimes ignore them, or as the Religion of the Law is a preparation for the higher Religion of the Spirit. Dionysius, nurtured in philosophy, passed beyond Philosophy without obscurantism, as St. Paul, nurtured in the Law, passed beyond the Law without disobedience. Finite things are good, for they point us on to the Infinite ; but if we chain ourselves to them they will become a hindrance to our journey, when they can no longer be a guide. And Dionysius

[1] *Hom.*, vii. 5.

would have us not destroy them but merely break our chains.

His doctrines are certainly dangerous. Perhaps that is a mark of their truth. For the Ultimate Truth of things is so self-contradictory that it is bound to be full of peril to minds like ours which can only apprehend one side of Reality at the time. Therefore it is not perhaps to be altogether desired that such doctrines should be very popular. They can only be spiritually discerned, through the intensest spiritual effort. Without this they will only too readily lead to blasphemous arrogance and selfish sloth. And yet the *Via Negativa*, for those who can scale its dizzy ascent, is after all but a higher altitude of that same royal road which, where it traverses more populous regions, we all recognize as the one true Pilgrim's Way. For it seeks to attain its goal through self-renunciation. And where else are the true principles of such a process to be found if it be not in the familiar virtues of Christian humility and Christian love?

X.—BIBLIOGRAPHY

[The writings of the Areopagite consist of four important treatises : *De divinis Nominibus, De mystica Theologia, De Cœlesti Hierarchia, De ecclesiatica Hierarchia ;* some letters ; and a number of lost documents referred to in the treatises. Little has been done as yet towards the provision of a critical text. The Syriac, Armenian and Arabic versions have not been investigated. Migne's text contains many manifest errors ; it is a reprint of the Venice edition of 1755–6.

The ideas of Dionysius's system are discussed in all books on Mysticism, and a multitude of magazine articles, mainly in German, deal with isolated points in the actual treatises besides the problem of author-ship. The brief list given below will suffice for the present purpose.

The Dionysian Documents have been critically in-vestigated by Hipler. His work was followed by J. Dräseke in an Essay entitled " Dionysiaca," in the *Zeitschrift für Wissenschaftliche Theologie*, 1887, pp. 300–333. Also by Nirschl. and by Styglmayr. in the *Historische Jahrbuch*, 1895. Criticism on the author-ship has been continued by Hugo Koch, "Pseudo-Dionysius Areopagita," in the *Forschungen zur Christlichen Litteratur-und Dogmengeschichte*, 1900. Ed. by Ehrhard and Kirsch. Hugo Koch's work is one of the best on the subject.

Colet, J. (Dean), *Two Treatises on The Hierarchies of Dionysius*, with introduction and translation, by J. H. Lupton (London, 1869).

Fowler, J., *The Works of Dionysius, especially in Reference to Christian Art* (London, 1872). J. Parker, English Translation (Oxford, 1897).

Sharpe, A. B., *Mysticism: Its True Nature and Value* (London, 1910). Contains a translation of the Mystical Theology and of the letters to Caius and Dorotheus.

Inge, W. R., *Christian Mysticism* (London, 1899), pp. 104–122.

Jones, Rufus M., *Studies in Mystical Religion* (London, 1909), Chap. IV.

Gardner, Edmund G., *Dante and the Mystics* (London, 1913), Chap. III.

For the general influence of Dionysius reference should be made to the following writers—

Bach, Josef, *Die Dogmengeschichte des Mittelalters*, 1 Theil., 1874, pp. 6–15.

Baur, F. C., *Die Christliche Lehre von der Dreiei-*

nigkeit und Menschwerdung Gottes, 1842, Bd. II., 207–251.

Dorner, *Development of the Doctrine of the Person of Christ*, English translation, Div. ii., Vol. I., pp. 157 ff.

Westcott, Essay on Dionysius the Areopagite in *Religious Thought in the West*, 1891, pp. 142–193.

Uebinger, J., *Die Gotteslehre des Nikolaus Cusanus*, 1888.—ED.]

THE DIVINE NAMES

THIS Treatise contains thirteen chapters. The following is a brief summary of their contents.

Chapter I. Introductory. The Purpose of the Treatise. Doctrine concerning God to be obtained from the Scriptures. But all the Names there given Him cannot represent Him who is Nameless. It is only Symbolical Theology.

Chapter II. On the Divine Unity and Distinction.

Chapter III. On the Approach to the Divine.

Chapter IV. On Goodness as a Name of Deity, including a discussion on the Nature of Evil.

Chapter V. On Deity as Being. The three degrees: Existence, Life, Intelligence.

Chapter VI. On Deity as Life.

Chapter VII. Deity considered as Wisdom, Reason, Truth.

Chapter VIII. Deity considered as Power.

Chapter IX. Deity considered as Great and as Small. Might be called, as Deity in relation to Space.

Chapter X. Deity as Omnipotent: the Ancient of Days. God in relation to Time.

Chapter XI. On God and Peace.

Chapter XII. On the Names Holy of holies, King of kings, Lord of lords, God of gods.

Chapter XIII. On the Divine Perfection and Unity.

CHAPTER I

Dionysius the Presbyter, to his fellow-Presbyter Timothy.[1]
*What is the purpose of the discourse, and what the
tradition concerning the Divine Names.*

1. NOW, Blessed Timothy, the *Outlines of Divinity*[2]
being ended, I will proceed, so far as in me lies, to an
Exposition of the Divine Names.   And here also let
us set before our minds the scriptural rule that in
speaking about God we should declare the Truth, not
with enticing words of man's wisdom, but in demon-
stration of the power which the Spirit[3] stirred up in
the Sacred Writers, whereby, in a manner surpassing
speech and knowledge,[4] we embrace those truths
which, in like manner, surpass them, in that Union
which exceeds our faculty, and exercise of discursive,
and of intuitive reason.[5]   We must not then dare to
speak, or indeed to form any conception, of the
hidden super-essential [6] Godhead, except those things
that are revealed to us from the Holy Scriptures.[7]

---

[1] The name of St. Paul's companion is intended to give colour to
the writer's pseudonym.   See Introduction, p. 1 ; cf. iii. 2.

[2] This work is lost.   [3] 2 Cor. ii. 4.

[4] τοῖς ἀφθέγκτοις καὶ ἀγνώστοις ἀφθέγκτως καὶ ἀγνώστως συναπτόμεθα.
See Intr. on "Unknowing," p. 32.

[5] κατὰ τὴν κρείττονα τῆς καθ᾽ ἡμᾶς λογικῆς καὶ νοερᾶς δυνάμεως καὶ
ἐνεργείας.   D. frequently distinguishes between the discursive and the
intuitive reason.   Together they cover the whole of the intellect, cf.
Wordsworth, *Prelude*, xiv. 119, 120 :
        " Hence endless occupation for the soul,
          Whether discursive or intuitive."
The former gives us deductions, the latter the axioms on which these
are based.   See Intr., p. 26.

[6] See Intr., p. 4.

[7] D. is here contrasting the Affirmative Path of Knowing with the
Negative Path of Unknowing.   The former has a value as leading up
to the latter ; but it is only safe so far as we keep within the bounds
of Scripture.   Unscriptural conceptions of God are false : Scriptural
conceptions are true so far as they go ; but their literal meaning must
be transcended.   See Intr., p. 41 f.

For a super-essential understanding of It is proper
to Unknowing, which lieth in the Super-Essence
Thereof surpassing Discourse, Intuition and Being ;
acknowledging which truth let us lift up our eyes
towards the steep height, so far as the effluent light
of the Divine Scriptures grants its aid, and, as we
strive to ascend unto those Supernal Rays, let us gird
ourselves for the task with holiness and the reverent
fear of God.   For, if we may safely trust the wise and
infallible Scriptures, Divine things are revealed unto
each created spirit in proportion to its powers, and
in this measure is perception granted through the
workings of the Divine goodness, the which in just
care for our preservation divinely tempereth unto
finite measure the infinitude of things which pass
man's understanding.   For even as things which are
intellectually discerned [1] cannot be comprehended or
perceived by means of those things which belong to
the senses, nor simple and imageless things by means
of types and images, nor the formless and intangible
essence of unembodied things by means of those
which have bodily form,[2] by the same law of truth
the boundless [3] Super-Essence surpasses Essences,
the Super-Intellectual Unity surpasses Intelligences,

[1] *i. e.* The Transcendent Truths which are beyond ordinary knowledge.

νοητά.   The word νοῦς = Mind in the sense not merely of abstract
intellect but of the spiritual personality.   Hence the word is often
used to = an angel ; and νοητός is often used as = spiritual, instead of
πνευματικός, which D. does not employ.   This use of νοῦς and its
derivatives is ultimately due to the influence of Aristotle.   (Cf. the
use of νοῦς in Plotinus.)   St. Thomas Aquinas regards *intellectus*
as = "personality."   But here the reference is perhaps rather to the
province of abstract intellect.

[2] Apparently this is the same thought repeated in three different
ways.   The formless essence (ἀμορφία) of a thing is simple and imageless—a Platonic *idea*—perceived by the mind ; things which have
bodily form are, as it were, types and symbols perceived by the
senses.

[3] Or "indeterminate."

the One which is beyond thought surpasses the
apprehension of thought, and the Good which is
beyond utterance surpasses the reach of words.[1]
Yea, it is an Unity which is the unifying Source of
all unity and a Super-Essential Essence,[2] a Mind
beyond the reach of mind [3] and a Word beyond
utterance, eluding Discourse, Intuition, Name, and
every kind of being. It is the Universal Cause of
existence while Itself existing not, for It is beyond
all Being and such that It alone could give, with
proper understanding thereof, a revelation of Itself.

2. Now concerning this hidden Super-Essential
Godhead we must not dare, as I have said, to speak,
or even to form any conception Thereof, except those
things which are divinely revealed to us from the
Holy Scriptures. For as It hath lovingly taught us
in the Scriptures concerning Itself [4] the understanding
and contemplation of Its actual nature is not acces-
sible to any being ; for such knowledge is super-
essentially exalted above them all. And many of
the Sacred Writers thou wilt find who have declared
that It is not only invisible and incomprehensible,
but also unsearchable and past finding out, since
there is no trace of any that have penetrated the
hidden depths of Its infinitude.[5] Not that the Good
is wholly incommunicable to anything ; nay, rather,
while dwelling alone by Itself, and having there

---

[1] Thus the three grades are : (1) the material world ; (2) the spiritual
world of truths, personality, etc. ; (3) the Godhead which is, so to
speak, supra-spiritual.

[2] *i. e.* A Supra-Personal Personality. See Intr., p. 4 f.

[3] νοῦς ἀνόητος. Probably not "Irrational Mind" (as Dr. Inge
translates it). Maximus takes it passively, as translated above.

[4] Ps. cxlv. 3 ; Matt. xi. 27 ; Rom. xi. 33 ; 1 Cor. ii. 11 ; Eph. iii. 8.

[5] ὡς οὐκ ὄντος ἴχνους οὐδενὸς τῶν ἐπὶ τὴν κρυφίαν αὐτῆς ἀπειρίαν
διεληλυθότων. Two interpretations of this passage are possible : (1)
Those who have penetrated the hidden Depths cannot describe the
Vision (cf. Dante, Par. xxxiii, 55–66) ; (2) Nobody has ever penetrated
into the ultimate Depths of Deity.

firmly fixed Its super-essential Ray, It lovingly
reveals Itself by illuminations corresponding to each
separate creature's powers, and thus draws upwards
holy minds into such contemplation, participation
and resemblance [1] of Itself as they can attain—
even them that holily and duly strive thereafter
and do not seek with impotent presumption the
Mystery beyond that heavenly revelation which is so
granted as to fit their powers, nor yet through their
lower propensity slip down the steep descent, [2] but
with unwavering constancy press onwards toward the
ray that casts its light upon them and, through the
love responsive to these gracious illuminations, speed
their temperate and holy flight on the wings of a
godly reverence.

3. In obedience to these divine behests which guide
all the holy dispositions [3] of the heavenly hosts, we
worship with reverent silence the unutterable Truths
and, with the unfathomable [4] and holy veneration of our
mind, approach that Mystery of Godhead which exceeds all Mind and Being. And we press upwards to
those beams which in the Holy Scripture shine upon
us; wherefrom we gain the light which leads us unto

---

[1] θεωριά, κοινωνία, ὁμοίωσις. These are three elements of one process.
Resemblance is the final goal, cf. 1 John iii. 2. D. defines
Deification as "a process whereby we are made like unto God
(ἀφομοίωσις) and are united unto Him (ἕνωσις) so far as these things
may be." (*Eccl. Hier.* I. 4. Migne, p. 376, A.)

[2] Two kinds of danger: (1) spiritual presumption; (2) the temptations of our earthly nature. In dealing with the first D. warns us
against leaving the Affirmative Path until we are ready. The Negative
Path goes on where the Affirmative Path stops. St. John of the Cross
and other spiritual writers insist that, though contemplation is a higher
activity than meditation through images, yet not all are called to it,
and that it is disastrous prematurely to abandon meditation. S. John
of the Cross, in the *Dark Night of the Soul*, explains the signs which
will show when the time has come for the transition. Note the spiritual
sanity of D. His Unknowing is not a blank.

[3] τὰς ὅλας . . . τῶν ὑπερουρανίων τάξεων ἁγίας διακοσμήσεις.

[4] A depth opens up in the heart of man corresponding to the depth
of the Godhead. Deep answers unto deep. Cf. 1 Cor. ii. 10, 11.

the Divine praises,[1] being supernaturally enlightened
by them and conformed unto that sacred hymnody,
even so as to behold the Divine enlightenments the
which through them are given in such wise as fits our
powers, and so as to praise the bounteous Origin of
all holy illumination in accordance with that Doctrine,
as concerning Itself, wherewith It hath instructed us
in the Holy Scriptures. Thus do we learn [2] that It is
the Cause and Origin and Being and Life of all creation.[3] And It is unto them that fall away from It a
Voice that doth recall them and a Power by which
they rise ; and to them that have stumbled into a
corruption of the Divine image within them, It is a
Power of Renewal and Reform ; and It is a sacred
Grounding to them that feel the shock of unholy
assault, and a Security to them that stand : an upward
Guidance to them that are being drawn unto It, and a
Principle of Illumination [4] to them that are being
enlightened : a Principle of Perfection to them that
are being perfected ; [5] a principle of Deity to them
that are being deified ; [6] and of Simplicity to them
that are being brought unto simplicity ; [7] and of Unity

[1] πρὸς τοὺς θεαρχικοὺς ὕμνους. Either (1) "leads us to declare the
Divine praises" ; or (2) "leads us to apprehend the Divine praises as
sung by angels," etc.

[2] In the whole of this passage God is spoken of as at the same time
Efficient, Formal and Final Cause of the soul's activity. D. teaches
that God is present in all things, but not equally in all. Cf. Intr.,
p. 14.

[3] Gen. i.

[4] Three stages may be traced here corresponding to Purgation,
Illumination and Union. I have tried to indicate the transitions from
one stage to the next by the punctuation.

[5] τῶν τελουμένων τελεταρχία. "Perfect" (τέλειος) and the words
connected with it were technical terms in the Greek Mysteries. Possibly
there are traces of this technical use in St. Paul's Epistles (e.g. 1 Cor.
ii. 6 ; Phil. iii. 15).

[6] τῶν θεουμένων θεαρχιά. See Intr., p. 39.

[7] The soul must turn away from the complex world of sense and
have only one desire—the desire for God. Thus it becomes concentrated
as it were, and so is in a simple and unified state. Cf. Matt. vi. 22.
See Intr., p. 25.

to them that are being brought unto unity. Yea, in a super-essential manner, above the category of origin, It is the Origin of all origin, and the good and bounteous Communication (so far as such may be [1]) of hidden mysteries; and, in a word, It is the life of all things that live and the Being of all that are, the Origin and Cause of all life and being through Its bounty which both brings them into existence and maintains them.

4. These mysteries we learn from the Divine Scriptures, and thou wilt find that in well-nigh all the utterances of the Sacred Writers the Divine Names refer in a Symbolical Revelation [2] to Its beneficent Emanations.[3] Wherefore, in almost all consideration of Divine things we see the Supreme Godhead celebrated with holy praises as One and an Unity, through the simplicity and unity of Its supernatural indivisibility, from whence (as from an unifying power) we attain to unity, and through the supernal conjunction of our diverse and separate qualities are knit together each into a Godlike Oneness, and all together into a mutual Godly union.[4] And It is called the Trinity because Its supernatural fecundity is revealed in a Threefold Personality,[5] wherefrom all Fatherhood in heaven and on earth exists and draws Its name. And It is called the Universal Cause [6] since all things came into being through Its

---

[1] *i. e.* So far as we are capable of receiving this communication.

[2] ἐκφαντορικῶς καὶ ὑμνητικῶς.

[3] *i. e.* God's differentiated activities. Since the ultimate Godhead is ineffable, Scripture can only hint at Its Nature by speaking of Its manifestations in the relative sphere. See Intr., p. 8.

[4] God is ineffable and transcends unity, see Intr., p. 5. But, since His presence in man produces an unity in each individual (and in human society), Scripture calls Him "One."

[5] The ineffable Godhead transcends our conception of the Trinity. But we call Him a Trinity because we experience His trinal working—as our ultimate Home, as an Individual Personality Who was once Incarnate, and as a Power within our hearts. See Intr., p. 7.

[6] God is not a First Cause, for a cause is one event in a temporal

bounty, whence all being springs; and It is called
Wise and Fair because all things which keep their
own nature uncorrupted are full of all Divine
harmony and holy Beauty;[1] and especially It is
called Benevolent[2] because, in one of Its Persons, It
verily and wholly shared in our human lot, calling
unto Itself and uplifting the low estate of man,
wherefrom, in an ineffable manner, the simple Being
of Jesus assumed a compound state,[3] and the Eternal
hath taken a temporal existence, and He who supernaturally transcends all the order of all the natural
world was born in our Human Nature without any
change or confusion of His ultimate properties. And
in all the other Divine enlightenments which the
occult Tradition of our inspired teachers hath, by
mystic Interpretation, accordant with the Scriptures,
bestowed upon us, we also have been initiated : appre-
hending these things in the present life (according to
our powers), through the sacred veils of that loving
kindness which in the Scriptures and the Hierarchical
Traditions,[4] enwrappeth spiritual truths in terms
drawn from the world of sense, and super-essential
truths in terms drawn from Being, clothing with
shapes and forms things which are shapeless and
formless, and by a variety of separable symbols,

---

series, and God is beyond Time and beyond the whole creation. Yet
in so far as He acts on the relative plane He may, by virtue of this
manifestation of Himself in the creation, be spoken of as a Cause.

[1] Beauty is a sacrament and only truly itself when it points to something beyond itself. That is why "Art for Art's sake" degrades art.
Beauty reveals God, but God is more than Beauty. Hence Beauty has
its true being *outside* itself in Him. Cf. Intr., p. 31.

[2] Love is the most perfect manifestation of God. Yet God is in a
sense beyond even love as we know it. For love, as we know it,
implies the distinction between "me" and "thee," and God is
ultimately beyond such distinction. See Intr., p. 35.

[3] ὁ ἁπλοῦς Ἰησοῦς συνετέθη. Cf. *Myst. Theol.* III., "Super-Essential
Jesus."

[4] ἱεραρχικῶν παραδόσεων, *i. e.* Ecclesiastical Tradition.

E

fashioning manifold attributes of the imageless and
supernatural Simplicity.   But hereafter, when we are
corruptible and immortal and attain the blessed lot of
being like unto Christ, then (as the Scripture saith),
we shall be for ever with the Lord,[1] fulfilled with His
visible Theophany in holy contemplations, the which
shall shine about us with radiant beams of glory
(even as once of old it shone around the Disciples at
the Divine Transfiguration) ; and so shall we, with our
mind made passionless and spiritual, participate in a
spiritual illumination from Him, and in an union
transcending our mental faculties, and there, amidst
the blinding blissful impulsions of His dazzling rays,
we shall, in a diviner manner than at present, be like
unto the heavenly Intelligences.[2]   For, as the infallible Scripture saith, we shall be equal to the angels
and shall be the Sons of God, being Sons of the
Resurrection.[3]   But at present we employ (so far as
in us lies), appropriate symbols for things Divine ;
and then from these we press on upwards according
to our powers to behold in simple unity the Truth perceived by spiritual contemplations, and leaving behind
us all human notions of godlike things, we still the
activities of our minds, and reach (so far as this may
be) into the Super-Essential Ray,[4] wherein all kinds
of knowledge so have their pre-existent limits (in a
transcendently inexpressible manner), that we cannot
conceive nor utter It, nor in any wise contemplate
the same, seeing that It surpasseth all things, and
wholly exceeds our knowledge, and super-essentially
contains beforehand (all conjoined within Itself) the
bounds of all natural sciences and forces (while yet

---

[1] I Thess. iv. 16.
[2] ἐν θειοτέρᾳ μιμήσει τῶν ὑπερουρανίων νοῶν—*i. e.* the angels.
[3] Luke xx. 36.
[4] Meditation leads on to Contemplation ; and the higher kind of
Contemplation is performed by the *Via Negativa.*

Its force is not circumscribed by any), and so possesses, beyond the celestial Intelligences,[1] Its firmly fixed abode. For if all the branches of knowledge belong to things that have being, and if their limits have reference to the existing world, then that which is beyond all Being must also be transcendent above all knowledge.[2]

5. But if It is greater than all Reason and all knowledge, and hath Its firm abode altogether beyond Mind and Being, and circumscribes, compacts, embraces and anticipates all things[3] while Itself is altogether beyond the grasp of them all, and cannot be reached by any perception, imagination, conjecture, name, discourse, apprehension, or understanding, how then is our Discourse concerning the Divine Names to be accomplished, since we see that the Super-Essential Godhead is unutterable and nameless? Now, as we said when setting forth our Outlines of Divinity, the One, the Unknowable, the Super-Essential, the Absolute Good (I mean the Trinal Unity of Persons possessing the same Deity and Goodness), 'tis impossible to describe or to conceive in Its ultimate Nature; nay, even the angelical communions of the heavenly Powers Therewith which we describe as either Impulsions or Derivations[4] from the Unknowable and blinding Goodness are themselves beyond utterance and knowledge, and belong to none but those angels who, in a manner beyond angelic knowledge, have been counted worthy

---

[1] *i. e.* The Angels. I have throughout translated ὑπερουράνιος "celestial" instead of "super-celestial." Presumably the meaning is "beyond the *material* sky," or "celestial in a *transcendent* sense."

[2] The whole of this passage shows that there is a positive element in Unknowing.

[3] παντῶν . . . προληπτική—*i.e.* contains them eternally before their creation.

[4] ἃς εἴτε ἐπιβολὰς εἴτε παραδοχὰς χρῆ φάναι—*i. e.* according as we describe the act from above or below. God sends the impulse, the angels receive it.

thereof. And godlike Minds,[1] angelically[2] entering (according to their powers) unto such states of union and being deified and united, through the ceasing of their natural activities, unto the Light Which surpasseth Deity, can find no more fitting method to celebrate its praises than to deny It every manner of Attribute.[3] For by a true and supernatural illumination from their blessed union Therewith, they learn that It is the Cause of all things and yet Itself is nothing, because It super-essentially transcends them all. Thus, as for the Super-Essence of the Supreme Godhead (if we would define the Transcendence of its Transcendent Goodness[4]) it is not lawful to any lover of that Truth which is above all truth to celebrate It as Reason or Power or Mind or Life or Being, but rather as most utterly surpassing all condition, movement, life, imagination, conjecture, name, discourse, thought, conception, being, rest, dwelling, union,[5] limit, infinity, everything that exists. And yet since, as the Subsistence[6] of goodness, It, by the very fact of Its existence, is the Cause of all things, in celebrating the bountiful Providence of the Supreme Godhead we must draw upon the whole creation. For It is both the central Force of all things, and also their final Purpose, and *is* Itself before them all, and they all subsist in It; and

[1] οἱ θεοειδεῖς . . . νόες—*i. e.* human minds.

[2] ἀγγελομιμήτως. "In a manner which imitates the angels." Cf. Wordsworth, *Prelude*, xiv. 108, 102: "Like angels stopped upon the wing by sound of harmony from heaven's remotest spheres."

[3] This shows that the *Via Negativa* is based on an experience and not on a mere speculation.

[4] ὅ τι ποτέ ἐστιν ἡ τῆς ὑπεραγαθότητος ὑπερύπαρξις.

[5] "Union" (ἕνωσις). This word has more than one meaning in D., and hence occasional ambiguity. It may = (1) Unity (*i. e.* that which makes an individual thing to be one thing); (2) Mental or Spiritual intercourse; (3) Physical intercourse; (4) Sense perception. Here it = either (1) or (2), probably (1).

[6] ἀγαθότητος ὕπαρξις—*i. e.* the ultimate Essence in which goodness consists.

through the fact of Its existence the world is brought into being and maintained ; and It is that which all things desire—those which have intuitive or discursive Reason seeking It through knowledge, the next rank of beings through perception, and the rest through vital movement or the property of mere existence belonging to their state.[1] Conscious of this, the Sacred Writers celebrate It by every Name while yet they call It Nameless.[2]

6. For instance, they call It Nameless when they say that the Supreme Godhead Itself, in one of the mystical visions whereby It was symbolically manifested, rebuked him who said : "What is thy name ? "[3] and, as though bidding him not seek by any means of any Name to acquire a knowledge of God, made the answer : "Why askest thou thus after My Name seeing it is secret ? " Now is not the secret Name precisely that which is above all names[4] and nameless, and is fixed beyond every name that is named, not only in this world but also in that which is to come ? On the other hand, they attribute many names to It when, for instance, they speak of It as declaring : "I am that I am,"[5] or "I am the Life,"[6] or "the Light,"[7] or "God,"[8] or "the Truth,"[9] and when the Inspired Writers themselves celebrate the Universal Cause with many titles drawn from the whole created

---

[1] Man—Animal—Vegetable—Inorganic Matter. For the thought of this whole passage, cf. Shelley, *Adonais* : "That Light whose smile kindles the universe." "The property of mere existence " = οὐσιώδη καὶ ἑκτικὴν ἐπιτηδειότητα. οὐσία = an individual existence. Its highest meaning is a "personality," its lowest a "thing." οὐσιώδης refers generally to its lowest meaning and = "possessing mere existence," *i. e.* "belonging to the realm of inorganic matter." See Intr., p. 4.

[2] This shows that there is a *positive* element in D.'s *Via Negativa*.

[3] Judges xiii. 18.

[4] Phil. ii. 9 ; Eph. i. 21.   [5] Ex. iii. 14.

[6] John xiv. 6.   [7] John viii. 12.

[8] Gen. xxviii. 13.   [9] John xiv. 6.

universe, such as " Good," [1] and " Fair," [2] and " Wise," [3] as " Beloved," [4] as " God of Gods " and " Lord of Lords " [5] and " Holy of Holies," [6] as " Eternal," [7] as " Existent " [8] and as " Creator of Ages," [9] as " Giver of Life," [10] as " Wisdom," [11] as " Mind," [12] as " Word," [13] as " Knower," [14] as " possessing beforehand all the treasures of knowledge," [15] as " Power," [16] as " Ruler," [17] as " King of kings," [18] as " Ancient of Days ; " [19] and as " Him that is the same and whose years shall not fail," [20] as " Salvation," [21] as " Righteousness," [22] as " Sanctification," [23] as " Redemption," [23] as " Surpassing all things in greatness," [24] and yet as being in " the still small breeze." [25]   Moreover, they say that He dwells within our minds, and in our souls [26] and bodies, [27] and in heaven and in earth, [28] and that, while remaining Himself, He is at one and the same time within the world around it and above it (yea, above the sky and above existence) ; and they call Him a Sun, [29] a Star, [30] and a Fire, [31] and Water, [32] a Wind or Spirit, [33] a Dew, [34] a Cloud, [35] an Archetypal Stone, [36] and a Rock, [37] and All Creation, [38] Who yet (they declare) is no created thing.

7. Thus, then, the Universal and Transcendent Cause must both be nameless and also possess the names of all things in order that It may truly be an universal Dominion, the Centre of creation on which all things depend, as on their Cause and

[1] Matt. xix. 17.   [2] Ps. xxvii. 4.   [3] Rom. xvi. 27.
[4] Isa. v. 1.   [5] Ps. cxxxvi. 2, 3.   [6] Isa. vi. 3.
[7] Deut. xxxiii. 27.   [8] Ex. iii. 14.   [9] Gen. i. 1–8.
[10] Gen. i. 20 ; ii. 7 ; Job x. 12 ; John x. 10.   [11] Prov. viii.
[12] 1 Cor. ii. 16.   [13] John i. 1.   [14] Ps. xliv. 21.   [15] Col. ii. 3.
[16] Rev. xix. 1.   [17] Rev. i. 5.   [18] Rev. xvii. 4.   [19] Dan. vii.
[20] Ps. cii. 25.   [21] Ex. xv. 2.   [22] Jer. xxiii. 6.   [23] 1 Cor. i. 30.
[24] Isa. xl. 15.   [25] 1 Kings xix. 12.   [26] John xiv. 17.
[27] 1 Cor. vi. 19.   [28] Isa. lxvi. 1.   [29] Ps. lxxxiv. 11.
[30] Rev. xxii. 16.   [31] Deut. iv. 24.   [32] Ps: lxxxiv. 6.
[33] John iv. 24 ; Acts ii. 2.   [34] Hosea xiv. 5.   [35] Ex. xiii. 21.
[36] Ps. cxviii. 22.   [37] Ps. xxxi. 2, 3.   [38] 1 Cor. xv. 28.

Origin and Goal; and that, according to the Scriptures, It may be all in all, and may be truly called the Creator of the world, originating and perfecting and maintaining all things; their Defence and Dwelling, and the Attractive Force that draws them: and all this in one single, ceaseless, and transcendent act.[1] For the Nameless Goodness is not only the cause of cohesion or life or perfection in such wise as to derive Its Name from this or that providential activity alone; nay, rather does It contain all things beforehand within Itself, after a simple and uncircumscribed manner through the perfect excellence of Its one and all-creative Providence, and thus we draw from the whole creation Its appropriate praises and Its Names.

8. Moreover, the sacred writers proclaim not only such titles as these (titles drawn from universal[2] or from particular[3] providences or providential activities[4]), but sometimes they have gained their images from certain heavenly visions[5] (which in the holy precincts or elsewhere have illuminated the Initiates or the Prophets), and, ascribing to the super-luminous nameless Goodness titles drawn from all manner of acts and functions, have clothed It in human (fiery or amber) shapes[6] or forms, and have spoken of Its Eyes,[7] and Ears,[8] and Hair,[9] and Face,[10] and Hands,[11] and Wings,[12] and Feathers,[13] and Arms,[14] and Back Parts,[15] and Feet;[16] and fashioned such mystical

---

[1] God is above Time.

[2] *e.g.* "I am that I am," "Good," "Fair."

[3] *e.g.* "Sun," "Star," "Rock," etc.

[4] ἀπὸ τῶν . . . προνοιῶν ἢ προνοουμένων. The first are the *faculties* of acting or being revealed in a certain way; the second are the *results* or manifestations of these faculties when in action.

[5] Thus the complete classification is: (1) Analogies drawn from the material world, (*a*) universal, (*b*) particular; (2) psychic visions.

[6] Ezek. i. 26, 27.	[7] Ps. x. 5.	[8] James v. 4.
[9] Dan. vii. 9.	[10] Ps. xxxiii. 17.	[11] Job x. 8.
[12] Ps. xci. 4.	[13] *Ibid.*	[14] Deut. xxxiii. 27.
[15] Ex. xxxiii. 23.	[16] Ex. xxiv. 10.	

conceptions as its Crown,[1] and Throne,[2] and Cup,[3] and Mixing Bowl,[4] etc., concerning which things we will attempt to speak when we treat of Symbolical Divinity. At present, collecting from the Scriptures what concerns the matter in hand, and employing as our canon the rule we have described, and guiding our search thereby, let us proceed to an exposition of God's Intelligible[5] Names; and as the Hierarchical Law directs us in all study of Divinity, let us approach these godlike contemplations (for such indeed they are[6]) with our hearts predisposed unto the vision of God, and let us bring holy ears to the exposition of God's holy Names, implanting holy Truths in holy instruments according to the Divine command, and withholding these things from the mockery and laughter of the uninitiate, or, rather, seeking to redeem those wicked men (if any such there be) from their enmity towards God. Thou, therefore, O good Timothy, must guard these truths according to the holy Ordinance, nor must thou utter or divulge the heavenly mysteries unto the uninitiate.[7] And for myself I pray God grant me worthily to declare the beneficent and manifold Names of the Unutterable and Nameless Godhead, and that He do not take away the word of Truth out of my mouth.

---

[1] Rev. xiv. 14.   [2] Ezek. i. 26, 27.
[3] Ps. lxxv. 8.   [4] Prov. ix. 5.

[5] τῶν νοητῶν θεωνυμιῶν—i. e. the Names belonging to God when revealed in the relative sphere; not those which belong to the ultimate Godhead as such. In fact, the Godhead, as such, is Nameless. See Intr., p. 7.

[6] κυρίως εἰπεῖν—i. e. actually godlike because man is deified by them.

[7] See *Myst. Theol.* I. 2 ; and cf. Matt. vii. 6.

CHAPTER II

Concerning the Undifferencing and the Differentiation in Divinity, and the Nature of Divine Unification and Differentiation.[1]

1. 'TIS the whole Being of the Supernal Godhead (saith the Scripture) that the Absolute Goodness hath defined and revealed.[2] For in what other sense may we take the words of Holy Writ when it tells us how the Godhead spake concerning Itself, and said: "Why asketh thou me concerning the good? None is good save one, that is, God."[3] Now this matter we have discussed elsewhere, and have shown that all the Names proper to God are always applied in Scripture not partially but to the whole, entire, full, complete Godhead, and that they all refer indivisibly, absolutely, unreservedly, and wholly to all the wholeness of the whole and entire Godhead. Indeed (as we made mention in the Outlines of Divinity), if any one deny that such utterance refers to the whole Godhead, he blasphemeth and profanely dares to divide the Absolute and Supreme Unity. We must, then, take them as referring unto the entire Godhead. For not only did the goodly Word Himself say: " I am Good,"[4] but

[1] περὶ ἡνωμένης καὶ διακεκριμένης θεολογίας καὶ τίς ἡ θεία ἕνωσις καὶ διάκρισις.

[2] The point of this section is that God's Nature is not a sum total of separate Attributes. Therefore when we say that the Scriptural titles of God are only symbols and that the ultimate Godhead transcends them, we do not mean that they express only a part of His Nature (for His Nature has no parts), but that they dimly suggest His whole Nature. Hence, too, we cannot say that some of God's titles belong only to one separate Person of the Trinity and others only to the other Persons severally—*e. g.* The Trinity, and not the Father alone, is the Creator of the world. "The one world was made by the Father, through the Son, in the Holy Ghost" (St. Aug., *Com. on St. John,* Tr. XX. 9).

[3] The title "Good" is applied to the whole Godhead. And if that title, then others too. Cf. Matt. xix. 17.

[4] John x. 11.

also one of the inspired prophets speaks of the Spirit
as Good.[1]   So, too, of the words " I Am that I Am."[2]
If, instead of applying these to the whole Godhead,
they wrest them to include only one part Thereof,
how will they explain such passages as : " Thus saith
He that is and was and is to come, the Almighty,"[3]
or : " Thou art the same,"[4] or " The Spirit of Truth
that is, and that proceedeth from the Father"?[5]
And if they deny that the whole Godhead is Life,
how can that Sacred Word be true Which declared :
" As the Father raiseth the dead and quickeneth
them, even so the Son quickeneth whom He will,"[6]
and also, " It is the Spirit that quickeneth "?[7]   And
as to the Dominion over the whole world belonging
to the whole Godhead, it is impossible, methinks, to
say (as far as concerns the Paternal and the Filial
Godhead) how often in the Scriptures the Name of
" Lord " is repeated as belonging both to the Father
and to the Son : moreover the Spirit, too, is Lord.[8]
And the Names " Fair " and " Wise " are given to
the whole Godhead ; and all the Names that belong
to the whole Godhead (*e.g.* " Deifying Virtue " and
" Cause ") Scripture introduces into all its praises of
the Supreme Godhead comprehensively, as when it
saith that "all things are from God,"[9] and more in
detail, as when it saith that " through Him are and to
Him are all things created,"[10] that " all things subsist
in Him," [11] and that " Thou shalt send forth Thy Spirit
and they shall be created."[12]   And, to sum it all in brief,

---

[1] Ps. cxliii. 10.   This is a further argument arising out of what has
been said above.   The point here is that we cannot limit the title
"Good" to one Person of the Trinity.   (The notion that the Father
is stern and the Son mollifies His sternness is false.)   The rest of the
section takes other titles and shows how they are common to all Three
Persons of the Trinity.

[2] Ex. iii. 14.
[3] Rev. i. 4.
[4] Ps. cii. 27.
[5] John xv. 26.
[6] John v. 21.
[7] John vi. 63.
[8] 2 Cor. iii. 17.
[9] 1 Chron. xxix. 14.
[10] Rom. xi. 36.
[11] *Ibid.*
[12] Ps. civ. 30.

the Divine Word Himself declared : "I and the Father are one," [1] and " All things that the Father hath are mine," [2] and " All mine are thine, and thine are mine." [3] And again, all that belongeth to the Father and to Himself He also ascribes in the Common Unity to the Divine Spirit, viz. the Divine operations, the worship, the originating and inexhaustible creativeness and the ministration of the bountiful gifts. And, methinks, that none of those nurtured in the Divine Scriptures will, except through perversity, gainsay it, that the Divine Attributes in their true and Divine signification all belong to the entire Deity. And, therefore, having here briefly and partially (and more at large elsewhere) given from the Scriptures the proof and definition of this matter, we intend that whatever title of God's Entire Nature we endeavour to explain be understood as referring to the Godhead in Its entirety.

2. And if any one say that we herein are introducing a confusion of all distinctions in the Deity,[4] we for our part opine that such his argument is not sufficient even to persuade himself. For if he is one utterly at enmity with the Scriptures, he will also be altogether far from our Philosophy ; and if he recks not of the Holy Wisdom drawn from the Scriptures, how can he reckon aught of that method by which we would conduct him to an understanding of things Divine ? But if he taketh Scriptural Truth as his Standard, this is the very Rule and Light by which we will (so far as in us lies) proceed straight to our defence, and will declare that the Sacred Science sometimes employs a method of Undifference and sometimes one of Differentiation ; and that we must neither disjoin those things which are Undifferenced

---

[1] John x. 30.   [2] John xvi. 15.   [3] John xvii. 10.
[4] *i. e.* That we are seeking to destroy the distinction between the Persons of the Trinity.

nor confuse those which are Differentiated; but following the Sacred Science to the best of our powers,
we must lift up our eyes towards the Divine Rays;
for, receiving thence the Divine Revelations as a
noble Standard of Truth, we strive to preserve its
treasure in ourselves without addition, diminution,
or distortion, and in thus preserving the Scriptures,
we also are preserved, and are moreover enabled by
the same to the end that we may still preserve them
and be by them preserved.

3. Now Undifferenced Names belong to the entire
Godhead [1] (as we showed more fully from the Scriptures in the Outlines of Divinity). To this class
belong the following: " Super-Excellent," " Super-
Divine," " Super-Essential," " Super-Vital," " Supra-
Sapient," and thereto all those titles wherein the
negative expresses excess; moreover, all those titles
which have a causal sense, such as " Good," " Fair,"
" Existent," " Lifegiving," " Wise," and whatever titles
are ascribed to the Cause of all good things from
Its bountiful gifts.[2] The differentiated Names, on
the other hand, are the Super-Essential names and
connotations of " Father," " Son," and " Spirit." In
these cases the titles cannot be interchanged, nor are
they held in common. Again, besides this, the perfect
and unchangeable subsistence of Jesus in our nature
is differentiated, and so are all the mysteries of Love
and Being therein displayed.[3]

[1] The method of Undifference applies to the *ultimate* Godhead, that
of Differentiation to the emanating Godhead. The absolute and the
relative planes of Being both belong to God. On the absolute plane
all distinctions are transcended, and the Persons exist in a manner in
which They would appear to us to be merged, but on the relative
plane we see that They are eternally distinct. See Intr., p. 8.

[2] Because we see things which are good, fair, existent, etc., we
apply to God, their ultimate Cause, the titles "Good," "Fair,"
"Existent," etc. See p. 36, n. 6.

[3] *i. e.* Only the Second Person was Incarnate, was crucified, etc.
"Mysteries of Love and Being" = Φιλανθρωπίας οὐσιώδη μυστήρια.

4. But needs must we, methinks, go deeper into the matter and thoroughly explain the difference between Undifference and Differentiation as concerning God, in order that our whole Discourse may be made clear, and, being free from all doubtfulness and obscurity, may (to the best of our powers) give a distinct, plain, and orderly statement of the matter. For, as I said elsewhere, the Initiates of our Divine Tradition designate the Undifferenced Attributes of the Transcendently Ineffable and Unknowable Permanence as hidden, incommunicable Ultimates, but the beneficent Differentiations of the Supreme Godhead, they call Emanations[1] and Manifestations; and following the Holy Scripture they declare that some Attributes belong especially to Undifference, and some, on the other hand, to Differentiation.[2] For instance, they say concerning the Divine Unity, or Super-Essence, that the undivided Trinity holds in a common Unity without distinction Its Subsistence beyond Being, Its Godhead beyond Deity, Its Goodness beyond Excel-

---

[1] προόδους τε καὶ ἐκφάνσεις,—sc. the Persons of the Trinity. See Intr., p. 16.

[2] The received text reads: Φᾶσι . . . καὶ τῆς εἰρημένης ἐνώσεως ἴδια καὶ αὖθις τῆς διακρίσεως εἶναί τινας ἰδικὰς καὶ ἑνώσεις καὶ διακρίσεις. This, as it stands, must be translated: "They say that certain qualities belong to the said Undifference, and that to Differentiation, on the other hand, belong certain principles of Unity and principles of Differentiation." This would mean that the Persons of the Trinity, though distinct from Each Other, yet have a Common Unity, or else that Each has a Unity of Its Own making It distinct from the Other Persons.

I have ventured, however, to emend the text by omitting the last six words and making the sentence end at εἶναι. I believe the last six words have crept in from a marginal gloss or variant, which ran (I imagine) as follows:—εἶναί τινας ἰδικὰς κ.τ.λ. If the MS. belonged to a family having seventeen or eighteen letters to a column the εἶναι after διακρίσεως would end a line, since there are 571 letters from the beginning of the chapter to the end of that word. Hence it would easily be confused with the εἶναι at the beginning of the gloss, which would thus creep into the text. And, since the added words amount to thirty-four letters, they would exactly fill two lines, thus making the interpolation easier. For the meaning, see Intr., p. 6 f.

lence; the Identity, surpassing all things, of Its transcendently Individual Nature; Its Oneness above Unity; Its Namelessness and Multiplicity of Names; Its Unknowableness and perfect Intelligibility; Its universal Affirmation [1] and universal Negation in a state above all Affirmation and Negation,[2] and that It possesses the mutual Abiding and Indwelling (as it were) of Its indivisibly supreme Persons in an utterly Undifferentiated and Transcendent Unity, and yet without any confusion [3] even as the lights of lamps (to use visible and homely similes) being in one house and wholly interpenetrating one another, severally possess a clear and absolute distinction each from each, and are by their distinctions united into one, and in their unity are kept distinct. Even so do we see, when there are many lamps in a house, how that the lights of them all are unified into one undifferentiated light, so that there shineth forth from them one indivisible brightness; and no one, methinks, could separate the light of one particular lamp from the others, in isolation from the air which embraces them all, nor could he see one light without another, inasmuch as, without confusion, they yet are wholly commingled.

Yea, if any one takes out of the dwelling one of the burning lamps, all its own particular light will therewith depart from the place without either carrying off in itself aught of the other lights or bequeathing any of its own brightness to the rest. For, as

---

[1] Cf. *Myst. Theol.* I. 2. This universal Affirmation is not pantheism because evil, as such, is held to be non-existent. It is only all goodness that is affirmed of God, though He surpasses it. God is present in all things, but not equally in all.

[2] "Yes" implies the possibility of "No," and "No" the possibility of "Yes." Thus "Yes" and "No" belong to the relative world. God's absolute existence is beyond such antithesis. See Intr., p. 4 f.

[3] The Persons, though fused, are yet not confused because the Godhead *transcends* unity. See Intr., p. 5.

I said, the entire and complete union of the lights
one with another brought no confusion or commixture
in any parts—and that though the light is literally
embodied in the air and streams from the material
substance of fire. The Super-Essential Unity of God,
however, exceedeth (so we declare) not only the
unions of material bodies, but even those of Souls
and of Intelligences, which these Godlike and celestial
Luminaries in perfect mutual interpenetration supernaturally and without confusion possess, through
a participation corresponding to their individual
powers of participating in the All-Transcendent
Unity.[1]

5. There is, on the other hand, a Differentiation
made in the Super-Essential Doctrine of God—not
merely such as I have just mentioned (viz. that in
the very Unity, Each of the Divine Persons possesses
without confusion Its own distinct existence), but also
that the Attributes of the Super-Essential Divine
Generation are not interchangeable.[2] The Father
alone is the Source of the Super-Essential Godhead,
and the Father is not a Son, nor is the Son a Father;
for the Divine Persons all preserve, Each without
alloy, His own particular Attributes of praise. Such,
then, are the instances of Undifference and of
Differentiation in the Ineffable Unity and Subsistence
of God. And if the term "Differentiation" be also
applied to the bounteous act of Emanation whereby
the Divine Unity, brimming Itself with goodness in
the excess of Its Undifferenced Unity thus enters

[1] Material things are merged by being united (e. g. drops of water).
Souls or angels being united through love (whereby they participate in
God) are not merged but remain distinct even while being, as it were,
fused into a single spiritual unity more perfect than the fusion of water
with wine. The Persons of the Trinity are still more perfectly united
and at the same time still more utterly distinct.

[2] Two kinds of Differentiation: (1) Distinctness of Existence,
(2) Difference of Functions.

into Multiplicity,[1] yet an undifferenced unity worketh even in those differentiated acts whereby, in ceaseless communications, It bestows Being, Life, and Wisdom, and those other gifts of the all-creative Goodness in respect of which (as we behold the communications and the participants thereof) we celebrate those things wherein the creatures supernaturally participate. Yea, 'tis a common and undifferenced activity of the whole Godhead that It is wholly and entirely communicated unto each of them that share It and unto none merely in part;[2] even as the centre of a circle is shared by all the radii which surround it in a circle;[3] and as there are many impressions of a seal all sharing in the seal which is their archetype while yet this is entire, nor is it only a part thereof that belongeth unto any of them. But the Incommunicable All-creative Godhead transcends all such symbols in that It is beyond Apprehension nor hath It any other mode of communion such as to join It unto the participants.[4]

Perhaps, however, some one will say : " The seal is not entire and the same in all the printed copies." I answer that this is not due to the seal itself (for it gives itself wholly and identically to each), but the difference of the substances which share it makes the impressions of the one, entire, identical archetype to be different. For instance, if they are soft, plastic, and smooth, and have no print already, and are neither hard and resistent, nor yet melting and unstable, the imprint will be clear, plain, and per-

---

[1] D. means that the Undifferentiated Godhead is actually present in all these creative activities. It is multiplied (as it were) in Its energies, and yet It remains indivisible. See Intr., p. 17.

[2] D. here touches on the fundamental difference between spiritual and material things. Cf. Shelley : "True love has this different from gold or clay that to divide is not to take away."

[3] Plotinus uses the same illustration (*Enn.* iv. 1).

[4] D. is always on his guard against Pantheism.

manent; but if the aforesaid fitness should in aught be lacking, then the material will not take the impression and reproduce it distinctly, and other such results will follow as an unsuitable material must bring about.

6. Again, it is by a Differentiated act of God's benevolence that the Super-Essential Word should wholly and completely take Human Substance of human flesh and do and suffer all those things which, in a special and particular manner, belong to the action of His Divine Humanity. In these acts the Father and the Spirit have no share, except of course that they all share in the loving generosity of the Divine counsels and in all that transcendent Divine working of unutterable mysteries which were performed in Human Nature by Him Who as God and as the Word of God is Immutable.[1] So do we strive to differentiate the Divine Attributes, according as these Attributes are Undifferenced or Differentiated.[2]

7. Now all the grounds of these Unifications, and Differentiations in the Divine Nature which the Scriptures have revealed to us, we have explained in the Outlines of Divinity, to the best of our abilities, treating separately of each. The latter class we have philosophically unravelled and unfolded, and so have sought to guide the holy and unspotted mind to contemplate the shining truths of Scripture, while the former class we have endeavoured (in accordance with Divine Tradition) to apprehend as Mysteries in a manner beyond the activities of our minds.[3] For

[1] Redemption is a work performed by the whole Trinity through the Second Person. (So, too, is Creation. Cf. p. 65, n. 2.)

[2] *i. e.* We strive to distinguish the two planes of Being in God. Cf. Athan. Creed: "Neither confounding the Persons," etc.

[3] Undifference belongs to the ultimate Godhead, Differentiation to the distinction between the Three Persons of the Trinity. The former is the sphere of Mystical Theology, the latter is that of Dogmatic Theology. The former implies the *Via Negativa* the latter the *Via Affirmativa.*

F

all Divine things, even those that are revealed to us,
are only known by their Communications. Their
ultimate nature, which they possess in their own
original being, is beyond Mind and beyond all Being
and Knowledge.[1] For instance, if we call the Super-
Essential Mystery by the Name of "God," or "Life,"
or "Being," or "Light," or "Word," we conceive of
nothing else than the powers that stream Therefrom
to us bestowing Godhead, Being, Life or Wisdom ;[2]
while that Mystery Itself we strive to apprehend by
casting aside all the activities of our mind, since
we behold no Deification,[3] or Life, or Being, which
exactly resembles the altogether and utterly Transcendent Cause of all things. Again, that the Father
is Originating Godhead while Jesus and the Spirit
are (so to speak) Divine Off-shoots of the Paternal
Godhead,and, as it were, Blossoms and Super-Essential
Shinings Thereof we learn from Holy Scripture ; but
how these things are so we cannot say, nor yet
conceive.

8. Just so far can the powers of our minds attain
as to see that all spiritual paternity and sonship is a
gift bestowed from the all-transcendent Archetypal
Fatherhood and Sonship both upon us and also upon
the celestial Powers : whereby Godlike Minds receive

[1] Even the Differentiations finally lead us up into the Undifferenced
Godhead Where they transcend themselves. (Cf. p. 70, n. 3 and the
passage in ii. 4 about the torches.) Into that region we cannot track
them. But on the other side they flow out into creative activity, and
thus are, in some degree, revealed.

[2] These terms may be thus classified :—

Sphere of Activity.	Nature of Gift.	Form under which Giver is manifested.
(i) *Grace*	. Godhead .	"God"
(ii) *Nature.*		
(1) Material existence . .	. Being	. "Being"
(2) Vegetable and animal existence .	Life	. "Life" }"Word."
(3) Human existence . .	. Wisdom	. "Light"

[3] The doctrine of "Deification" is not a mere speculation. It
embodies an experienced fact. See Intr., p. 43.

the states and names of Gods, and Sons of Gods, and
Fathers of Gods, such paternity and sonship being
perfected in a spiritual manner (*i. e.* incorporeally,
immaterially, and invisibly) because the Divine Spirit
setteth above all invisible Immateriality and Deification, and the Father and the Son, supernaturally
transcend all spiritual fatherhood and sonship.[1] For
there is no exact similitude between the creatures
and the Creative Originals ; [2] for the creatures possess
only such images of the Creative Originals as are
possible to them, while the Originals Themselves
transcend and exceed the creatures by the very
nature of Their own Originality. To employ human
examples, we say that pleasant or painful conditions
produce in us feelings of pleasure or pain while yet
they possess not these feelings themselves ; and we
do not say that the fire which warms and burns is
itself burnt or warmed. Even so if any one says that
Very Life lives, or that Very Light is enlightened, he
will be wrong (according to my view) unless, perchance,
he were to use these terms in a different sense from
the ordinary one to mean that the qualities of created
things pre-exist, after a superlative manner as touching
their true Being in the Creative Originals.[3]

9. Even the plainest article of Divinity, namely the

[1] The act by which one spirit or soul imparts spiritual life to another
is a manifestation in time of a Mystery which is eternally perfect in the
Trinity, and would be impossible were it not ultimately rooted in that
Mystery. Just as all life draws its existence from the Divine *supra-
vitality*, so all spiritual paternity draws its existence from the Divine
supra-paternity.

[2] τὰ αἴτια—*i. e.* The Persons of the Godhead.

[3] So St. Augustine constantly teaches that God acts not in the
manner which we call activity, but by causing the creature itself to
perform the action. Thus he explains God's rest on the Seventh Day
to mean not that God Himself rested but that the creation now rested
in Him. Aristotle and his disciple, St. Thomas, teach that God
moves all things simply through being desired by them. So God
causes action without Himself acting (somewhat as fire causes warmth
without feeling it). Cf. p. 87, n. 1.

Incarnation and Birth of Jesus in Human Form, cannot be expressed by any Language or known by any Mind—not even by the first of the most exalted angels. That He took man's substance is a mysterious truth, the which we have received ; but we know not how from the Virgin's seed He was formed in another manner than is natural, nor how His dry feet supporting the solid weight of His material body He walked upon the unstable substance of the water, nor understand we any of the other things which belong to the Supernatural Nature of Jesus. Of these things I have spoken enough elsewhere ; and our renowned Teacher hath wonderfully [1] declared, in his *Elements of Divinity*, what he hath either learnt directly from the Sacred Writers, or else hath discovered from his cunning research concerning Scriptural truths through the much toil and labour which he bestowed thereon, or else hath had revealed unto him by some diviner inspiration wherein he received not only true spiritual *notions* but also true spiritual *motions*,[2] and by the kinship of his mind with them (if I may so express it) was perfected to attain without any other teacher to a mystical communion with these verities and a belief therein.[3] And to put before them in briefest compass the many blessed speculations of his ingenious mind thus speaketh he concerning Jesus in his compilation of the *Elements of Divinity*.

10. *From the* ELEMENTS OF DIVINITY, *by S. Hierotheus.*

The Universal Cause which filleth all things is the Deity of Jesus, whereof the parts are in such wise tempered to the whole that It is neither whole nor part, and yet is at the same time whole and also part,

---

[1] ὑπερφυῶς. The proper meaning of ὑπερφυής in the Dionysian writings appears to be "supernatural."

[2] οὐ μόνον μαθὼν ἀλλὰ καὶ παθὼν τὰ θεῖα.

[3] πρὸς τὴν ἀδίδακτον αὐτῶν καὶ μυστικὴν ἀποτελεσθεὶς ἕνωσιν καὶ πίστιν.

containing in Its all-embracing unity both part and whole, and being transcendent and antecedent to both.[1] This Deity is perfect in those Beings that are imperfect as a Fount of Perfection ; [2] It is Perfectionless [3] in those that are perfect as transcending and anticipating their Perfection ; It is the Form producing Form in the formless, as a Fount of every form ; and it is Formless in the Forms, as being beyond all form ; It is the Being that pervades all beings at once though not affected by them ; [4] and It is Super-Essential, as transcending every being ; It sets all bounds of Authority and Order, and yet It has Its seal beyond all Authority and Order.[5] It is the Measure of the Universe ; [6] and it is Eternity, and above Eternity and before Eternity.[7] It is an

---

[1] Being beyond Unity the Godhead is, of course, beyond the categories of whole and part. The Godhead is not a Whole because It is indivisible, nor a Part because there is nothing, on the ultimate plane, outside It. Yet It is a Whole because It includes the true existence of all things, and is Partitive because It contains the principle of separate Individuality whereby Christ possesses a Human Soul distinct from all other human souls, and whereby, too, we possess distinct and separate souls.

[2] God is in us even before we are in Him. Cf. Luke xvii. 21. Cf. St. Aug., "Thou wast within ; I was without." Also cf. c. i. 3 ; c. iii. i : "For the Trinity," etc. See Intr., p. 6 on the use of the word "outside."

[3] Perfection implies an object or purpose achieved. Hence it implies a distinction between self and not self. The Godhead is beyond such a distinction. Compared with imperfection, It is perfect ; compared with perfection, It is perfectionless ($\dot{\alpha}\tau\epsilon\lambda\dot{\eta}s$), or, rather, beyond Perfection ($\dot{\upsilon}\pi\epsilon\rho\tau\epsilon\lambda\dot{\eta}s$) and before it ($\pi\rho\sigma\tau\epsilon\lambda\epsilon\iota\sigma s$), just as compared with impersonal things It is personal, and compared with personality It is non-personal, or, rather, supra-personal.

[4] Cf. p. 75, n. 3.

[5] Cf. St. Paul on the Law and the Spirit. The Law is deposited, as it were, by the Spirit : and yet the Law cramps the Spirit, and the Spirit must break loose from this bondage.

[6] i. e. It gives the universe its bounds and distinctions.

[7] Eternity, in the sense of "Very Eternity" ($\alpha\dot{\upsilon}\tau\sigma\alpha\iota\dot{\omega}\nu$), is an Emanation of the Godhead—a distinct view of Its transcendent state (cf. Intr., p. 17). It is the Divine Rest taken in the abstract, as Very Life is

Abundance in those Beings that lack, and a Super-
Abundance in those that abound; unutterable,
ineffable; beyond Mind, beyond Life, beyond Being;
It supernaturally possesses the supernatural and
super-essentially possesses the super-essential.[1] And
since that Supra-Divine Being hath in loving kindness
come down from thence unto the Natural Estate, and
verily took substance and assumed the name of Man
(we must speak with reverence of those things which
we utter beyond human thought and language), even
in this act He possesses His Supernatural and Super-
Essential Existence—not only in that He hath
without change or confusion of Attributes shared
in our human lot while remaining unaffected by that
unutterable Self-Emptying as regards the fullness of
His Godhead, but also because (most wonderful of all
wonders!) He passed in His Supernatural and Super-
Essential state through conditions of Nature and
Being, and receiving from us all things that are ours,
exalted them far above us.[2]

11. So much for these matters. Now let us
proceed to the object of our discussion and endeavour
to explain the Common and Undifferenced Names
belonging to God's Differentiated Being.[3] And, that
the subject of our investigation may be clearly defined beforehand, we give the name of Divine Differen-

---

perhaps the Divine Motion taken in the abstract. The Godhead includes both Rest and Motion by transcending them.

[1] Behind Nature are certain higher supernatural possibilities (which
are manifested, *e. g.*, in the Miracles of·Christ and His Disciples), and
beyond our personalities there is a mystery which is greater than our
finite selves, and yet, in a sense, is our true selves. The Godhead
possesses in Itself the supernatural possibilities of Nature and the
supra-personal possibilities of our personalities.

[2] *i. e.* Christ did not merely keep His Godhead parallel, as it were,
with His Manhood, but brought It into His Manhood and so exalted
the Manhood.

[3] *i. e.* Let us explain what are the Names which belong indivisibly to
all Three Persons of the Trinity.

tiation (as was said) to the beneficent Emanations of the Supreme Godhead.[1] For bestowing upon all things and supernally infusing Its Communications unto the goodly Universe, It becomes differentiated without loss of Undifference ;[2] and multiplied without loss of Unity ; from Its Oneness it becomes manifold while yet remaining within Itself. For example, since God is super-essentially Existent and bestows existence upon all things that are, and brings the world into being, that single Existence of His is said to become manifold through bringing forth the many existences from Itself, while yet He remains One in the act of Self-Multiplication ; Undifferenced throughout the process of Emanation, and Full in the emptying process of Differentiation ; Super-Essentially transcending the Being of all things, and guiding the whole world onwards by an indivisible act, and pouring forth without diminution His indefectible bounties. Yea, being One and communicating of His Unity both unto every part of the world and also unto the whole, both unto that which is one and unto that which is many, He is One in an unchangeable and super-essential manner, being neither an unit in the multiplicity of things nor yet the sum total of such units. Indeed, He is not an unity in this sense, and doth not participate in unity nor possess it ;[3] but He is an Unity in a manner far

---

[1] The word "Emanation" is here used in its very widest sense as including (1) the Persons of the Trinity, (2) Their creative activity as manifested in the Universal and the Particular stream of energy. See Intr., p. 17. The Differentiated Being of the Trinity underlies all the Differentiations of the creative process. The Trinity is differentiated on the plane of Eternity ; then It emanates or energizes on the temporal plane, and thus It is manifested in all the differentiations of the universe, (especially in deified souls).

[2] God is indivisibly present in each separate deified soul (see *supra*, p. 71), the sentence beginning : "And if the term 'Differentiation' be also applied to the bounteous act," etc.

[3] These two phrases well express the meaning of the title "Beyond

different from this, above all unity which is in the world; yea, He is an Indivisible Plurality, insatiable yet brim-full, producing, perfecting, and maintaining all unity and plurality. Moreover, since many, through Deification from Him, are made Gods [1] (so far as the Godlike capacity of each allows), there thus appears to be what is called a Differentiation [2] and a Reduplication of the One God, yet none the less He is the primal God, the Supra-Divine and Super-Essentially One God, who dwells Indivisibly within the separate and individual things, being an Un-differenced Unity in Himself and without any com-mixture or multiplication through His contact with the Many. [3] And supernaturally perceiving this, thus speaketh (by inspiration, in his holy writings) that Guide unto Divine illumination by whom both we and our teacher are led, that mighty man in things Divine, that Luminary of the world. For though (saith he) there be that are called gods, whether in heaven or in earth (as there be gods many and lords many). But to us there is but one God, the Father, of whom are all things, and we in Him, and one Lord Jesus Christ, by whom are all things, and we by Him. For in divine things the undifferenced Unities are of more might than the Differentiations [4] and hold the foremost place and retain their state of Undifference even after the One has, without departing from Its oneness, entered into Differentiation. These Differ-entiations or beneficent Emanations of the whole

Unity " (ὑπερηνωμένη), which I have generally translated, like ἡνωμένη, as "Undifferenced."

[1] τῇ ἐξ αὐτοῦ θεώσει . . . θεῶν πολλῶν γιγνομένων. See Intr., p. 43.

[2] Cf. p. 71, n. 1.

[3] The fullness of God's Unity is manifested, (1) in all the multiplicity of the material world, (2) after a higher manner in the deified souls of men and in angels.

[4] Each deified soul is a differentiation of God (cf. p. 71, n. 1); yet the Unity of God transcends them all, even after God has thus poured Himself into them.

Godhead—whereby Its Undifferenced Nature is
shared in common [1]—we shall (so far as in us lies)
endeavour to describe from the Divine Names which
reveal them in the Scriptures, having now made this
clear beforehand (as hath been said) : that every Name
of the Divine beneficent Activity unto whichever of
the Divine Persons it is applied, must be taken as
belonging, without distinction, to the whole entirety
of the Godhead. [2]

CHAPTER III

*What is the power of Prayer ?   Also concerning the Blessed
Hierotheus and concerning Reverence and the Writing of
Divinity.*

1. AND first of all, if it like thee, let us consider the
highest Name, even " Goodness," by which all the
Emanations of God are conjointly revealed. [3]   And
let us begin with an invocation of the Trinity, the
Which, as It surpasseth Goodness, and is the Source
of all goodness, doth reveal all conjoined together Its
own good providences. [4]   For we must first lift up our
minds in prayer unto the Primal Goodness, and by
drawing nearer Thereunto, we must thus be initiated
into the mystery of those good gifts which are rooted
in Its being.   For the Trinity is nigh unto all things,
and yet not all things are nigh unto It. [5]   And when
we call upon It with holy prayers and unspotted

---

[1] *i. e.* These active Manifestations whereby God enters into each part
of the universe, yet without loss of Unity.

[2] See the beginning of this chapter.

[3] All God's activities are good.

[4] The particular activities of God exist as one Act in Him, cf. p. 79,
n. 2.   So St. Thomas (following Aristotle) calls Him *Actus Purus.*

[5] Cf. p. 77, n. 1.

mind and with our souls prepared for union with
God, then are we also nigh Thereto ; for It is not in
space, so as to be absent from any spot, or to move
from one position to another.[1]   Nay, to speak of It
as omnipresent doth not express Its all-transcendent
all-embracing Infinitude.[2]   Let us then press on in
prayer, looking upwards to the Divine benignant
Rays, even as if a resplendent cord were hanging
from the height of heaven unto this world below, and
we, by seizing it with alternate hands in one advance,
appeared to pull it down ; but in very truth
instead of drawing down the rope (the same being
already nigh us above and below), we were ourselves
being drawn upwards to the higher Refulgence of the
resplendent Rays.   Or even as, having embarked on
a ship and clinging to the cables, the which being
stretched out from some rock unto us, presented
themselves (as it were) for us to lay hold upon them,
we should not be drawing the rock towards ourselves,
but should, in very truth, be drawing ourselves and
the vessel towards the rock ; as also, conversely, if
any one standing upon the vessel pushes away the
rock that is on the shore, he will not affect the rock
(which stands immovable) but will separate himself
therefrom, and the more he pushes it so much the
more will he be staving himself away.   Hence, before
every endeavour, more especially if the subject be
Divinity, must we begin with prayer : not as though
we would pull down to ourselves that Power which is

---

[1] This is profound.   Spatial metaphors are always dangerous, though
unavoidable, in Theology.   In space if A is touching B then B must be
touching A.   In the spiritual world this is not so.   God is near me (or
rather *in* me), and yet I may be far from God *because I may be far from
my own true self.*   I must seek my true self where it *is*, in God.   It is
the paradox of Personality that my true self is outside my self and I can
only gain it by casting aside this counterfeit " self."   Cf. p. 77, n. 1,
and Intr., p. 15.

[2] Even the word " omnipresent" suggests that God is in space,
whereas really His existence is non-spatial.

nigh both everywhere and nowhere, but that, by these remembrances and invocations of God, we may commend and unite ourselves Thereunto.

2. Now perhaps there is need of an explanation why, when our renowned teacher Hierotheus hath compiled[1] his wonderful *Elements of Divinity*, we have composed other Tractates of Divinity, and now are writing this present as if his work were not sufficient. Now if he had professed to deal in an ordered system with all questions of Divinity, and had gone through the whole sum of Divinity with an exposition of every branch, we should not have gone so far in madness or folly as to suppose that we could touch these problems with a diviner insight than he, nor would we have cared to waste our time in a vain repetition of those same truths; more especially since it would be an injury to a teacher whom we love were we thus to claim for ourselves the famous speculations and expositions of a man who, next to Paul the Divine, hath been our chief preceptor. But since, in his lofty " Instructions on Divinity," he gave us comprehensive and pregnant definitions fitted to our understanding, and to that of such amongst us as were teachers of the newly initiated souls, and bade us unravel and explain with whatever powers of reason we possessed, the comprehensive and compact skeins of thought spun by his mighty intellect; and since thou hast thyself oftentimes urged us so to do, and hast remitted his treatise to us as too sublime for comprehension, therefore we, while setting him apart (as a teacher of advanced and perfect spirits) for those above the commonalty, and as a kind of second Scriptures worthy to follow the Inspired Writings, will yet teach Divine Truths, according to our capacity, unto those who are our peers. For if solid food is suited

---

[1] τὰς θεολογικὰς στοιχειώσεις ὑπερφυῶς συναγαγόντος.

only to the perfect, what degree of perfection would it need to give this food to others? Wherefore we are right in saying that the direct study of the spiritual [1] Scriptures and the comprehensive teaching of them need advanced capacities, while the understanding and the learning of the matter which contribute thereto is suited to the inferior Initiators and Initiates.[2] We have, however, carefully observed the principle : Whatsoever things our Divine Preceptor has throughly dealt with and made clearly manifest we have never in any wise ventured thereon, for fear of repetition, nor given the same explanation of the passage whereof he treated. For [3] even among our inspired Hierarchs (when, as thou knowest, we with him and many of our holy brethren met together to behold that mortal body, Source of Life, which received the Incarnate God,[4] and James, the brother of God, was there, and Peter, the chief and highest of the Sacred Writers, and then, having beheld it, all the Hierarchs there present celebrated, according to the power of each, the omnipotent goodness of the Divine weakness): on that occasion, I say, he surpassed all the Initiates next to the Divine Writers,

---

[1] Or "intelligible" (νοητῶν). Cf. p. 52, n. 1. The Scriptures are expressed in symbolic terms which our minds can grasp. Hierotheus was inspired to penetrate to the ultimate truth enshrined in these symbols. Thus he was able not only to assimilate this solid food himself but also to give it to others. Apparently Hierotheus passed through certain extraordinary psychic experiences, which are described in his writings. These particular experiences D. has not himself passed through. But he believes that his own teaching may clear the ground, and so be a preliminary to such flights. He is chiefly explaining principles, but these principles may lead the way to a true experience. St. Paul and other Scriptural writers experienced such extraordinary psychic states, though they do not speak of them in the extravagant terms apparently used by Hierotheus. Cf. 2 Cor. xii. 2–4.

[2] τοῦ ὑφειμένοις καθιερωταῖς καὶ ἱερωμένοις.

[3] sc. It would be an impiety to do so, for he is almost equal to the Scriptural Writers, as he showed when he met with them to view the body of the B. V. M.

[4] Cf. p. 1, n. 1.

yea, he was wholly transported, was wholly outside of himself, and was so moved by a communion with those Mysteries he was celebrating, that all who heard him and saw him and knew him (or rather knew him not) deemed him to be rapt of God and endued with utterance Divine. But why should I tell thee of the divine things that were uttered in that place ? For, unless I have forgotten who I am, I know that I have often heard from thee certain fragments of those enraptured praises ; so earnest hast thou been with all thy soul to follow heavenly things.

3. But, to say nothing of those mystical experiences (since they cannot be told unto the world, and since thou knowest them well), when it behoved us to communicate these things unto the world and to bring all whom we might unto that holy knowledge we possessed, how he surpassed nearly all the holy teachers in the time he devoted to the task, in pureness of mind, in exactness of exposition, and in all other holy qualities, to such a degree that we could not attempt to gaze upon such spiritual radiance. For we are conscious in ourselves and well aware that we cannot sufficiently perceive those Divine Truths which are granted to man's perception, nor can we declare and utter those elements of Divine Knowledge which are given unto man to speak. We fall very short of that understanding which the Divine men possessed concerning heavenly truths, and verily, from excess of reverence, we should not have ventured to listen, or give utterance to any truths of Divine philosophy, were it not that we are convinced in our mind that such knowledge of Divine Truth as is possible must not be disregarded. This conviction was wrought within us, not only by the natural impulse of our minds, which yearn and strive for such vision of supernatural things as may be

attained, but also by the holy ordinance of Divine
Law itself, which, while it bids us not to busy ourselves
in things beyond us because such things are both
beyond our merits and also unattainable,[1] yet
earnestly exhorts us to learn all things within our
reach, which are granted and allowed us, and also
generously to impart these treasures unto others.[2]
In obedience to these behests we, ceasing not through
weariness or want of courage in such search for
Divine Truth as is possible, yea, and not daring to
leave without assistance those who possess not a
greater power of contemplation than ourselves, have
set ourselves to the task of composition, in no vain
attempt to introduce fresh teaching, but only seeking
by more minute and detailed investigations to make
more clear and plain that which the true Hierotheus
hath said in brief.

CHAPTER IV

*Concerning "Good," "Light," "Beautiful," "Desire,"
"Ecstasy," "Jealousy." Also that Evil is neither existent
nor sprung from anything existent nor inherent in existent
things.*

1. Now let us consider the name of "Good" which
the Sacred Writers apply to the Supra-Divine Godhead in a transcendent manner, calling the Supreme
Divine Existence Itself "Goodness" (as it seems to
me) in a sense that separates It from the whole
creation, and meaning, by this term, to indicate that
the Good, under the form of Good-Being,[3] extends
Its goodness by the very fact of Its existence unto all

---

[1] Ecclus. iii. 21 ; Ps. cxxxi. 1.   [2] 2 Tim. ii. 2.
[3] ὡς οὐσιῶδες ἀγαθόν.

things.[1] For as our sun, through no choice or deliberation, but by the very fact of its existence, gives light to all those things which have any inherent power of sharing its illumination, even so the Good (which is above the sun, as the transcendent archetype by the very mode of its existence is above its faded image) sends forth upon all things according to their receptive powers, the rays of Its undivided Goodness. Through these all Spiritual Beings and faculties and activities (whether perceived or percipient[2]) began; through these they exist and possess a life incapable of failure or diminution, and are untainted by any corruption or death or materiality or birth, being separate above all instability and flux and restlessness of change. And whereas they are bodiless and immaterial they are perceived by our minds, and whereas they are minds themselves, they possess a supernatural perception and receive an illumination (after their own manner) concerning the hidden nature of things,[3] from whence they pass on their own knowledge to other kindred spirits. Their rest is in the Divine Goodness, wherein they are grounded, and This Goodness maintains them and protects them and feasts them with Its good things. Through desiring this they possess their being and their blessedness, and, being conformed thereto (according

---

[1] God's activity cannot be distinguished from Himself. Cf. p. 81, n. 4. God acts simply by being what He is—by being Good. This fits in with the doctrine that He creates the world as being the Object of its desire. He *attracts* it into existence.

[2] αἱ νοηταὶ καὶ νοεραὶ πᾶσαι καὶ οὐσίαι καὶ δυνάμεις καὶ ἐνέργειαι. Angels and men are percipient Essences; their powers when quiescent or dormant on the one hand and active on the other are respectively percipient faculties and activities. But angels and men with their faculties and activities can also be perceived. Cf. next sentence.

[3] This doctrine may be based on some psychic experience enjoyed by D. or recounted to him. George Fox received an experience of this kind in which he had an intuitive knowledge concerning the hidden properties of plants. See his Diary near the beginning.

to their powers), they are goodly, and, as the Divine Law commands, pass on to those that are below them, of the gifts which have come unto them from the Good.

2. Hence have they their celestial orders, their self-unities, their mutual indwellings, their distinct Differences, the faculties which raise the lower unto the higher ranks, the providences of the higher for those beneath them; their preservation of the properties belonging to each faculty, their unchanging introversions,[1] their constancy and elevation in their search for the Good, and all the other qualities which we have described in our book concerning the Properties and Orders of the Angels.[2] Moreover all things appertaining to the Celestial Hierarchy, the angelic Purifications, the Illuminations and the attainments which perfect them in all angelic perfection and come from the all-creative and originating Goodness, from whence it was given to them to possess their created goodness, and to manifest the Secret Goodness in themselves, and so to be (as it were) the angelic Evangelists of the Divine Silence and to stand forth as shining lights revealing Him that is within the shrine. And next those sacred and holy Minds, men's souls and all the excellences that belong to souls derive their being from the Super-Excellent Goodness. So do they possess intelligence; so do they preserve their living being[3] immortal; so is it they exist at all, and can, by straining towards the living angelic powers, through

---

[1] Lit. "Revolutions." (αἱ . . . περὶ ἑαυτὰς ἀμετάπτωτοι συνελίξεις.) In Dante's *Paradiso* the souls of the Redeemed all move with a circular motion. This symbolizes an activity of spiritual concentration. Cf. iv. 8, 9.

[2] The *Celestial Hierarchy* is among D.'s extant works. It is referred to by Dante and was the chief source of mediæval angelology.

[3] τὴν οὐσιώδη ζωήν—*i. e.* life as such, mere life, the life which they share with animals and plants.

their good guidance mount towards the Bounteous Origin of all things ; so can they (according to their measure) participate in the illuminations which stream from above and share the bounteous gift (as far as their power extends) and attain all the other privileges which we have recounted in our book, *Concerning the Soul.* Yea, and the same is true, if it must needs be said, concerning even the irrational souls, or living creatures, which cleave the air, or tread the earth, or crawl upon the ground, and those which live among the waters or possess an amphibious life, and all that live buried and covered in the earth—in a word all that possess a sensitive soul or life. All these are endowed with soul and life because the Good exists. And all plants derive from the Good that life which gives them nourishment and motion, and even whatsoever has no life or soul exists through the Good, and thus came into the estate of being.[1]

3. Now if the Good is above all things (as indeed It is) Its Formless Nature produces all-form ; and in It alone Not-Being is an excess of Being,[2] and Lifelessness an excess of Life and Its Mindless state is an excess of Wisdom,[3] and all the Attributes of

---

[1] The existence of the whole creation—angels, men, animals, and vegetables, dead matter—is in the Good. It has not, in the ordinary sense, made them, but they are grounded in It and draw their existence from it and would not exist but for it. They exist not through any particular activity It exerts but solely because It *Is.*

[2] "Being" implies finite relations ; for one thing must be distinguished from another. If a thing is itself, it is not something else ; this thing is not that. The Good is beyond this distinction, for nothing (on the ultimate plane) is outside It. See Intr., p. 5.

[3] This apparently profitless speculation really suggests profound spiritual mysteries. Love is the one reality and love is self-realization through self-sacrifice. We must lose our life to find it. We must, through the excess of spiritual life within us, seek to be (as it were) lifeless, so that this excess of life may still be ours. And such was the Incarnate Life of Christ and such is the Life of God in eternity. So too the wisdom of Christ is, from a worldly point of view, foolishness.

G

the Good we express in a transcendent manner by
negative images.[1] And if it is reverent so to say,
even that which *is not* desires the all-transcendent
Good and struggles itself, by its denial of all things,
to find its rest in the Good which verily transcends
all being.

4. Nay, even the foundation and the boundaries of the heavens (as we forgot to say while

---

For worldly wisdom = self-seeking, but the Wisdom of Christ = self-
abandonment. In fact Heavenly Wisdom = Love. Cf. 1 Cor. i. 25 ;
iii. 18, 19.

[1] That which *Is Not* = Evil (*vide infra* in this chapter). Cf. Intr.,
p. 20. The Good is Non-Existent as being beyond existence ; evil is
non-existent as being contrary to it. Thus evil is by its very nature
trying as it were to be Good.

This also looks like a barren paradox and yet it may contain a spiritual
truth. Evil is, in the words of Goethe, "the spirit that denies" : It
is destructive, *e.g.* injustice, cruelty, immorality, etc., undermine or
overwhelm civilization and so destroy it. But the Good supersedes
civilization and so in a sense destroys it. Cf. the eschatological teaching of Christ. Civilization, art, morality, etc., are good so far as they
go, but imperfect. Being halfway, as it were, between Good and
evil, and being of necessity neither wholly the one nor wholly the
other, they must disappear wherever the one or the other completely
triumphs. Christ's teaching on Marriage illustrates this. Marriage
is sacred, and divorce is wrong, because it seeks to abolish Marriage.
And yet Marriage is finally abolished in heaven. St. Paul's antithesis
of Law and Spirit is another example. The Law is good and yet is
not the Good. Sin is contrary to the Law, but the Spirit is contrary
to the Law in another sense and so supersedes it. So too with art. A
modern vandal is indifferent to beauty because he is below it, a
Mediæval Saint became sometimes indifferent to beauty by rising to a
super-sensuous plane above it. Greek idolatry is a higher thing than
Calvinism, but the Christianity of the New Testament is a higher
thing than Greek idolatry. The Saints sometimes employ negatives
in one sense and those who are not saints employ the same negatives
in another ; whence disaster. Much of Nietzsche's language (*e. g.*
the phrase "Beyond Good and Evil") might have been used by a
Mediæval Christian Mystic ; but Nietzsche did not generally mean
what the Christian Mystic would have meant by it. Soo too with
pain. All pain is in itself bad, being a negation of our personality.
And yet a self-abnegation springing from Love which bravely bears
pain is the highest kind of Good. "The devil . . . put it into the heart
of Judas to betray" Christ, and yet the Passion was in accordance with
"the determinate counsel and foreknowledge of God."

thinking of other matters) owe their origin to
the Good. Such is this universe, which lessens not
nor grows, and such the noiseless movements (if
noiseless they be)[1] of the vast heavenly revolution,
and such the starry orders whose light is fixed as
an ornament of heaven, and such the various wander-
ings of certain stars—especially the repeated and
returning orbits of those two luminaries to which
the Scripture giveth the name of "Great,"[2] whereby
we reckon our days and nights and months and
years; which define the round of time and temporal
events and give them measurement, sequence, and
cohesion. And what shall I say concerning the
sun's rays considered in themselves? From the
Good comes the light which is an image of Goodness; wherefore the Good is described by the name
of "Light," being the archetype thereof which is
revealed in that image. For as the Goodness of the
all-transcendent Godhead reaches from the highest
and most perfect forms of being unto the lowest,
and still is beyond them all, remaining superior to
those above and retaining those below in its embrace,
and so gives light to all things that can receive It,
and creates and vitalizes and maintains and perfects
them, and is the Measure[3] of the Universe and its
Eternity,[4] its Numerical Principle,[5] its Order, its

---

[1] εἰ οὕτω χρὴ φάναι. D. is alluding to the ancient belief in the
Music of the Spheres.

[2] Gen. i. 16.

[3] μέτρον. All things have their pre-existent limits in the Super-
Essence.

[4] αἰών—i.e. The Permanent Principle underlying its temporal process.
This and the next phrase explain what is meant by the words "the
Measure of the universe." The Good sets bounds to the world
(1) temporally, because Eternity is the Fount of Time, (2) spatially,
because Transcendent Unity is the Fount of Number. All temporal
things are permanent in God; and all diversities are one in Him.

[5] All number has its roots in the Good. Elsewhere D. says that
the Good being *beyond* Unity, is a Multiplicity as well as an Unity.
Cf. Intr., p. 5.

Embracing Power, its Cause and its End:[1] even so this great, all-bright and ever-shining sun, which is the visible image of the Divine Goodness, faintly re-echoing the activity of the Good, illumines all things that can receive its light while retaining the utter simplicity of light, and expands above and below throughout the visible world the beams of its own radiance. And if there is aught that does not share them, this is not due to any weakness or deficiency in its distribution of the light, but is due to the unreceptiveness of those creatures which do not attain sufficient singleness to participate therein. For verily the light passeth over many such substances and enlightens those which are beyond them, and there is no visible thing unto which the light reacheth not in the exceeding greatness of its proper radiance.[2] Yea, and it contributes to the birth of material bodies and brings them unto life, and nourishes them that they may grow, and perfects and purifies and renews them. And the light is the measure and the numerical principle of seasons and of days and of all our earthly Time; for 'tis the selfsame light (though then without a form) which, Moses the Divine declares, marked even that first period of three days which was at the beginning of time. And like as Goodness draweth all things to Itself, and is the great Attractive Power which unites things that are sundered[3] (being as It is: the Godhead and the Supreme Fount and Producer of Unity);

---

[1] Here we get once more the Aristotelian classification of causes. The Good is:—

(i) Formal Cause (1) immanent *in* the world (Order—τάξις); (2) containing the world (Embracing Power—περιοχή).

(ii) Efficient Cause (Cause—αἰτία).

(iii) Final Cause (End—τέλος).

[2] The light permeates water but it does not permeate a stone. It passes over the stone and permeates the water beyond it.

[3] ἀρχισυνάγωγος ἐστι τῶν ἐσκεδασμένων.

and like as all things desire It as their beginning,
their cohesive power and end; and like as 'tis the
Good (as saith the Scripture) from which all things
were made and are (having been brought into existence thence as from a Perfect Cause); and like as in
the Good all things subsist, being kept and controlled
in an almighty Receptacle;[1] and like as unto the
Good all things are turned (as unto the proper End
of each); and like as after the Good all things do
yearn—those that have mind and reason seeking It
by knowledge, those that have perception seeking
It by perception, those that have no perception seeking It by the natural movement of their vital instinct,
and those that are without life and have mere
existence seeking It by their aptitude for that bare
participation whence this mere existence is theirs[2]—
even so doth the light (being as it were Its visible
image) draw together all things and attract them
unto Itself: those that can see, those that have
motion, those that receive Its light and warmth,
those that are merely held in being by Its rays;[3]
whence the sun is so called because it summeth[4] all
things and uniteth the scattered elements of the world.
All material things desire the sun, for they desire
either to see or to move and to receive light and
warmth and to be maintained in existence by the
light. I say not (as was feigned by the ancient
myth) that the sun is the God and Creator of this
Universe, and therefore takes the visible world
under his special care; but I say that the "invisible
things of God from the creation of the world
are clearly seen, being understood by the things

---

[1] ὡς ἐν παντοκρατορικῷ πυθμένι.

[2] (1) Man, (2) Animal, (3) Vegetable, (4) Matter.

[3] This seems to imply that matter itself could not exist without the
influence of the light.   Perhaps this belief rests on Gen. i. 1, 2.

[4] ἥλιος ὅτι πάντα ἀολλῆ ποιεῖ.   With the *naïf* etymology cf. iv. 5.

that are made, even His eternal power and God-head." [1]

5. But these things are dealt with in the "Symbolic Divinity." Here I desire to declare what is the spiritual meaning of the name "Light" as belonging to the Good.[2] The Good God is called Spiritual Light because He fills every heavenly mind with spiritual light, and drives all ignorance and error from all souls where they have gained a lodgment, and giveth them all a share of holy light and purges their spiritual eyes from the mist of ignorance that surrounds them, and stirs and opens the eyes which are fast shut and weighed down with darkness, and gives them first a moderate illumination, then (when they taste the Light and desire It more) He giveth Himself in greater measure and shineth in more abundance on them "because they have loved much," and ever He constraineth them according to their powers of looking upwards.

6. And so that Good which is above all light is called a Spiritual Light because It is an Originating Beam and an Overflowing Radiance, illuminating with its fullness every Mind above the world, around it, or within it,[3] and renewing all their spiritual powers, embracing them all by Its transcendent compass and exceeding them all by Its transcendent elevation. And It contains within Itself, in a simple form, the entire ultimate principle of light;[4] and is

---

[1] Rom. i. 20. The sun is not personal or supra-personal. But its impersonal activity is an emblem, as it were, of God's supra-personal activity.

[2] Two worlds : (1) Nature, (2) Grace. God is revealed in both ; the former was apparently the subject of the *Symbolic Divinity*; the latter is that of the present treatise.

[3] *i.e.* Men and different orders of angels.

[4] Material light is diffused in space and hence is divisible. The Spiritual Light is indivisible, being totally present to each illuminated mind. Hence the Spiritual Light is simple in a way that the material light is not.

the Transcendent Archetype of Light; and, while bearing the light in its womb, It exceeds it in quality and precedes it in time; and so conjoineth together all spiritual and rational beings, uniting them in one.[1] For as ignorance leadeth wanderers astray from one another, so doth the presence of Spiritual Light join and unite together those that are being illuminated, and perfects them and converts them toward that which truly Is—yea, converts them from their manifold false opinions and unites their different perceptions, or rather fancies, into one true, pure and coherent knowledge, and filleth them with one unifying light.

7. This Good is described by the Sacred Writers as Beautiful and as Beauty, as Love or Beloved, and by all other Divine titles which befit Its beautifying and gracious fairness. Now there is a distinction between the titles " Beautiful " and " Beauty " applied to the all-embracing Cause. For we universally distinguish these two titles as meaning respectively the qualities shared and the objects which share therein. We give the name of " Beautiful " to that which shares in the quality of beauty, and we give the name of " Beauty " to that common quality by which all beautiful things are beautiful. But the Super-Essential Beautiful is called " Beauty " because of that quality which It imparts to all things severally according to their nature,[2] and because It is the Cause of the harmony and splendour in all things, flashing forth upon them all, like light, the beautifying communications of Its originating ray; and because It summons all things to *fare* unto Itself (from whence It hath the name of " Fairness "[3]), and because It

---

[1] All our spiritual and mental powers are due to the same Spiritual Light working in each one of us. Cf. Wordsworth: "Those mysteries of Being which have made and shall continue evermore to make of the whole human race one brotherhood."

[2] Cf. ii. 8.

[3] ὡς πάντα πρὸς ἑαυτὸ καλοῦν (ὅθεν καὶ κάλλος λέγεται). Cf. iv. 4.

draws all things together in a state of mutual inter-penetration. And it is called "Beautiful" because It is All-Beautiful and more than Beautiful, and is eternally, unvaryingly, unchangeably Beautiful; incapable of birth or death or growth or decay; and not beautiful in one part and foul in another; nor yet at one time and not at another; nor yet beautiful in relation to one thing but not to another; nor yet beautiful in one place and not in another (as if It were beautiful for some but were not beautiful for others); nay, on the contrary, It is, in Itself and by Itself, uniquely and eternally beautiful, and from beforehand It contains in a transcendent manner the originating beauty of everything that is beautiful. For in the simple and supernatural nature belonging to the world of beautiful things,[1] all beauty and all that is beautiful hath its unique and pre-existent Cause. From this Beautiful all things possess their existence, each kind being beautiful in its own manner, and the Beautiful causes the harmonies and sympathies and communities of all things. And by the Beautiful all things are united together and the Beautiful is the beginning of all things, as being the Creative Cause which moves the world and holds all things in existence by their yearning for their own Beauty. And It is the Goal of all things, and their Beloved, as being their Final Cause (for 'tis the desire of the Beautiful that brings them all into existence), and It is their Exemplar[2] from which they derive their definite limits; and hence the Beautiful is the

---

[1] The ultimate nature of all beautiful things is a simple and supernatural Element common to them all and manifested in them all. The law of life is that it has its true and ultimate being outside it. The true beauty of all beautiful things is outside them in God. Hence all great art (even when not directly religious) tends towards the Supernatural or has a kind of supernatural atmosphere.

[2] παραδειγματικόν—i.e. the ultimate Law of their being, the *Idea* or Type.

same as the Good, inasmuch as all things, in all causation, desire the Beautiful and Good ; nor is there anything in the world but hath a share in the Beautiful and Good. Moreover our Discourse will dare to aver that even the Non-Existent[1] shares in the Beautiful and Good, for Non-Existence[2] is itself beautiful and good when, by the Negation of all Attributes, it is ascribed Super-Essentially to God. This One Good and Beautiful is in Its oneness the Cause of all the many beautiful and good things. Hence comes the bare existence of all things, and hence their unions,[3] their differentiations, their identities, their differences,[4] their similarities, their dissimilarities, their communions of opposite things,[5] the unconfused distinctions of their interpenetrating elements ;[6] the providences of the Superiors,[7] the interdependence of the Co-ordinates, the responses of the Inferiors,[8] the states of permanence wherein all keep their own identity. And hence again the intercommunion of all things according to the power of each ; their harmonies and sympathies (which do not merge them) and the co-ordinations of the whole

---

[1] τὸ μὴ ὅν—*i.e.* that mere nothingness which is manifested either as (1) formless "matter" or (2) evil. See Intr., p. 20.

[2] Evil is non-existent in one sense. The Good is Non-Existent in another. Cf. p. 90, n. 1.

[3] ἑνώσεις, διακρίσεις, ταὐτότητες, ἑτερότητες.

[4] Hence parts are united into wholes and wholes articulated into parts, and hence each thing is identical with itself and distinct from everything else.

[5] *e.g.* Moisture interpenetrates the solid earth.

[6] *e.g.* In a piece of wet ground the water is water and the earth is earth.

[7] αἱ πρόνοιαι τῶν ὑπερτέρων. Lit. "the providences," etc., *e.g.* the influence of the light without which, D. holds, the material world could not exist. Or this and the following may refer to different ranks of angels, or to angels and men.

[8] αἱ ἐπιστροφαί τῶν καταδεεστέρων. Lit. "the conversions," etc. *e.g.* Matter (according to his theory) responds to the influence of the light. And men are influenced by angels, and the lower angels by the higher.

universe;[1] the mixture of elements therein and the indestructible ligaments of things; the ceaseless succession of the recreative process in Minds and Souls and in Bodies; for all have rest and movement in That Which, above all rest and all movement, grounds each one in its own natural laws and moves each one to its own proper movement.[2]

8. And the Heavenly Minds are spoken of as moving (1) in a circular manner, when they are united to the beginningless and endless illuminations of the Beautiful and Good;[3] (2) straight forward, when they advance to the providential guidance of those beneath them and unerringly accomplish their designs;[4] and (3) with spiral motion, because, even while providentially guiding their inferiors, they remain immutably in their self-identity,[5] turning unceasingly around the Beautiful and Good whence all identity is sprung.

9. And the soul hath (1) a circular movement—viz. an introversion[6] from things without and the unified concentration[7] of its spiritual powers—which gives it a kind of fixed revolution, and, turning it from the multiplicity without, draws it together first into itself,[8] and then (after it has reached this unified condition) unites it to those powers which are a

[1] The point of this section is that besides the particular and partial harmonies already mentioned, there is a universal harmony uniting the whole world in one system.

[2] In the two following sections the difference between angelic and human activity is that the angels confer spiritual enlightenment and men receive it. Angels are in a state of attainment and men are passing through a process of attainment.

[3] *Vide supra* on Introversion (p. 88, n. 1).

[4] They are united to God in the centre of their being, by ceaselessly entering into themselves. They help us by going forth, as it were, from themselves.

[5] Their true self-identity is rooted in God. See Intr., pp. 31 f.

[6] ἡ εἰς ἑαυτὴν εἴσοδος.

[7] In souls being unified and simplified. See Intr., p. 25.

[8] Cf. St. Aug. "ascendat per se supra se."

perfect Unity,[1] and thus leads it on unto the Beautiful and Good Which is beyond all things, and is One and is the Same, without beginning or end. (2) And the soul moves with a spiral motion whensoever (according to its capacity) it is enlightened with truths of Divine Knowledge, not in the special unity of its being[2] but by the process of its discursive reason and by mingled and alternative activities.[3] (3) And it moves straight forward when it does not enter into itself to feel the stirrings of its spiritual unity (for this, as I said, is the circular motion), but goes forth unto the things around it and feels an influence coming even from the outward world, as from a rich abundance of cunning tokens, drawing it unto the simple unity of contemplative acts.[4]

10. These three motions, and also the similar motions we perceive in this material world and (far anterior to these) the individual permanence, rest and

---

[1] *i. e.* To the Angels and the perfected Saints. There is a somewhat similar thought in Wordsworth's *Prelude:* "To hold fit converse with the spiritual world / and with the generations of mankind / spread over time past, present, and to come / age after age till time shall be no more." This thought in Wordsworth and in D. is an experience and not a speculation.

[2] This spiritual unity was by later Mystical writers called the apex of the soul, or the ground, or the spark. Another name is *synteresis* or *synderesis.*

[3] There is an element of intuition in all discursive reasoning because all argument is based on certain axioms which are beyond proof (*e. g.* the law of universal causation). In fact the validity of our laws of thought is an axiom and therefore perceived by intuition. In the present passage D. means something deeper. He means that formal Dogmatic Theology advances round a central core of spiritual experience by which it must constantly be verified, *Pectus facit theologum.* Whenever theology even attempts to be purely deductive it goes wrong (*e. g.* Calvinism). If it is not rooted in intuition it will be rooted in fancies.

[4] In D.'s classification Introversion and Sensation are both unmixed movements, for each leads to a kind of perception. Discursive reasoning is a mixed movement because it does not lead to a direct perception and yet it must contain an element of perception.

grounding of each Kind[1] have their Efficient, Formal, and Final Cause in the Beautiful and Good ; Which is above all rest and motion ; through Which all rest and motion come ; and from Which, and in Which, and unto Which, and for the sake of Which they are. For from It and through It are all Being and life of spirit and of soul ; and hence in the realm of nature magnitudes both small, co-equal and great ; hence all the measured order and the proportions of things, which, by their different harmonies, commingle into wholes made up of co-existent parts ; hence this universe, which is both One and Many ; the conjunctions of parts together ; the unities underlying all multiplicity, and the perfections of the individual wholes ; hence Quality, Quantity, Magnitude and Infinitude ; hence fusions[2] and differentiations, hence all infinity and all limitation ; all boundaries, ranks, transcendences,[3] elements and forms, hence all Being, all Power, all Activity, all Condition,[4] all Perception, all Reason, all Intuition, all Apprehension, all Understanding, All Communion[5]—in a word, all that *is* comes from the Beautiful and Good, hath its very existence in the Beautiful and Good, and turns towards the Beautiful and Good. Yea, all that exists and that comes into being, exists and comes into being because of the Beautiful and Good ; and unto this Object all things gaze and by It are moved and are conserved, and for the sake of It, because of It and in It, existeth every originating Principle—be

---

[1] *i. e.* The types of things existent in the permanent spiritual world before the things were created in this transitory material world ; the Platonic *Ideas.* There was also a Jewish belief in such a pre-existence of things. Cf. Rev. iv. 11 (R. V.).

[2] συγκρίσεις.

[3] ὑπεροχαί.   [4] ἕξις.

[5] ἕνωσις. The word is here used in the most comprehensive manner to include physical communion, sense-perception, and spiritual communion of souls with one another and with God.

this Exemplar,[1] or be it Final or Efficient or Formal or Material Cause—in a word, all Beginning, all Conservation, and all Ending, or (to sum it up) all things that have being are derived from the Beautiful and Good. Yea, and all things that have no substantial being[2] super-essentially exist in the Beautiful and Good : this is the transcendent Beginning and the transcendent Goal of the universe. For, as Holy Scripture saith : " Of Him, and through Him, and to Him, are all things : to whom be glory for ever. Amen."[3] And hence all things must desire and yearn for and must love the Beautiful and the Good. Yea, and because of It and for Its sake the inferior things yearn for the superior under the mode of attraction, and those of the same rank have a yearning towards their peers under the mode of mutual communion ; and the superior have a yearning towards their inferiors under the mode of providential kindness ; and each hath a yearning towards itself under the mode of cohesion,[4] and all things are moved by a longing for the Beautiful and Good, to accomplish every outward work and form every act of will. And true reasoning will also dare to affirm that even the Creator of all things Himself yearneth after all things, createth all things, perfecteth all things, conserveth all things, attracteth all things, through

[1] The exemplar is the formal cause before this is actualized in the object embodying it. The principle in an oak tree constituting it an oak is the formal cause. But before there were any oak trees this principle existed as an exemplar. The final cause is the beneficent purpose the oak tree serves. In the Aristotelian classification exemplar and final cause would be classed together as final cause.

[2] This means either (1) that *actually* non-existent things (*e. g.* the flowers of next year which have not yet appeared, or those of last year, which are now dead) have an eternal place in God ; or else (2) that *evil* things have their true being, under a different form, in Him.

[3] Rom. xi. 36.

[4] In the whole of this passage D. is thinking primarily of Angels and men, or at least of sentient creatures. But he would see analogies of such activity in the inanimate material world.

nothing but excess of Goodness. Yea, and the Divine Yearning is naught else than a Good Yearning towards the Good for the mere sake of the Good. For the Yearning which createth all the goodness of the world, being pre-existent abundantly in the Good Creator, allowed Him not to remain unfruitful in Himself, but moved Him to exert the abundance of His powers in the production of the universe.[1]

11. And let no man think we are contradicting the Scripture when we solemnly proclaim the title of "Yearning." For 'tis, methinks, unreasonable and foolish to consider the phrases rather than the meaning ; and such is not the way of them that wish for insight into things Divine, but rather of them that receive the empty sounds without letting them pass beyond their ears, and shut them out, not wishing to know what such and such a phrase intends, nor how they ought to explain it in other terms expressing the same sense more clearly. Such men are under the dominion of senseless elements and lines, and of uncomprehended syllables and phrases which penetrate not into the perception of their souls, but make a dumb noise outside about their lips and hearing :

---

[1] εἰς τὸ πρακτικεύεσθαι κατὰ τὴν ἀπάντων γεννητικὴν ὑπερβολήν. Desire = want. And want in us = imperfection ; but in God it = that excess of perfection, whereby God is "Perfectionless." Thus the words "super-excellence," "super-unity," etc., are not meaningless superlatives. They imply an impulse towards motion within the Divine Stillness, a Thirst in the Divine Fullness. Cf. Julian of Norwich : *Revelations*, ch. xxxi. ". . . There is a property in God of thirst and longing." The categories of Greek Philosophy are static. The superlatives of D. imply something dynamic, though the static element remains. In much modern philosophy (the Pragmatists and also Bergson) dynamic conceptions are prominent ; but the tendency here is for the static to disappear instead of being subsumed as it is in D. The result, or the cause, is that Grace is lost sight of and only Nature is perceived. Really Absolutism and Pragmatism are not mutually exclusive ; for Rest and Motion co-exist as transcended elements in God. This is the paradox of perfect Love which is both at rest and in motion, both satisfied and unsatisfied. Cf. Julian of Norwich : "I had Him and I wanted Him" (*Revelations*, ch. x.).

holding it unlawful to explain the number "four" by
calling it "twice two," or a straight line by calling it
a "direct line" or the "Motherland" by calling it the
"Fatherland," or so to interchange any other of those
terms which under varieties of language possess all
the same signification. Need is there to understand
that in proper truth we do but use the elements and
syllables and phrases and written terms and words as
an aid to our senses; inasmuch as when our soul is
moved by spiritual energies unto spiritual things, our
senses, together with the thing which they perceive,
are all superfluous; even as the spiritual faculties are
also such when the soul, becoming Godlike,[1] meets in
the blind embraces of an incomprehensible union the
Rays of the unapproachable Light.[2] Now when
the mind, through the things of sense, feels an eager
stirring to mount towards spiritual contemplations,[3]
it values most of all those aids from its perceptions
which have the plainest form, the clearest words, the
things most distinctly seen, because, when the objects
of sense are in confusion, then the senses themselves
cannot present their message truly to the mind. But
that we may not seem, in saying this, to be setting
aside Holy Scripture, let those who blame the title
of "Yearning" hear what the Scripture saith:
"Yearn for her and she shall keep thee; exalt her and
she shall promote thee; she shall bring thee to honour
when thou dost embrace her."[4] And there are many

---

[1] θεοειδής.

[2] This clause can only have been written by one for whom Unknowing was a personal experience. The previous clause shows how there
is a negative element even in the Method of Affirmation. Sense-perception must first give way to spiritual intuition, just as this must finally
give way to Unknowing. (Cf. St. John of the Cross's *Dark Night*, on
three kinds of night.) All progress is a transcendence and so, in a
sense, a *Via Negativa.* Cf. St. Aug., *Transcende mundum et sape
animum, transcende animum et sape Deum.*

[3] This shows that the *Via Negativa* starts from something positive.
It is a transcendence, not a mere negation.   [4] Prov. iv. 6, 8.

other such Scriptural passages which speak of this yearning.

12. Nay, some of our writers about holy things have thought the title of "Yearning" diviner than that of "Love." Ignatius the Divine writes: "He whom I yearn for is crucified." [1] And in the "Introductions" of Scripture [2] thou wilt find some one saying concerning the Divine Wisdom: "I yearned for her beauty." Let us not, therefore, shrink from this title of "Yearning," nor be perturbed and affrighted by aught that any man may say about it. For methinks the Sacred Writers regard the titles "Love" and "Yearning" as of one meaning; but preferred, when speaking of Yearning in a heavenly sense, to qualify it with the world "real" [3] because of the inconvenient pre-notion of such men. For whereas the title of "Real Yearning" is employed not merely by ourselves but even by the Scriptures, mankind (not grasping the unity intended when Yearning is ascribed to God) fell by their own propensity into the notion

---

[1] ὁ ἐμὸς Ἔρως ἐσταύρωται. Ignatius Ep. ad Rom. § 6. But possibly St. Ignatius means: "My earthly affections are crucified." St. Ignatius wrote just before being martyred, at the beginning of the second century. This reference would alone be sufficient to make the authenticity of the Dionysian writings improbable.

[It is perhaps impossible to determine whether Ignatius meant by the words "my Love is crucified" to refer to Jesus or to himself. The latter is supported by Zahn and by Lightfoot, the former by Origen, Prologue to Commentary on Canticles. "Nec puto quod culpari possit, si quis Deum, sicut Joannis, charitatur, ita ipse amorem nominit. Denejire memini, aliquem sanctorum dixisse Ignatium nomine de Christo: Mens autem amor crucifixus est: nec reprehendi eum per hoc dignum judico." Much further evidence is given in Jacobson's *Apostolic Fathers* (p. 377). Jacobson himself supports it, observing that the Greek commemoration of Ignatius takes the words in this sense. Whether Dionysius followed Origen or not, his exposition is very interesting and is quite possibly the true. See also the translator's note on ἔρως. ED.]

[2] ἐν ταῖς προεισαγωγαῖς τῶν λογίων. Apparently this was a title of the books ascribed to Solomon. The present reference is Wisdom viii. 2.

[3] τοῖς θείοις μᾶλλον ἀναθεῖναι τὸν ὄντως ἔρωτα.

of a partial, physical and divided quality, which is not true Yearning but a vain image of Real Yearning, or rather a lapse therefrom.[1]   For mankind at large cannot grasp the simplicity of the one Divine Yearning, and hence, because of the offence it gives to most men, it is used concerning the Divine Wisdom to lead and raise them up to the knowledge of the Real Yearning until they are set free from all offence thereat ; and often on the other hand when it was possible that base minds should suppose that which is not convenient, the word that is held in greater reverence is used concerning ourselves.[2]   " Thy love," says some one, "came upon me like as the love of women."[3]   To those who listen aright to Holy Scripture, the word " Love " is used by the Sacred Writers in Divine Revelation with the same meaning as the word " Yearning."   It means a faculty of unifying and conjoining and of producing a special commingling together[4] in the Beautiful and Good : a faculty which pre-exists for the sake of the Beautiful and Good, and is diffused from this Origin and to this End, and holds together things of the same order by a mutual connection, and moves the highest to take thought for those below and fixes the inferior in a state which seeks the higher.

13. And the Divine Yearning brings ecstasy, not allowing them that are touched thereby to belong unto themselves but only to the objects of their affection.   This principle is shown by superior things

---

[1] Earthly desire is below static conditions, the Divine Desire is above them.

[2] i. e. The word ἔρως is sometimes used concerning God to stimulate our minds by its unexpectedness and so to make us penetrate beyond the word to the mystery hinted at by it.   On the other hand ἀγάπη or ἀγάπησις is sometimes used concerning human relationships to prevent any degrading associations from entering in.

[3] 2 Sam. i. 26.

[4] καί ἐστι τοῦτο δυνάμεως ἐνοποιοῦ καὶ συνδετικῆς καὶ διαφερόντως συγκρατικῆς.

H

through their providential care for their inferiors, and by those which are co-ordinate through the mutual bond uniting them, and by the inferior through their diviner tendency towards the highest. And hence the great Paul, constrained by the Divine Yearning, and having received a share in its ecstatic power, says, with inspired utterance, " I live, and yet not I but Christ liveth in me " : true Sweetheart that he was and (as he says himself) being beside himself unto God, and not possessing his own life but possessing and loving the life of Him for Whom he yearned. And we must dare to affirm (for 'tis the truth) that the Creator of the Universe Himself, in His Beautiful and Good Yearning towards the Universe, is through the excessive yearning of His Goodness, transported outside of Himself in His providential activities towards all things that have being, and is touched by the sweet spell of Goodness, Love and Yearning, and so is drawn from His transcendent throne above all things, to dwell within the heart of all things, through a super-essential and ecstatic power whereby He yet stays within Himself.[1] Hence Doctors call Him " jealous," because He is vehement in His Good Yearning towards the world, and because He stirs men up to a zealous search of yearning desire for Him, and thus shows Himself zealous inasmuch as zeal is always felt concerning things which are desired, and inasmuch as He hath a zeal concerning the creatures for which He careth. In short, both the Yearning and its Object belong to the Beautiful and the Good, and have therein their pre-existent roots and because of it exist and come into being.

14. But why speak the Sacred Writers of God sometimes as Yearning and Love, sometimes as the

---

[1] This finely suggests that the " Selfhood " of God is selfless. *Vide* Intr., p. 9. Note also the combination of rest and motion alluded to here.

Object of these emotions? In the one case He is the Cause and Producer and Begetter of the thing signified, in the other He is the Thing signified Itself. Now the reason why He is Himself on the one hand moved by the quality signified, and on the other causes motion by it,[1] is that He moves and leads onward Himself unto Himself.[2] Therefore on the one hand they call Him the Object of Love and Yearning as being Beautiful and Good, and on the other they call Him Yearning and Love as being a Motive-Power leading all things to Himself, Who is the only ultimate Beautiful and Good—yea, as being His own Self-Revelation and the Bounteous Emanation of His own Transcendent Unity, a Motion of Yearning simple, self-moved, self-acting, pre-existent in the Good, and overflowing from the Good into creation, and once again returning to the Good. And herein the Divine Yearning showeth especially its beginningless and endless nature, revolving in a perpetual circle for the Good, from the Good, in the Good, and to the Good, with unerring revolution, never varying its centre or direction, perpetually advancing and remaining and returning to Itself. This by Divine inspiration our renowned Initiator hath declared in his *Hymns of Yearning*, which it will not be amiss to quote and thus to bring unto a holy consummation our Discourse concerning this matter.

15. Words of the most holy Hierotheus from the *Hymns of Yearning*. "Yearning (be it in God or Angel, or Spirit, or Animal Life, or Nature) must be

---

[1] Yearning is a movement in the soul; the Object of Yearning causes such movement in the soul.

[2] Cf. St. Thomas Aquinas: *Deus movet sicut desideratum a Se Ipso.* Cf. Spenser: "He loved Himself because Himself was fair." Cf. Plato's Doctrine of ἔρως. This Yearning is eternally fulfilled in the Trinity. Cf. Dante: "O somma luce che sola in Te sidi / sola T' intendi e da Te intelletta / ed intendente Te ami ed arridi." It is struggling towards actualization in this world.

conceived of as an uniting and commingling power
which moveth the higher things to a care for those
below them, moveth co-equals to a mutual communion,
and finally moveth the inferiors to turn towards their
superiors in virtue and position."

16. Words of the same, from the same *Hymns of
Yearning.* "Forasmuch as we have set down in
order the manifold yearnings springing from the One,
and have duly explained what are the powers of
knowledge and of action belonging to the yearnings
springing from the One, and have duly explained
what are the powers of knowledge and of action
proper to the Yearnings within [1] the world and
above [2] it (wherein, as hath been already explained,
the higher place belongeth unto those ranks and
orders of Yearning which are spiritually felt and
perceived, and highest amongst these are the Divine
Yearnings in the very core of the Spirit towards those
Beauties which have their veritable Being Yonder),[3]
let us now yet further resume and compact them all
together into the one and concentrated Yearning
which is the Father of them all, and let us collect
together into two kinds their general desiderative

---

[1] *i. e.* The social instinct in men and animals, and the impulse of
mutual attraction in the inanimate world.

[2] The manifold yearnings of the spirit for Truth, Beauty, Spiritual
Love, etc.

[3] *i. e.* Of the two classes just alluded to the second is the higher ;
and of those yearnings which belong to this class the most transcendent
are the highest. Religion is higher than secular life, and the highest
element in Religion is other-worldly.

The received text reads—

"The Divine Yearnings in the very core," etc., οἱ αὐτονόητοι καὶ
θεῖοι τῶν ὄντως ἐκεῖ καλῶς ἐρώτων. I have ventured to amend ἐρώτων
to ἔρωτες. If the MS from which the received text is derived belonged
to a family having seventeen or eighteen letters to a line then this
word would probably come at the end of a line (since there are
260 letters to the end of it, from the beginning of the section), and
would have the ὀν- of ὄντως just above it and the -ον- of αὐτονόητοι just
above that, and ἐρώτων at the end of the line next but one above that.
This would make the corruption of ἔρωτες into ἐρώτων very natural.

powers, over which the entire mastery and primacy is in that Incomprehensible Causation of all yearning which cometh from Beyond them all, and whereunto the universal yearning of all creatures presseth upwards according to the nature of each."

17. Words of the same, from the same *Hymns of Yearning.* "Let us once more collect these powers into one and declare that there is but One Simple Power Which of Itself moveth all things to be mingled in an unity, starting from the Good and going unto the lowest of the creatures and thence again returning through all stages in due order unto the Good, and thus revolving from Itself, and through Itself and upon Itself[1] and towards Itself, in an unceasing orbit."

18. Now some one, perhaps, will say: "If the

---

[1] "That which is not" = formless matter. Plotinus (*Enn.* i. 8. 3) defines the Non-Existent as the world of sense-perception. It is, as it were, the stuff of which all things perceived by the senses are made. This stuff cannot exist without some kind of "form," and therefore, if entirely bereft of all "form," would simply disappear into nothingness. Thus, apart from that element of "form" which it derives from the Good, it is sheer Non-Entity.

Each individual thing consists of "matter" and "form"—*i. e.* of this indeterminate "stuff" and of the particular qualities belonging to that thing. Remove those qualities and the thing is destroyed : *e.g.* remove the colours, shape, etc., of a tree, and the tree becomes non-existent. It crumbles into dust, and thus the "stuff" takes on a new form. If, as M. Le Bon maintains, material particles sometimes lose their material qualities and are changed into energy, in such a case the "stuff" takes on yet another kind of form. The individual thing, in every case, becomes non-existent when it loses its "form," or the sum total of its individual qualities, but the "stuff" persists because it at once assumes another "form."

Hence this "stuff," being non-existent *per se*, draws its existence from the Good Which is the Source of all "form." And thus the existence of this non-existent stuff is ultimately *contained* in the Good.

D. tries to prove that evil is non-existent by showing that there is nothing that can have produced it. Good cannot have produced it because a thing cannot produce its own opposite ; evil cannot have produced itself because evil is always destructive and never productive. All things that exist are produced by the Good or the desire for the Good—which comes to the same thing.

Beautiful and Good is an Object of Yearning and
desire and love to all (for even that which *is not* longs
for It, as was said,[1] and strives to find its rest therein,
and thus It creates a form even in formless things and
thus is said super-essentially to *contain*, and does so
contain, the non-existent)[2]—if this is so, how is it that
the company of the devils desires not the Beautiful
and Good, but, being inclined towards matter and
fallen far from the fixed angelic state of desire for the
Good, becomes a cause of all evils to itself and to all
other beings which we describe as becoming evil?
How is it that the devils, having been produced
wholly out of the Good, are not good in disposition?
Or how is it that, if produced good from out of the
Good, they became changed?[3] What made them

[1] The "matter" or stuff of which the universe is made, exists
ultimately in the Good, but evil does not. All force exists ultimately
in the Good, but the warping of it, or the lawlessness of it (which is
the evil of it), does not exist in the Good. Force, or energy, as such is
a relative embodiment of the Absolute: evil as such is a contradiction
of the Absolute.

[2] *i. e.* There is an element of good in evil things enabling them to
cohere and so to exist. In this passage "Non-Existent" is used in
three senses: (1) "Matter," or force, cannot exist without some form
(which is its complement) and therefore is technically called non-
existent. (2) Evil cannot exist at all on the ultimate plane of Being,
nor in this world without an admixture of good (which is its contrary)
and therefore is in an absolute sense non-existent. (3) The Good is
beyond all existence and therefore is by transcendence Non-Existent.

[3] The Good is beyond this world and beyond the stuff, or force, of
which this world is made.

Evil, on the other hand, is below this world and the stuff composing
it. Get rid of the limitations in this world (*sc.* the difference between
one quality and another) and you have an energy or force possessing
all the particular qualities of things fused in one. Get rid of the
limitations inherent in this (*i. e.* intensify it to infinity) and you have
the Good. On the other hand, destroy some particular object (*e.g.* a
tree), and that object, being now actually non-existent, has still a
potential existence in the world-stuff. Destroy that potential existence
and you have absolute non-existence, which is Evil.

Thus the three grades may be tabulated as follows:

(i) Transcendent Non-Existence (= the Good).

(ii) Actual Non-Existence (= the world stuff, force or energy, of

evil, and indeed what is the nature of evil? From what origin did it arise and in what thing doth it lie? Why did He that is Good will to produce it? And how, having so willed, was He able so to do?[1] And if evil comes from some other cause, what other cause can anything have excepting the Good? How, if there is a Providence, doth evil exist, or arise at all, or escape destruction? And why doth anything in the world desire it instead of Good?"

19. Thus perhaps will such bewildered discourse speak. Now we will bid the questioner look towards the truth of things, and in the first place we will venture thus to answer: "Evil cometh not of the Good; and if it cometh therefrom it is not evil. For even as fire cannot cool us, so Good cannot produce the things which are not good. And if all things that have being come from the Good (for it is natural to the Good to produce and preserve the creatures, and natural to evil to corrupt and to destroy them) then nothing in the world cometh of evil. Then evil can-

which material particles are a form. Modern science teaches that atoms have no actual existence. Thus the atomic theory has worked round to something very much like D.'s theory of the non-existent world stuff).

(iii) Absolute Non-Existence (= Evil).

The three grades might be expressed by a numerical symbol as follows: If finite numbers represent the various forms of existence, the Infinity (which contradicts the laws of finite numbers) = the Good: Unity (which is a mere abstraction and cannot exist apart from multiplicity since every finite unit is divisible into parts) = the world stuff: Zero (which annihilates all finite numbers that are multiplied by it) = Evil.

[1] The argument in the rest of the section is as follows:

Evil exists, for there is a radical difference between virtue and vice. Evil is, in fact, not merely negative, but positive: not merely destructive, but also productive. And hence it is necessary to the perfection of the world. To which D. replies in the next section that evil does not exist *qua* evil, nor is it positive or productive *qua* evil. It exists and is positive and productive solely through an admixture of the Good. (We might illustrate this by the fact that Zero, multiplied by Infinity, produces finite number.)

not even in any wise exist, if it act as evil upon itself. And unless it do so act, evil is not wholly evil, but hath some portion of the Good whereby it can exist at all. And if the things that have being desire the Beautiful and Good and accomplish all their acts for the sake of that which seemeth good, and if all that they intend hath the Good as its Motive and its Aim (for nothing looks unto the nature of evil to guide it in its actions), what place is left for evil among things that have being, or how can it have any being at all bereft of such good purpose? And if all things that have being come of the Good and the Good is Beyond things that have being, then, whereas that which exists not yet hath being in the Good; evil contrariwise hath none (otherwise it were not wholly evil or *Non-Ens;* for that which is wholly *Non-Ens* can be but naught except this be spoken Super-Essentially of the Good). So the Good must have Its seat far above and before that which hath mere being and that which hath not; but evil hath no place either amongst things that have being or things that have not, yea it is farther removed than the Non-Existent from the Good and hath less being than it. 'Then' (saith one perchance) 'whence cometh evil? For if' (saith he) 'evil is not, virtue and vice must needs be the same both in their whole entirety and in their corresponding particulars,'—*i.e.* even that which fighteth against virtue cannot be evil. And yet temperance is the opposite of debauchery, and righteousness of wickedness. And I mean not only the righteous and the unrighteous man, or the temperate and intemperate man ; I mean that, even before the external distinction appeared between the virtuous man and his opposite, the ultimate distinction between the virtues and the vices hath existed long beforehand in the soul itself, and the passions war against the reason, and hence we must assume something evil

which is contrary to goodness.   For goodness is not
contrary to itself, but, being come from One Beginning
and being the offspring of One Cause, it rejoices in
fellowship, unity, and concord.   Even the lesser Good
is not contrary to the greater, for that which is less
hot or cold is not contrary to that which is more so.
Wherefore evil lieth in the things that have being and
possesseth being and is opposed and contrary to goodness.   And if evil is the destruction of things which
have being, that depriveth it not of its own being.   It
itself still hath being and giveth being to its offspring.
Yea, is not the destruction of one thing often the
birth of another?   And thus it will be found that evil
maketh contribution unto the fullness of the world,
and through its presence, saveth the universe from
imperfection."

20. The true answer whereunto will be that evil
(*qua* evil) causes no existence or birth, but only
debases and corrupts, so far as its power extends, the
substance of things that have being.   And if any one
says that it is productive, and that by the destruction
of one thing it giveth birth to somewhat else, the true
answer is that it doth not so *qua* destructive.   *Qua*
destructive and evil it only destroys and debases; but
it taketh upon it the form of birth and essence through
the action of the Good.   Thus evil will be found to
be a destructive force in itself, but a productive force
through the action of the Good.   *Qua* evil it neither
hath being nor confers it; through the action of the
Good, it hath being (yea, a good being) and confers
being on good things.   Or rather (since we cannot
call the same thing both good and bad in the same
relations, nor are the destruction and birth of the
same thing the same function or faculty, whether productive or destructive, working in the same relations),
Evil in itself hath neither being, goodness, productiveness, nor power of creating things which have being

and goodness; the Good, on the other hand, wherever It becomes perfectly present, creates perfect, universal and untainted manifestations of goodness; while the things which have a lesser share therein are imperfect manifestations of goodness and mixed with other elements through lack of the Good. In fine, evil is not in any wise good, nor the maker of good; but every thing must be good only in proportion as it approacheth more or less unto the Good, since the perfect Goodness penetrating all things reacheth not only to the wholly good beings around It, but extendeth even unto the lowest things, being entirely present unto some, and in a lower measure to others, and unto others in lowest measure, according as each one is capable of participating therein.[1] Some creatures participate wholly in the Good, others are lacking in It less or more, and others possess a still fainter participation therein, while to others the Good is present as but the faintest echo. For if the Good were not present only in a manner proportioned unto each, then the divinest and most honourable things would be no higher than the lowest! And how, pray, could all things have a uniform share in the Good, since not all are equally fit to share entirely therein? But in truth the exceeding greatness of the power of the Good is shown by this—that It giveth power even to the things which lack It, yea even unto that very lack itself, inasmuch as even here is to be found some kind of participation in It.[2] And, if we must needs

---

[1] D. is no pantheist. According to Pantheism God is *equally* present in all things. Thus Pantheism is a debased form of the Immanence doctrine, as Calvinism is a debased form of the Transcendence doctrine. In the one case we get Immanence without Transcendence: in the other Transcendence without Immanence. D. holds a Transcendent Immanence (cf. Bradley, *Appearance and Reality*, rebutting charge of Pantheism).

[2] *e. g.* The cruelty of Nature seems to show Intelligence; and Intelligence *per se* is a good thing.

boldly speak the truth, even the things that fight
against It possess through Its power their being and
their capability to fight.   Or rather, to speak shortly,
all creatures in so far as they have being are good and
come from the Good, and in so far as they are deprived
of the Good, neither are good nor have they being.[1]
For in the case of other qualities, such as heat or cold,
the things which have been warmed have their being
even when they lose their warmth, and many of the
creatures there are which have no life or mind ; and
in like manner God transcendeth all being and so is
Super-Essential ;[2] and generally, in all other cases,
though the quality be gone or hath never been
present, the creatures yet have being and can subsist ;
but that which is utterly bereft of the Good never had,
nor hath, nor ever shall have, no nor can have any sort
of being whatever.   For instance, the depraved sinner,
though bereft of the Good by his brutish desire, is in
this respect unreal and desires unrealities ; but still he
hath a share in the Good in so far as there is in him a
distorted reflection of true Love and Communion.[3]
And anger hath a share in the Good, in so far as it is
a movement which seeks to remedy apparent evils,
converting them to that which appears to be fair.
And even he that desires the basest life, yet in so far
as he feels desire at all and feels desire for life, and
intends what he thinks the best kind of life, so far
participates in the Good.   And if you wholly destroy
the Good, there will be neither being, life, desire, nor
motion, or any other thing.   Hence the birth of fresh

[1] All evil things contain the seed of their own decay, and so tend to
non-existence.   The arrogance and cruelty of the Germans has been
their weakness, as discipline and self-sacrifice has been their strength.

[2] God exists without Essence, as an object can exist without this
particular quality or that.

[3] D. is thinking especially of carnal sin.   Such sin is a depraved
form of that which, in its true purity, is a mystery, symbolizing the
Unitive Life.

life out of destruction is not the function of evil but is the presence of Good in a lesser form, even as disease is a disorder, yet not the destruction of all order, for if this happen the disease itself will not exist.[1] But the disease remains and exists. Its essence is order reduced to a *minimum ;* and in this it consists. For that which is utterly without the Good hath neither being nor place amongst the things that are in being ; but that which is of mixed nature owes to the Good its place among things in being, and hath this place amongst them and hath being just so far as it participates in the Good. Or rather all things in being will have their being more or less in proportion as they participate in the Good. For so far as mere Being is concerned, that which hath not being in any respect will not exist at all ; that which hath being in one respect but not in another doth not exist in so far as it hath fallen away from the everlasting Being ; while in so far as it hath a share of being, to that extent it exists ; and thus both an element of existence and an element of non-existence in it are kept and preserved. So too with evil. That which is utterly fallen from Good can have no place either in the things which are more good or in the things which are less so. That which is good in one respect but not in another is at war with some particular good but not with the whole of the Good. It also is preserved by the admixture of the Good, and thus the Good giveth existence to the lack of Itself through some element of Itself being present there. For if the Good be entirely removed, there will not remain aught at all, either good or mixed or absolutely bad. For if evil is imperfect Goodness, the perfect absence of the Good will remove both the perfect and the imperfect Good, and evil will only exist and appear because, while it is evil in relation to one kind of good (being the contrary

[1] A diseased body still lives. Death ends the disease.

thereof), yet it depends for its existence on another kind of good and, to that extent, is good itself. For things of the same kind cannot[1] be wholly contradictory to one another in the same respects.[2] Hence evil is Non-Existent.

21. Neither inhereth evil in existent creatures.[3] For if all creatures are from the Good, and the Good is in them all and embraces them all, either evil can have no place amongst the creatures, or else it must have a place in the Good.[4] Now it cannot inhere in the Good, any more than cold can inhere in fire; just so the quality of becoming evil cannot inhere in that which turns even evil into good. And if evil doth inhere in the Good, what will the mode of its inherence be? If you say: It cometh of the Good, I answer: That is absurd and impossible. For (as the infallible Scriptures say), a good tree cannot bring forth evil fruit, nor yet is the converse possible. But if it cometh not of the Good, it is plainly from another origin and cause. Either evil must come from the Good, or the Good from evil, or else (if this is impossible) both the Good and evil must be from another origin or cause. For no duality can be an origin: some unity must be the origin of all duality. And yet it is absurd to suppose that two entirely

---

[1] Exuberant vitality is *per se* a good thing and the more exuberant the better, though, like all good things, it is dangerous, and unless properly directed is disastrous.

[2] If good and evil are both existent, they are, to that extent, both of the same kind ; which is impossible.

[3] So far D. has been showing that evil is not an *ultimate* principle, being neither (1) identical with the Good, nor (2) self-subsistent. Now he argues that it is not a necessary element in any created thing : neither in their existence as such, nor in any particular kind of creature.

[4] D. rambles characteristically, but the general argument is plain. All existence is from the Good. Hence, if evil is inherent in the nature of existence, evil is from the Good. Thus D. meets again and proceeds to lay the ghost of a theory which he has already elaborately slain in the previous section.

opposite things can owe their birth and their being to the same thing. This would make the origin itself not a simple unity but divided, double, self-contradictory and discordant. Nor again is it possible that the world should have two contradictory origins, existing in each other and in the whole and mutually at strife. For,[1] were this assumed, God[2] cannot be free from pain, nor without a feeling of ill, since there would be something causing Him trouble, yea, all things must in that case be in a state of disorder and perpetual strife; whereas the Good imparts a principle of harmony to all things and is called by the Sacred Writers Peace and the Bestower of Peace. And hence it is that all good things display a mutual attraction and harmony, and are the offspring of one Life and are disposed in fellowship towards one Good, and are kindly, of like nature, and benignant to one another. And so evil is not in God,[3] and is not divine. Nor cometh it of God. For either He is not good, or else He worketh goodness and bringeth good things unto

---

[1] Having just given a metaphysical argument for the non-existence of evil, D. now gives an argument drawn from the actual nature of the universe and of God's creative activity.

This argument is not so satisfactory as the metaphysical one, for, under all the harmony of the world, there is perpetual strife, and the Cross of Christ reveals God as suffering pain. "Christ is in an agony and will be till the end of the world" (*Pascal*).

The metaphysical argument is sound because metaphysics deal with ultimate ideals, and evil is ultimately or ideally non-existent. The argument from actual facts is unsound because evil is actually existent. Much wrong thinking on the subject of evil is due to a confusion of ideal with actual non-existence. D. here seems to fall into this mistake.

[2] D. here uses the name "God" because he is thinking of the Absolute or the Good, not in Its ultimate Nature, but in Its emanating or creative activity, in which the Personal Differentiations of the Trinity appear. See II. 7.

[3] *i. e.* Evil does not arise through the passage of the Good from Super-Essence into Essence. It is not in the Good through the Good submitting to the conditions of existence (D. has already shown that evil has no place in the ultimate Super-Essential Nature of the Good).

existence. Nor acts He thus only at some times and
not at others, or only in the case of some things but
not of all. For were He to act thus, He must suffer
a change and alteration, and that in respect of the
divinest quality of all—causality. And if the Good
is in God as His very substance, God must, in changing from the Good, sometimes exist and sometimes
not exist. Doubtless if you feign that He hath the
Good by mere participation therein, and derives It
from another, in that case He will, forsooth, sometimes
possess It and sometimes not possess It.[1] Evil, therefore, doth not come from God, nor is it in God either
absolutely or temporally.[2]

22. Neither inhereth evil in the angels.[3] For if the
good angel declares the Divine Goodness, he is in
a secondary manner and by participation that which
the Subject of his message is in a primary and causal
manner.[4] And thus the angel is an image of God,
a manifestation of the invisible light, a burnished
mirror, bright, untarnished, without spot or blemish,
receiving (if it is reverent to say so) all the beauty
of the Absolute Divine Goodness, and (so far as may
be) kindling in itself, with unallowed radiance, the
Goodness of the Secret Silence. Hence evil inhereth
not in the angels; they are evil only in so far as they
must punish sinners. But in this respect even those
who chastise wrong-doers are evil, and so are the
priests who exclude the profane man from the Divine

---

[1] This is a *reductio ad absurdum*. D. considers it obvious that God
possesses the Good as His Substance and not by participation. The
Persons of the Trinity are not products of the Absolute but Emanations
or Differentiations of It.

[2] The argument is as follows : No evil is from God. All existence
is from God. Therefore no existence is evil.

[3] Having shown that existence as such is not inherently evil, D. now
takes various forms of existence and shows that none of them is, as
such, inherently evil.

[4] Cf. Old Testament title, "Sons of God," and D. on Deification.
Cf. also "I have said, Ye are Gods."

Mysteries.   But, indeed, 'tis not the suffering of the punishment that is evil but the being worthy thereof; nor yet is a just exclusion from the sacrifices evil, but to be guilty and unholy and unfit for those pure mysteries is evil.

23. Nor are the devils naturally evil.   For, were they such, they would not have sprung from the Good, nor have a place amongst existent creatures, nor have fallen from Goodness (being by their very nature always evil). Moreover, are they evil with respect to themselves or to others?   If the former [1] they must also be self-destructive; if the latter, how do they destroy, and what do they destroy? [2]   Do they destroy Essence, or Faculty, or Activity? [3]   If Essence, then, first, they cannot destroy it contrary to its own nature; for they cannot destroy things which by their nature are indestructible, but only the things which are capable of destruction.   And, secondly, destruction itself is not evil in every case and under all circumstances.   Nor can any existent thing be destroyed so far as its being and nature act; for its destruction is due to a failure of its natural order, whereby the principle of harmony and symmetry grows weak and so cannot remain unchanged. [4]   But

[1] *i. e.* If *totally* and *essentially by very nature* evil with respect to themselves.   In so far as they continue to exist they are good with respect to themselves.

[2] Evil is the contrary of the Good.   Hence since the Good is by Its very nature productive, evil must be destructive.   Hence the devils, if essentially evil, must be essentially destructive.   Now they are not essentially self-destructive, for, were they such, they could not exist.   Therefore, if essentially evil, they must under all circumstances be destructive of other things.

[3] The essence of (*e. g.*) an apple-tree is self-identity; its faculty is its latent power of producing leaves, apples, etc.; its activity is the actual production of the leaves, apples, etc.

[4] (1) The devils do not destroy *all* things (*e. g.* they do not annihilate the human soul).   Therefore they are not *essentially* evil.   Evil passions are good things misdirected.   (2) Often the destruction of a thing is beneficial (*e. g.* the falling of the faded leaf).   In fact, nothing could be

the weakness is not complete ; for, were it complete, it would have annihilated both the process of destruction and the object which suffers it : and such a destruction as this must be self-destructive. Hence such a quality is not evil but imperfect good ; for that which is wholly destitute of the Good can have no place among things that have being.[1] And the same is true of destruction when it works upon a faculty or activity. Moreover, how can the devils be evil since they are sprung from God ? For the Good produceth and createth good things. But it may be said that they are called evil not in so far as they exist (for they are from the Good and had a good existence given them), but in so far as they do not exist, having been unable (as the Scripture saith) to keep their original state. For in what, pray, do we consider the wickedness of the devils to consist except their ceasing from the quality and activity of divine virtues ? Otherwise, if the devils are naturally evil, they must be always evil. But evil is unstable.[2] Hence if they are always in the same condition, they are not evil ; for to remain always the same is a property of the Good. But if they are not always evil, then they are not evil by their natural constitution, but only through a lack of angelic virtues.[3] Hence they are not utterly without the Good, seeing that they exist and live and form intuitions and have

---

destroyed if it had not grown feeble and so become worthy to be destroyed. (D. here, in his zeal to explain evil away, countenances the base doctrine that might is right. What is wrong with the whole system of the universe is that its underlying law is the survival of the fittest. The enlightened conscience of humanity rebels against this law.)

[1] The weakness is an imperfect good, and therefore the process of destruction which co-operates with the weakness is an imperfect good.

[2] The Good is permanent. Hence its contrary must be unstable.

[3] Evil is essentially a negative and self-contradictory thing. Its very permanence would be opposed to its own nature and would be due to an element of the Good within it.

I

within them any movement of desire at all; but they are called evil because they fail in the exercise of their natural activity. The evil in them is therefore a warping, a declension from their right condition; a failure, an imperfection, an impotence, and a weakness, loss and lapse of that power which would preserve their perfection in them. Moreover what is the evil in the devils? Brutish wrath, blind desire, headstrong fancy. But these qualities, even though they exist in the devils, are not wholly, invariably, and essentially evil. For in other living creatures, not the possession of these qualities but their loss is destructive of the creature and hence is evil; while their possession preserves the creature and enables the creature possessing them to exist. Hence the devils are not evil in so far as they fulfil their nature, but in so far as they do not. Nor hath the Good bestowed complete upon them been changed; rather have they fallen from the completeness of that gift. And we maintain that the angelic gifts bestowed upon them have never themselves suffered change, but are unblemished in their perfect brightness, even if the devils themselves do not perceive it through blinding their faculties of spiritual perception.[1] Thus, so far as their existence is concerned, they possess it from the Good, and are naturally good, and desire the Beautiful and Good in desiring existence, life, and intuition, which are existent things. And they are called evil through the deprivation and the loss whereby they have lapsed from their proper virtues. And hence they are evil in so far as they do not exist; and in desiring evil they desire that which is non-existent.

24. But perhaps some one will say that human

---

[1] There is a timeless ground in all personalities, and this ground is good. Eckhart and Tauler say that even the souls in hell possess eternally the divine root of their true being. Ruysbroeck says, this divine root does not of itself make us blessed, but merely makes us exist.

souls are the seat of evil. Now if the reason alleged
is that they have contact with evil temptations when
they take forethought to preserve themselves therefrom, this is not evil but good and cometh from the
Good that turns even evil into good. But if we mean
the depravation which souls undergo, in what do they
undergo depravation except in the deficiency of good
qualities and activities and in the failure and fall
therefrom due to their own weakness? Even so we
say that the air is darkened around us by a deficiency
and absence of the light; while yet the light itself is
always light and illuminates the darkness. Hence
the evil inhereth not in the devils or in us, as evil,
but only as a deficiency and lack of the perfection of
our proper virtues.

25. Neither inhereth evil in the brute beasts. For
if you take away the passions of anger, desire, etc.
(which are not in their essential nature evil, although
alleged to be so), the lion, having lost its savage
wildness, will be a lion no longer; and the dog, if it
become gentle to all, will cease to be a dog, since
the virtue of a dog is to watch and to allow its own
masters to approach while driving strangers away.
Wherefore 'tis not evil for a creature so to act as
preserveth its nature undestroyed; evil is the destruction of its nature, the weakness and deficiency
of its natural qualities, activities, and powers. And
if all things which the process of generation produces
have their goal of perfection in time, then even that
which seemeth to be their imperfection is not wholly
and entirely contrary to nature.[1]

26. Neither inhereth evil in nature as a whole. For
if all natural laws together come from the universal
system of Nature, there is nothing contrary to Nature.[2]

---

[1] *i. e.* That which is imperfect in them is capable of being made
perfect.

[2] The sum total of natural laws comes from the ultimate unity of

'Tis but when we consider the nature of particular things, that we find one part of Nature to be natural and another part to be unnatural. For one thing may be unnatural in one case, and another thing in another case; and that which is natural in one is unnatural in another.[1]   Now the evil taint of a natural force is something unnatural.   It is a lack of the thing's natural virtues.   Hence, no natural force is evil : the evil of nature lies in a thing's inability to fulfil its natural functions.[2]

27. Neither inhereth evil in our bodies.   For ugliness and disease are a deficiency in form and a want of order.   But this is not wholly evil, being rather a lesser good.   For were there a complete destruction of beauty, form, and order, the very body must disappear.   And that the body is not the cause of evil in the soul is plain in that evil can be nigh at hand even without a body, as it is in the devils. Evil in spirits' souls and bodies is a weakness and lapse in the condition of their natural virtues.

28. Nor is the familiar notion true that "Evil inheres in matter *qua* matter."   For matter, too, hath a share in order, beauty, and form.   And if matter is without these things, and in itself hath no quality or form, how can it produce anything, since in that case it hath not of itself even the power of suffering any affection?   Nay, how can matter be

---

Nature, which comes from the Good.   Thus the sum total of natural laws is not, as such, opposed to the ultimate unity of Nature, and therefore is not as such opposed to the Good.   It is not *essentially* evil.

[1] Cf. Section 30.

[2] The argument of the whole passage is that evil is not inherent in the essential nature of things as a whole or of any particular thing.   It arises in particular things (accidentally, as it were) through their failure to fulfil their true nature.   But what of this accident?   Is it inherent? Perhaps we might answer, "Not inherent because capable of being eliminated."

evil? For if it hath no being whatever, it is neither good nor evil; but if it hath a kind of being, then (since all things that have being come from the Good) matter must come from the Good. And thus either the Good produces evil (*i. e.* evil, since it comes from the Good, is good), or else the Good Itself is produced by evil (*i. e.* the Good, as coming thus from evil, is evil). Or else we are driven back again to two principles. But if so, these must be derived from some further single source beyond them. And if they say that matter is necessary for the whole world to fulfil its development, how can that be evil which depends for its existence upon the Good? For evil abhors the very nature of the Good. And how can matter, if it is evil, produce and nourish Nature? For evil, *qua* evil, cannot produce or nourish anything, nor create or preserve it at all. And if they reply that matter causes not the evil in our souls, but that it yet draws them down towards evil, can that be true? For many of them have their gaze turned towards the Good. And how can that be, if matter doth nothing except drag them down towards evil? Hence evil in our souls is not derived from matter but from a disordered and discordant motion. And if they say that this motion is always the consequence of matter; and if the unstable medium of matter is necessary for things that are incapable of firm self-subsistence, then *why* is it that evil is thus necessary or that this necessary thing is evil? [1]

29. Nor is the common saying true that Deprivation or Lack fights by its natural power against the Good. For a complete lack is utterly impotent; and that

[1] Matter, it is argued, is *evil* because the discordant motion of the soul springs from matter. But, replies D., matter is *necessary* for certain kinds of existence. Hence it follows that evil is necessary. But this is impossible.

which is partial hath its power, not in so far as it is a lack, but in so far as it is not a perfect lack. For when the lack of the Good is partial, evil is not as yet; and when it becomes perfect, evil itself utterly vanishes.

30. In fine, Good cometh from the One universal Cause; and evil from many partial deficiencies. God knows evil under the form of good, and with Him the causes of evil things are faculties productive of good. And if evil is eternal, creative, and powerful, and if it hath being and activity, whence hath it these attributes? Come they from the Good? Or from the evil by the action of the Good? Or from some other cause by the action of them both? All natural results arise from a definite cause; and if evil hath no cause or definite being, it is unnatural. For that which is contrary to Nature hath no place in Nature, even as unskilfulness hath no place in skilfulness. Is the soul, then, the cause of evils, even as fire is the cause of warmth? And doth the soul, then, fill with evil whatsoever things are near it? Or is the nature of the soul in itself good, while yet in its activities the soul is sometimes in one state, and sometimes in another?[1] Now, if the very existence of the soul is naturally evil, whence is that existence derived? From the Good Creative Cause of the whole world? If from this Origin, how can it be, in its essential nature, evil? For all things sprung from out this Origin are good. But if it is evil merely in its activities, even so this condition is not fixed. Otherwise (*i.e.* if it doth not itself also assume a good quality) what is the origin of the virtues?[2]

[1] D. is here alluding to the mystical doctrine of the timeless self—the ultimate root of goodness in each individual which remains unchanged by the failures and sins of the temporal self.

[2] D. is arguing with those who hold that evil is in some sense necessary to the existence of the world, and therefore has a permanent place in it. Sin is, they hold, a necessary self-realization of human

There remains but one alternative: Evil is a weakness and deficiency of Good.

31. Good things have all one cause. If evil is opposed to the Good, then hath evil many causes. The efficient causes of evil results, however, are not any laws and faculties, but an impotence and weakness and an inharmonious mingling of discordant elements. Evil things are not immutable and unchanging but indeterminate and indefinite : the sport of alien influences which have no definite aim. The Good must be the beginning and the end even of all evil things. For the Good is the final Purpose of all things, good and bad alike. For even when we act amiss we do so from a longing for the Good ; for no one makes evil his definite object when performing any action. Hence evil hath no substantial being, but only a shadow thereof ; since the Good, and not itself, is the ultimate object for which it comes into existence.

32. Unto evil we can attribute but an accidental kind of existence. It exists for the sake of something else, and is not self-originating. And hence our action appears to be right (for it hath Good as its object) while yet it is not really right (because we mistake for good that which is not good). 'Tis proven, then, that our purpose is different from our action. Thus evil is contrary to progress, purpose, nature, cause, principle, end, law, will, and being. Evil is, then, a lack, a deficiency, a weakness, a disproportion, an error, purposeless, unlovely, lifeless, unwise, unreasonable, imperfect, unreal, causeless, indeterminate, sterile, inert, powerless, disordered, incongruous, indefinite, dark, unsubstantial, and never in itself possessed of any existence whatever. How,

---

souls which are in their ultimate essence sinless. D. replies that, if this is so, we cannot explain how goodness can ever be (as it is) a form of self-realization for human souls.

then, is it that an admixture of the Good bestows any
power upon evil ?   For that which is altogether destitute of Good is nothing and hath no power.   And
if the Good is Existent and is the Source of will,
power, and action, how can Its opposite (being destitute of existence, will, power, and activity), have any
power against It?   Only because evil things are not
all entirely the same in all cases and in all relations.[1]
In the case of a devil evil lieth in the being contrary
to spiritual goodness ; in the soul it lieth in the being
contrary to reason ; in the body it lieth in the being
contrary to nature.

33. How can evil things have any existence at all
if there is a Providence?   Only because evil (as such)
hath no being, neither inhereth it in things that have
being.   And naught that hath being is independent
of Providence ; for evil hath no being at all, except
when mingled with the Good.   And if no thing in
the world is without a share in the Good, and evil is
the deficiency of Good and no thing in the world is
utterly destitute of Good, then the Divine Providence
is in all things, and nothing that exists can be without It.   Yea, even the evil effects that arise are turned
by Providence to a kindly purpose, for the succour
of themselves or others (either individually or in
common), and thus it is that Providence cares individually for each particular thing in all the world.
Therefore we shall pay no heed to the fond argument
so often heard that "Providence shall lead us unto
virtue even against our will."   'Tis not worthy of
Providence to violate nature.   Wherefore Its Providential character is shown herein : that It preserves
the nature of each individual, and, in making provision for the free and independent, it hath respect
unto their state, providing, both in general and in

---

[1] *i. e.* Evil things are not *entirely* bad, but are bad only in some
partial aspect.

particular, according as the nature of those It cares
for can receive Its providential benefactions, which
are bestowed suitably on each by Its multiform and
universal activity.

34. Thus evil hath no being, nor any inherence in
things that have being. Evil is nowhere *qua* evil ;
and it arises not through any power but through
weakness. Even the devils derive their existence
from the Good, and their mere existence is good.
Their evil is the result of a fall from their proper
virtues, and is a change with regard to their individual state, a weakness of their true angelical
perfections. And they desire the Good in so far
as they desire existence, life, and understanding ; and
in so far as they do not desire the Good, they desire
that which hath no being. And this is not desire,
but an error of real desire.

35. By "men who sin knowingly" Scripture means
them that are weak in the *exercised* knowledge[1] and
performance of Good ; and by "them that know the
Divine Will and do it not,"[2] it means them that have
heard the truth and yet are weak in faith to trust the
Good or in action to fulfil it.[3] And some desire not
to have understanding in order that they may do
good, so great is the warping or the weakness
of their will. And, in a word, evil (as we have
often said) is weakness, impotence, and deficiency of

---

[1] περὶ τὴν ἄλησστον τοῦ ἀγαθοῦ γνῶσιν.

[2] Luke xii. 47.

[3] In the previous section D has maintained that all people ultimately
desire the Good. Hence it follows that all sin is due to ignorance ; for
could we all recognize that which we desire we would follow it. This
raises the question : What, then, does Scripture mean by speaking of
men who sin knowingly ? To this D. replies that wilful sin is wilful
ignorance. It is the failure to exercise the knowledge we possess : as
when we know a fact which yet is not actually present to our minds.
We know (having been taught it) the desirableness of the Good, but
we can shut this desirableness out from our minds and refuse to dwell
upon it. In such a case we refuse to exercise our knowledge.

knowledge (or, at least, of exercised knowledge), or of faith, desire, or activity as touching the Good. Now, it may be urged that weakness should not be punished, but on the contrary should be pardoned. This would be just were the power not within man's grasp; but if the power is offered by the Good that giveth without stint (as saith the Scripture) that which is needful to each, we must not condone the wandering or defection, desertion, and fall from the proper virtues offered by the Good. But hereon let that suffice which we have already spoken (to the best of our abilities) in the treatise *Concerning Justice and Divine Judgment:*[1] a sacred exercise wherein the Truth of Scripture disallowed as lunatic babbling such nice arguments as despitefully and slanderously blaspheme God. In this present treatise we have, to the best of our abilities, celebrated the Good as truly Admirable, as the Beginning and the End of all things, as the Power that embraces them, as That Which gives form to non-existent things, as That which causes all good things and yet causes no evil things, as perfect Providence and Goodness surpassing all things that are and all that are not, and turning base things and the lack of Itself unto good, as That Which all must desire, yearn for, and love; and as possessed of many other qualities the which a true argument hath, methinks, in this chapter expounded.

[1] This treatise is lost.

CHAPTER V

Concerning "Existence" and also concerning "Exemplars."

1. Now must we proceed to the Name of "Being" which is truly applied by the Divine Science to Him that truly Is. But this much we must say, that it is not the purpose of our discourse to reveal the Super-Essential Being in its Super-Essential Nature[1] (for this is unutterable, nor can we know It, or in anywise express It, and It is beyond even the Unity[2]), but only to celebrate the Emanation of the Absolute Divine Essence into the universe of things. For the Name of "Good" revealing all the emanations of the universal Cause, extends both to the things which

---

[1] The ultimate Godhead is reached only by the Negative Path, and known only by Unknowing. The Affirmative Path of philosophical knowledge leads only to the differentiated manifestations of the Godhead: *e.g.* the Trinity, in Its creative and redemptive activities, is known by the Affirmative Method, but behind these activities and the faculty for them lies an ultimate Mystery where the Persons transcend Themselves and are fused (though not confused).

[2] In spiritual Communion, the mind, being joined with God, distinguishes itself from Him as Self from Not-Self, Subject from Object. And this law was fulfilled even in the Human Soul of Christ, Who distinguished Himself from His Father. The Persons of the Trinity, though they lie deeper than this temporal world (being, in Their eternal emanative Desire, the Ground of its existence), were manifested through the Incarnation. Hence the distinction of Father, Son, and Spirit, revealed in the Human Soul of Christ, exists eternally in the Trinity. And those who reach the Unitive State, since they reach it only through the Spirit of Christ and are one spirit with Him, must in a lesser degree reveal the Personal Differentiations of the Trinity in their lives. But because the eternal Differentiations of the Trinity transcend Themselves in the Super-Essence, therefore Their manifestations in the Unitive State lead finally to a point beyond Union where all distinctions are transcended. At that point the distinction between Self and Not-Self, Subject and Object, vanishes in the unknowable Mystery of the Divine Darkness. The Self has disappeared and been, in a sense, merged. But in another sense the Self remains. This is the paradox of Personality—that it seeks (and attains) annihilation in the Supra-personal plane, and yet on the relative plane retains its own particular being. This is the paradox of Love. See Intr., p. 28 f., and p. 8.

are, and to the things which are not, and is beyond
both categories.[1] And the title of " Existent " extends to all existent things and is beyond them.
And the title " Life " extends to all living things
and is beyond them. And the title of " Wisdom "
extends to the whole realm of Intuition, Reason, and
Sense-Perception, and is beyond them all.[2]

2. These Names which reveal the Providence of
God our Discourse would now consider. For we
make no promise to express the Absolute Super-
Essential Goodness and Being and Life and Wisdom
of the Absolute Super-Essential Godhead which (as
saith the Scripture) hath Its foundation in a
secret place [3] beyond all Goodness, Godhead, Being,
Wisdom, and Life ; but we are considering the benignant Providence which is revealed to us and are
celebrating It as Transcendent Goodness and Cause
of all good things, and as Existent as Life and as
Wisdom, and as productive Cause of Existence and
of Life and the Giver of Wisdom, in those creatures
which partake of Existence, Life, Intelligence, and

---

[1] *i.e.* Extends both to good things and to bad things and is beyond
the opposition between good and bad. The Good extends to bad
things because evil is a mere distortion of good, and no evil thing could
exist but for an element of good holding it together : its existence, *qua*
existence, is good. See ch. iv.

The Good is beyond the opposition between good and evil because
on the ultimate plane nothing exists outside It. It is beyond relationships. Hence also beyond Existence, Life, and Wisdom, since these
(as we know them) imply relationships.

[2] Sense-perception is a direct apprehension of that which we
actually touch, see, hear, taste, or smell ; Reason or Inference is an
indirect apprehension of that which we do not actually touch, see, etc.
Intuition is a direct apprehension of that which (by its very nature) we
do not touch, see, etc. Sense perception, Reason, and Intuition are
refractions from the perfect Light of Divine Wisdom ; but the Divine
Wisdom is beyond them because God apprehends all things, not as
existent outside Himself, but as existent in Himself, under the form of
a single Unity which is identical with His own Being.

The Godhead is a Single Desire wherein all the souls eternally exist
as fused and inseparable elements.   [3] See Ps. xvii. 12.

Perception. We do not regard the Good as one thing, the Existent as another, and Life or Wisdom as another ; nor do we hold that there are many causes and different Godheads producing different effects and subordinate one to another ; but we hold that one God is the universal Source of the emanations,[1] and the Possessor of all the Divine Names we declare ; and that the first Name expresses the perfect Providence of the one God, and the other names express certain more general or more particular modes of His Providence.[2]

3. Now, some one may say : "How is it, since Existence transcends Life, and Life transcends Wisdom, that living things are higher than things which merely exist, and sentient things than those which merely live, and reasoning things than those which merely feel, and intelligences than those which have only reason ?[3] Why do the creatures rise in this order to the Presence of God and to a closer relationship with Him ? You would have expected those which participate in God's greater gifts to be the higher, and to surpass the rest." Now if intelligent beings were defined as having no

[1] *i. e.* Is the Source of Goodness, existence, life, wisdom, etc.

[2] The title "Good" applies to all God's providential activity, for everything that He makes is good. And even evil is good depraved ; and exists *as* good in the Good (see p. 132, n. 1). Or, rather, evil possesses not an existence but a *non-existence* in the Good. It is (according to D.) a kind of non-existent good. Hence the title "Existent" is not quite so general as the title "Good." "Living" is a less general title still (since a stone, for instance, has no life), and "Wise" is yet less general (since a plant is not wise). Thus we get the following table of emanating activity :

(1) Good (including and transcending *existent* and non-existent things, viz. "good," and "evil").
(2) Existent (*existent* things, viz. good).
(3) Life (plants, animals, men, angels).
(4) Wisdom (men and angels).

[3] Intuition is the faculty of the Intelligences or Angels, by which are meant, of course, angels and *spiritual* men ; Discursive Reason is that of *natural* men.

Existence or Life, the argument would be sound ; but since the divine Intelligences do exist in a manner surpassing other existences, and live in a manner surpassing other living things, and understand and know in a manner beyond perception and reason, and in a manner beyond all existent things participate in the Beautiful and Good, they have a nearer place to the Good in that they especially participate therein, and have from It received both more and greater gifts, even as creatures possessed of Reason are exalted, by the superiority of Reason, above those which have but Perception, and these are exalted through having Perception and others through having Life. And the truth, I think, is that the more anything participates in the One infinitely-bountiful God the more is it brought near to Him and made diviner than the rest.[1]

[1] The more universal a Title is, the more truly it is applicable to God (see end of Section 2). Thus Existence is more applicable than Life, and Life than Wisdom, as involving in each case less that needs to be discarded. Thus Wisdom implies both a time-process and also a certain finite mode of consciousness, neither of which belong to the eternal and infinite God : Life implies a time-process though not a finite consciousness : Existence implies neither time-process nor finite consciousness. Thus we reach the highest conception of God by a process of abstraction in which we cast aside all particular elements (cf. St. Augustine on the *Bonum bonum*).

This is the philosophical basis of the *Via Negativa*. But this abstraction is not mere abstraction nor this negation mere negation. Existence in God subsumes and so includes all that is real in Life ; and Life in Him subsumes all that is real in Wisdom. Hence the creatures, as they advance in the scale of creation, draw from Him more and more particular qualities and progress by becoming more concrete and individual instead of more abstract. All the rich variety of creation exists as a simple Unity in God, and the higher a creature stands in the scale, the more does it draw fresh forces from this simple Unity and convert them into its own multiplicity. D. would have understood Evolution very well. This passage exactly fits in with D's. psychological doctrine of the *Via Negativa*. That which is reached by the spiritual act of Contemplation explains the principles underlying the whole creative process, the growing diversity of the world-process and of human life. In God there is a rich Unity, and we must leave all diversity behind to reach It. Thus we shall have richness without diversity.

4. Having now dealt with this matter, let us consider the Good as that which really Is and gives their being to all things that exist. The Existent God is, by the nature of His power, super-essentially above all existence ; He is the substantial Cause and Creator of Being, Existence, Substance and Nature, the Beginning and the Measuring Principle of ages ; the Reality underlying time and the Eternity underlying existences ; the time in which created things pass,[1] the Existence of those that have any kind of existence, the Life-Process of those which in any way pass through that process. From Him that Is come Eternity, Essence, Being, Time, Life-Process, and that which passes through such Process, the things which inhere in existent things[2] and those which under any power whatever possess an independent subsistence. For God is not Existent in any ordinary sense, but in a simple and undefinable manner embracing and anticipating all existence in Himself. Hence He is called "King of the Ages," because in Him and around Him all Being is and subsists, and He neither was, nor will be, nor hath entered the life-process, nor is doing so, nor ever will, or rather He doth not even exist, but is the Essence of existence in things that exist ; and not only the things that exist but also their very existence comes from Him that Is before the ages. For He Himself is the Eternity of the ages and subsists before the ages.

---

[1] Eternity is a *totum simul*. It may thus be symbolized by a point revolving round a centre at infinite speed. Time would be symbolized by a point revolving round a centre at a finite speed. Thus eternity is time made perfect. Time is thus subsumed in eternity as the incomplete in the complete. Hence time, like existence, life, etc., exists in God as transcended. Hence the temporal-process is a manifestation of Him. This might lead to Pantheism, but D. is saved from such a result by his hold on the complementary truth of Transcendence. All the properties, etc., of each thing exist *outside that thing* as an element in the Transcendent Being of God.

[2] *i. e.* The qualities of things.

5. Let us, then, repeat that all things and all ages derive their existence from the Pre-Existent. All Eternity and Time are from Him, and He who is Pre-Existent is the Beginning and the Cause of all Eternity and Time and of anything that hath any kind of being. All things participate in Him, nor doth He depart from anything that exists; He is before all things, and all things have their maintenance in Him ; and, in short, if anything exists under any form whatever, 'tis in the Pre-Existent that it exists and is perceived and preserves its being. Antecedent[1] to all Its other participated gifts is that of Being. Very Being is above Very Life, Very Wisdom, Very Divine Similarity and all the other universal Qualities, wherein all creatures that participate must participate first of all in Being Itself; or rather, all those mere Universals wherein the creatures participate do themselves participate in very Being Itself. And there is no existent thing whose essence and eternal nature is not very Being.[2] Hence God receives His Name from the most primary of His gifts when, as is meet, He is called in a special manner above all things, " He which Is." For, possessing in a transcendent manner Pre-Existence and Pre-Eminence, He caused beforehand all Existence (I mean Very Being) and in that Very Being caused all the particular modes of existence. For all the principles of existent things derive from their participation in Being the fact that they are existent and that they are principles and that the former quality precedes the latter. And if it like thee to say that Very Life is the Universal Principle of living things as such, and Very Similarity of similar things as such, and Very Unity of unified things as such, and Very

---

[1] *sc.* Logically not temporally.
[2] Cf. St. Augustine, "Homini bono tolle hominem, et Deum invenis." Cf. Section 8.

Order of orderly things as such, and if it like thee
to give the name of Universals to the Principles of
all other things which (by participating in this quality
or in that or in both or in many) *are* this, that, both
or many thou wilt find that the first Quality in which
they participate is Existence, and that their existence
is the basis, (1) of their permanence, and (2) of their
being the principles of this or that ; and also that only
through their participation in Existence do they exist
and enable things to participate in them.   And if
these Universals exist by participating in Existence,
far more is this true of the things which participate
in them.

6. Thus the first gift which the Absolute and
Transcendent Goodness bestows is that of mere
Existence, and so It derives its first title from the
chiefest of the participations in Its Being.   From It
and in It are very Being and the Principles of the
world, and the world which springs from them and
all things that in any way continue in existence.
This attribute belongs to It in an incomprehensible
and concentrated oneness.   For all number pre-
exists indivisibly in the number One, and this number
contains all things in itself under the form of unity.
All number exists as unity in number One, and only
when it goes forth from this number is it differenced
and multiplied.[1]   All the radii of a circle are concentrated into a single unity in the centre, and this
point contains all the straight lines brought together
within itself and unified to one another, and to the
one starting-point from which they began.   Even so
are they a perfect unity in the centre itself, and,
departing a little therefrom they are differenced a
little, and departing further are differenced further,
and, in fact, the nearer they are to the centre, so

---

[1] The number One, being infinitely divisible, contains the potentiality of all numbers.

K

much the more are they united to it and to one another, and the more they are separated from it the more they are separated from one another.[1]

7. Moreover, in the Universal Nature of the world all the individual Laws of Nature are united in one Unity without confusion; and in the soul the individual faculties which govern different parts of the body are united in one. And hence it is not strange that, when we mount from obscure images to the Universal Cause, we should with supernatural eyes behold all things (even those things which are mutually contrary) existing as a single Unity in the Universal Cause. For It is the beginning of all things, whence are derived Very Being, and all things that have any being, all Beginning and End, all Life, Immortality, Wisdom, Order, Harmony, Power, Preservation, Grounding, Distribution, Intelligence, Reason, Perception, Quality, Rest, Motion, Unity, Fusion, Attraction, Cohesion, Differentiation, Definition, and all other Attributes which, by their mere existence, qualify all existent things.

8. And from the same Universal Cause come those godlike and angelical Beings, which possess Intelligence and are apprehended by Intelligence; and from It come our souls and the natural laws of the whole universe, and all the qualities which we speak of as existing in other objects or as existing merely in our thoughts. Yea, from It come the all-holy and most reverent Powers, which possess a real existence[2] and are grounded, as it were, in the fore-court of the Super-Essential Trinity, possessing from It and in It their existence and the godlike nature thereof; and, after them, those which are inferior to them, possessing their inferior existence from the same Source; and

[1] Cf. Plotinus.
[2] sc. In contradistinction to the Godhead, which (being beyond essence) does not literally exist.

the lowest, possessing from It their lowest existence
(*i. e.* lowest compared with the other angels, though
compared with us it is above our world). And human
souls and all other creatures possess by the same
tenure their existence, and their blessedness, and exist
and are blessed only because they possess their
existence and their blessedness from the Pre-existent,
and exist and are blessed in Him, and begin from
Him and are maintained in Him and attain in Him
their Final Goal. And the highest measure of
existence He bestows upon the more exalted Beings,
which the Scripture calls eternal; [1] but also the mere
existence of the world as a whole is perpetual; and
its very existence comes from the Pre-existent. He
is not an Attribute of Being, but Being is an Attribute
of Him; He is not contained in Being, but Being is
contained in Him; He doth not possess Being, but
Being possesses Him; He is the Eternity, the Beginning, and the Measure of Existence, being anterior to
Essence and essential Existence and Eternity, because
He is the Creative Beginning, Middle, and End of all
things. And hence the truly Pre-existent receives
from the Holy Scripture manifold attributions drawn
from every kind of existence; and states of being
and processes (whether past, present, or future) are
properly attributed to Him; for all these attributions,
if their divine meaning be perceived, signify that He
hath a Super-Essential Existence fulfilling all our
categories, and is the Cause producing every mode of
existence. For He is not This without being That;
nor doth He possess this mode of being without
that. On the contrary He *is* all things as being the
Cause of them all, and as holding together and
anticipating in Himself all the beginnings and all the
fulfilments of all things; and He is above them all
in that He, anterior to their existence, super-essentially

[1] 2 Cor. iv. 18.

transcends them all.   Hence all attributes may be affirmed at once of Him, and yet He is No Thing.[1] He possesses all shape and form, and yet is formless and shapeless, containing beforehand incomprehensibly and transcendently the beginning, middle, and end of all things, and shedding upon them a pure radiance of that one and undifferenced causality whence all their fairness comes.[2]   For if our sun, while still remaining one luminary and shedding one unbroken light, acts on the essences and qualities of the things which we perceive, many and various though they be, renewing, nourishing, guarding, and perfecting them; differencing them, unifying them, warming them and making them fruitful, causing them to grow, to change, to take root and to burst forth ; quickening them and giving them life, so that each one possesses in its own way a share in the same single sun—if the single sun contains beforehand in itself under the form of an unity the causes of all the things that participate in it ; much more doth this truth hold good with the Cause which produced the sun and all things ; and all the Exemplars [3] of existent thnigs must pre-exist in It under the form of one Super-Essential Unity.[4]   For It produces Essences only by an outgoing from Essence.   And we give the name of "Exemplars" to those laws which, pre-existent in God [5] as an Unity, produce the essences of things : laws which are called in Divine Science

[1] Cf. *Theol. Germ.* passim.   Hence the soul possessing God is in a state of "having nothing and yet possessing all things."   Cf. Dante, *cio che per l'universa si squaderna*, etc.

[2] Cf. Section 5.

[3] *i. e.* The Platonic ideas of things—their ultimate essences.   But see below.

[4] Cf. Blake.   "Jerusalem," *ad fin.*

[5] *i. e.* If It produces the essences of things, It must first contain Essence.   D. here uses the term "God" because he is thinking of the Absolute in Its emanating activity (wherein the Differentiations of the Trinity appear).

" Preordinations " or Divine and beneficent Volitions,
laws which ordain things and create them, laws
whereby the Super-Essential preordained and brought
into being the whole universe.

9. And whereas the philosopher Clement[1] maintains
that the title " Exemplar " may, in a sense, be applied
to the more important types in the visible world, he
employs not the terms of his discourse in their proper,
perfect and simple meaning.[2]   But even if we grant

[1] This is apparently the Bishop of Rome (*c.* A.D. 95), writer of the
well-known Epistle to the Corinthians, which is the earliest Christian
writing outside the New Testament, and is published in Lightfoot's
Apostolic Fathers.   But no such passage as D. alludes to occurs in the
Epistle, which is his one extant writing.

[2] Cf. St. Augustine, *Commentary on St. John*, Tr. XXI., § 2 : " Ubi
demonstrat Filio Pater quod facit nisi in ipso Filio per quem facit?
. . . . Si quid facit Pater per Filium facit ; si per sapientiam suam et
virtutem suam facit ; non extra illi ostendit quod videat . . . in ipso illi
ostendit quod facit. . . . (3) Quid videt Pater, vel potius quid videt
Filius in Patre . . . et ipse."   (The Son beholds all things in Himself,
and is Himself in the Father.)

All things ultimately and timelessly exist in the Absolute.   It is
their Essence (or Super-Essence).   Their creation from the Absolute
into actual existence is performed by the Differentiated Persons of the
Trinity : the Father working by the Spirit through the Son.   Thus
the Differentiated Persons (to which together is given the Name of
God) being the *manifested* Absolute, contain eternally those fused yet
distinct essences of things which exist in the Absolute as a single yet
manifold Essence.   This Essence they, by their mutual operation, pour
forth, so that while ultimately contained in (or, rather identified with)
the Absolute, it is in this world of relationships distinct and separate
from the Differentiated Persons Which together are God, being in
fact, a created manifestation of the Absolute, as God is an Uncreated
Manifestation Thereof.

This created Essence of the world itself becomes differentiated into
the separate creatures (water, earth, plants, animals, etc.), having this
tendency because it contains within itself their separate generic forms
which seek expression in the various particular things.   Wherever we
can trace a law or purpose it is due to the presence of a generic form.
Thus vapour condenses into water in obedience to the generic form of
water, and an oak-tree grows to its full stature in obedience to the
generic form of the oak.   So too with works of art.   A cathedral is
built in accordance with a plan or purpose, and this plan is the pre-
existent generic form of the building ; whereas a fortuitous heap of
stones does not (as such) manifest any plan, and therefore has no
generic form.

the truth of his contention, we must remember the Scripture which saith : " I did not show these things unto thee that thou mightest follow after them," but that through such knowledge of these as is suited to our faculties we may be led up (so far as is possible) to the Universal Cause. We must then attribute unto It all things in one All-Transcendent Unity, inasmuch as, starting from Being, and setting in motion the creative Emanation and Goodness, and penetrating all things, and filling all things with Being from Itself, and rejoicing in all things, It anticipates all things in Itself, in one exceeding simplicity rejecting all reduplication ; and It embraces all things alike in the Transcendent Unity of Its infinitude, and is indivisibly shared by all (even as a sound, while remaining one and the same, is shared *as* one by several pairs of ears).

10. Thus the Pre-existent is the Beginning and the End of all things : the Beginning as their Cause, the End as their Final Purpose. He bounds all things and yet is their boundless Infinitude, in a manner that transcends all the opposition between the Finite and the Infinite.[1] For, as hath been often

---

D. attributing to Clement (perhaps fictitiously) the view that generic forms can in themselves—*i. e.* in their created essence—be properly called Exemplars, maintains that this is not strictly accurate. Properly speaking, he says, they are Exemplars only as existent in God, and not as projected out from Him. If, by a licence, we call them Exemplars, yet we must not let our minds rest in them, but must pass on at once to find their true being in God.

This apparent hair-splitting is really of the utmost practical importance. D. is attacking the irreligious attitude in science, philosophy, and life. We must seek for all things (including our own personalities) not in themselves but in God. The great defect of Natural Science in the nineteenth century was its failure to do this. It was, perhaps, the defect of Gnosticism in earlier days, and is the pitfall of Occultism to-day.

[1] *i. e.* He gives each thing its distinctness while yet containing infinite possibilities of development for it.

said, He contains beforehand and did create all things in One Act, being present unto all and everywhere, both in the particular individual and in the Universal Whole, and going out unto all things while yet remaining in Himself. He is both at rest and in motion,[1] and yet is in neither state, nor hath He beginning, middle, or end ; He neither inheres in any individual thing, nor is He any individual thing.[2] We cannot apply to Him any attribute of eternal things nor of temporal things. He transcends both Time and Eternity, and all things that are in either of them; inasmuch as Very Eternity[3] and the world with its standard of measurement and the things which are measured by those standards have their being through Him and from Him. But concerning these matters let that suffice which hath been spoken more properly elsewhere.

[1] He is always yearning yet always satisfied. Cf. St. Augustine, *Confessions, ad in.* A reproduction of this state has been experienced by some of the Saints. Cf. Julian of Norwich : "I had Him and I wanted Him."

[2] He is the ultimate Reality of all beings, and is not one Being among others.

[3] Very Eternity perhaps corresponds to the *aeternitas* of St. Thomas and Eternity to his *aevum* (with which cf. Bergson's *durée*). Eternity is a *totum simul* without beginning or end, *aevum* is a *totum simul* with beginning but no end. It is eternity reached through Time, or Time accelerated to the stillness of infinite motion and so changed into Eternity, as in human souls when finally clothed with perfected immortality.

The Absolute, or Godhead, is beyond Very Eternity, because this latter is a medium of differentiated existence (for the differentiated Persons of the Trinity exist in it), whereas the Godhead is undifferentiated and beyond relationships. This world of Time springs out of Very Eternity and is rooted therein, being made by the differentiated Persons.

CHAPTER VI

Concerning " Life."

1. Now must we celebrate Eternal Life as that whence cometh very Life and all life,[1] which also endues every kind of living creature with its appropriate meed of Life.   Now the Life of the immortal Angels and their immortality, and the very indestructibility of their perpetual motion, exists and is derived from It and for Its sake.   Hence they are called Ever-living and Immortal, and yet again are denied to be immortal, because they are not the source of their own immortality and eternal life, but derive it from the creative Cause which produces and maintains all life.   And, as, in thinking of the title " Existent," we said that It is an Eternity of very Being, so do we now say that the Supra-Vital or Divine Life is the Vitalizer and Creator of Life.   And all life and vital movement comes from the Life which is beyond all Life and beyond every Principle of all Life.   Thence have souls their indestructible quality, and all animals and plants possess their life as a far-off reflection of that Life. When this is taken away, as saith the Scripture, all life fades ;[2] and those which have faded, through being unable to participate therein, when they turn to It again revive once more.

2. In the first place It gives to Very Life its vital quality, and to all life and every form thereof It gives the Existence appropriate to each.   To the celestial forms of life it gives their immaterial, godlike, and

---

[1] The Godhead, though called Eternal Life, is really supra-vital, because life implies differentiations, and the Godhead as such is undifferentiated.   This Supra-Vitality passes out through the Differentiated Persons of the Trinity into Very Life, whence life is derived to all the creatures.

[2] Ps. civ. 29, 30.

unchangeable immortality and their unswerving and
unerring perpetuity of motion ; and, in the abundance
of Its bounty, It overflows even into the life of the
devils, for not even diabolic life derives its existence
from any other source, but derives from This both its
vital nature and its permanence. And, bestowing
upon men such angelic life as their composite nature
can receive, in an overflowing wealth of love It turns
and calls us from our errors to Itself, and (still
Diviner act) It hath promised to change our whole
being (I mean our souls and the bodies linked
therewith) to perfect Life and Immortality, which
seemed to the ancients unnatural, but seems to me and
thee and to the Truth a Divine and Supernatural
thing : Supernatural, I say, as being above the visible
order of nature around us, not as being above the
Nature of Divine Life. For unto this Life (since it is
the Nature of all forms of life,[1] and especially of those
which are more Divine) no form of life is unnatural
or supernatural. And therefore fond Simon's cap-
tious arguments[2] on this subject must find no entry
into the company of God's servants or into thy
blessed soul. For, in spite of his reputed wisdom, he
forgot that no one of sound mind should set the
superficial order of sense-perception against the Invisible Cause of all things.[3] We must tell him that
if there is aught " against Nature " 'tis his language.
For naught can be contrary to the Ultimate Cause.

3. From this Source all animals and plants receive
their life and warmth. And wherever (under the
form of intelligence, reason, sensation, nutrition,
growth, or any mode whatsoever) you find life or the

---

[1] *i. e.* The ultimate Principle.
[2] Simon denied the Resurrection of the Body.   *Vide* Irenæus,
Origen, Hippolytus, Epiphanius.
[3] Physical life has behind it Eternal Life, by which it is in the true
sense natural for it to be renewed and transformed.

Principle of life or the Essence of life, there you find
that which lives and imparts life from the Life transcending all life, and indivisibly [1] pre-exists therein as
in its Cause.   For the Supra-Vital and Primal Life is
the Cause of all Life, and produces and fulfils it and
individualizes it.   And we must draw from all life the
attributes we apply to It when we consider how It
teems with all living things, and how under manifold
forms It is beheld and praised in all Life and lacketh
not Life or rather abounds therein, and indeed hath
Very Life, and how it produces life in a Supra-Vital
manner and is above all life [2] and therefore is
described by whatsoever human terms may express
that Life which is ineffable.

CHAPTER VII

Concerning "Wisdom," "Mind," "Reason," "Truth," "Faith."

1. Now, if it like thee, let us consider the Good and
Eternal Life as Wise and as Very Wisdom, or rather
as the Fount of all wisdom and as Transcending all
wisdom and understanding.   Not only is God so overflowing with wisdom that there is no limit to His
understanding, but He even *transcends* all Reason,
Intelligence, and Wisdom.[3]   And this is supernaturally perceived by the truly divine man (who hath

[1] Since Eternal Life is undifferentiated, all things have in It a
common or identical life, as all plants and animals have a common life
in the air they breathe.

[2] See p. 144, n. 1.

[3] All wisdom or knowledge implies the distinction between thinker
and object of thought.   The undifferentiated Godhead is beyond this
distinction ; but (in a sense) it exists in the Persons of the Trinity and
between them and the world, and hence from Them comes Absolute
Wisdom, though the Godhead transcends it.

been as a luminary both to us and to our teacher)
when he says : " The foolishness of God is wiser than
men." [1]   And these words are true not only because
all human thought is a kind of error when compared
with the immovable permanence of the perfect
thoughts which belong to God, but also because it is
customary for writers on Divinity to apply negative
terms to God in a sense contrary to the usual one.
For instance, the Scripture calls the Light that shines
on all things "Terrible," and Him that hath many Titles
and many Names " Ineffable " and " Nameless," and
Him that is present to all things and to be discovered
from them all " Incomprehensible " and " Unsearchable."   In the same manner, it is thought, the divine
Apostle, on the present occasion, when he speaks of
God's " foolishness," is using in a higher sense the apparent strangeness and absurdity implied in the word,
so as to hint at the ineffable Truth which is before all
Reason.   But, as I have said elsewhere, we misinter-
pret things above us by our own conceits and cling to
the familiar notions of our senses, and, measuring
Divine things by our human standards, we are led
astray by the superficial meaning of the Divine and
Ineffable Truth.   Rather should we then consider
that while the human Intellect hath a faculty of
Intelligence, whereby it perceives intellectual truths,
yet the act whereby the Intellect communes with the
things that are beyond it transcends its intellectual
nature. [2]   This transcendent sense, therefore, must be
given to our language about God, and not our human
sense.   We must be transported wholly out of ourselves and given unto God.   For 'tis better to belong
unto God and not unto ourselves, since thus will the

---

[1] 1 Cor. i. 25.
[2] This is the Doctrine of Unknowing.
   Cf. " Through love, through hope, and faith's transcendent dower,
     We feel that we are mightier than we know."

Divine Bounties be bestowed, if we are united to God.[1] Speaking, then, in a transcendent manner of this "Foolish Wisdom,"[2] which hath neither Reason nor Intelligence, let us say that It is the Cause of all Intelligence and Reason, and of all Wisdom and Understanding, and that all counsel belongs unto It, and from It comes all Knowledge and Understanding, and in It "are hid all the treasures of wisdom and knowledge."[3] For it naturally follows from what hath already been said that the All-wise (and more than Wise) Cause is the Fount of Very Wisdom and of created wisdom both as a whole and in each individual instance.[4]

2. From It the intelligible and intelligent powers of the Angelic Minds derive their blessed simple perceptions, not collecting their knowledge of God in partial fragments or from partial activities of Sensation or of discursive Reason, nor yet being circumscribed by aught that is akin to these,[5] but rather, being free from all taint of matter and multiplicity, they perceive the spiritual truths of Divine things in a single immaterial and spiritual intuition. And their intuitive faculty and activity shines in its unalloyed and undefiled purity and possesses its Divine intuitions all together in an indivisible and immaterial manner, being by that Godlike unification made similar (as far as may be) to the Supra-Sapient Mind and Reason of

---

[1] The term "God" is rightly used here because the *manifested* Absolute is meant.

[2] 1 Cor. i. 25.   [3] Col. ii. 3.

[4] (1) Very Wisdom = Wisdom in the abstract.

    (2) Wisdom as a whole = Wisdom embodied in the universe as a whole.

    (3) Wisdom in each individual instance = Wisdom as shown in the structure of some particular plant or animal, or part of a plant or animal.

        (1) Is an Emanation ; (2) and (3) are created.

[5] *i. e.* They are not limited by the material world, which, with its laws, is known through sensation and discursive reason.

God through the working of the Divine Wisdom.[1]
And human souls possess Reason, whereby they turn
with a discursive motion round about the Truth of
things, and, through the partial and manifold activities
of their complex nature, are inferior to the Unified
Intelligences : yet they too, through the concentration
of their many faculties, are vouchsafed (so far as their
nature allows) intuitions like unto those of the
Angels. Nay, even our sense-perceptions themselves
may be rightly described as an echo of that Wisdom ;
even diabolic intelligence, *qua* intelligence, belongs
thereto, though in so far as it is a distraught intelligence, not knowing how to obtain its true desire, nor
wishing to obtain it, we must call it rather a declension from Wisdom. Now we have already said that
the Divine Wisdom is the Beginning, the Cause, the
Fount, the Perfecting Power, the Protector and the
Goal of Very Wisdom and all created Wisdom, and of
all Mind, Reason, and Sense-Perception. We must
now ask in what sense God,[2] Who is Supra-Sapient,
can be spoken of as Wisdom, Mind, Reason, and
Knowledge ? How can He have an intellectual intuition of intelligible things when He possesses no
intellectual activities ? Or how can He know the
things perceived by sense when His existence transcends all sense-perception ? And yet the Scripture
says that He knoweth all things and that nothing
escapes the Divine Knowledge. But, as I have often
said, we must interpret Divine Things in a manner

[1] This speculation is, no doubt, based on experience. A concentration of the spiritual faculties in the act of contemplation produces that
unity of the soul of which all mystics often speak. The angels are
conceived of as being always in such a state of contemplation.

[2] God is the Manifested Absolute. Hence *qua* Absolute He is
supra-sapient, *qua* Manifested He is wise (cf. ch. i, § 1). The Persons
of the Trinity possess one common Godhead (= the Absolute) which
is supra-sapient, and in that Godhead. They *are* One. Yet they are
known by us only in their differentiation wherein Supra-Sapience is
revealed as Wisdom.

suitable to their nature. For the lack of Mind and Sensation must be predicated of God by excess and not by defect.[1] And in the same way we attribute lack of Reason to Him that is above Reason, and Imperfectibility to Him that is above and before Perfection; and Intangible and Invisible Darkness we attribute to that Light which is Unapproachable because It so far exceeds the visible light. And thus the Mind of God embraces all things in an utterly transcendent knowledge and, in Its causal relation to all things, anticipates within Itself the knowledge of them all—knowing and creating angels before the angels were, and knowing all other things inwardly and (if I may so put it) from the very beginning, and thus bringing them into existence. And methinks this is taught by the Scripture when it saith "Who knoweth all things before their birth."[2] For the Mind of God gains not Its knowledge of things from those things; but of Itself and in Itself It possesses, and hath conceived beforehand in a causal manner, the cognizance and the knowledge and the being of them all. And It doth not perceive each class specifically,[3] but in one embracing casuality It knows and maintains all things—even as Light possesses beforehand in itself a causal knowledge of the darkness, not knowing the darkness in any other way than from the Light.[4] Thus the Divine Wisdom in knowing Itself

---

[1] *Via Negativa.* It is not *mere* negation.

[2] Susannah 42.

[3] "According to its idea," "according to the law of its species." We perceive that this is a rose and that is a horse because we have two separate notions in our minds—one the notion of a rose and the other that of a horse. But in the Divine Knowledge there is only one Notion wherein such specific notions are elements, as the activities of several nerves are elements in one indivisible sensation of taste, or touch, or smell.

[4] *i. e.* Suppose the light were conscious, and knew its own nature, it would know that if it withheld its brightness there would be darkness (for the very nature of light is that it dispels, or at least prevents,

will know all things : will in that very Oneness know
and produce material things immaterially, divisible
things indivisibly, manifold things under the form of
Unity. For if God, in the act of causation, imparts
Existence to all things, in the same single act of causation He will support all these His creatures the
which are derived from Him and have in Him their
forebeing, and He will not gain His knowledge of
things from the things themselves, but He will bestow
upon each kind the knowledge of itself and the knowledge of the others. And hence God doth not possess
a private knowledge of Himself and as distinct therefrom a knowledge embracing all the creatures in
common ; for the Universal Cause, in knowing Itself,
can scarcely help knowing the things that proceed
from it and whereof It is the Cause. With this knowledge, then, God knoweth all things, not through a
mere understanding of the things but through an
understanding of Himself. For the angels, too, are
said by the Scripture to know the things upon earth
not through a sense-perception of them (though they
are such as may be perceived this way), but through
a faculty and nature inherent in a Godlike Intelligence.

3. Furthermore, we must ask how it is that we know
God when He cannot be perceived by the mind or
the senses and is not a particular Being. Perhaps
'tis true to say that we know not God by His Nature
(for this is unknowable and beyond the reach of all
Reason and Intuition), yet by means of that ordering
of all things which (being as it were projected out of

---

darkness). On the other hand, the light could not directly know the
darkness, because darkness cannot exist where there is light. The
simile is capable of being applied to illustrate God's knowledge of the
world, because the world is imperfect. It applies more fundamentally
to God's knowledge of evil, and is so employed by St. Thomas Aquinas,
who quotes this passage and says (*Summa*, xiv. 10) that, since evil is
the lack of good, God knows evil things in the act by which He knows
good things, as we know darkness through knowing light.

Him) possesses certain images and semblances of His Divine Exemplars, we mount upwards (so far as our feet can tread that ordered path), advancing through the Negation and Transcendence of all things and through a conception of an Universal Cause, towards That Which is beyond all things.[1] Hence God is known in all things and apart from all things; and God is known through Knowledge and through Unknowing, and on the one hand He is reached by Intuition, Reason, Understanding, Apprehension, Perception, Conjecture, Appearance, Name, etc.; and yet, on the other hand, He cannot be grasped by Intuition, Language, or Name, and He is not anything in the world nor is He known in anything. He is All Things in all things and Nothing in any,[2] and is known from all things unto all men, and is not known from any unto any man. 'Tis meet that we employ such terms concerning God, and we get from all things (in proportion to their quality) notions of Him Who is their Creator. And yet on the other hand, the Divinest Knowledge of God, the which is received through Unknowing, is obtained in that communion which transcends the mind, when the mind, turning away from all things and then leaving even itself behind, is united to the Dazzling Rays, being from them and in them, illumined by the unsearchable depth of Wisdom.[3] Nevertheless, as I said, we must

---

[1] God, being the Manifested Absolute, exists on two planes at once: that of Undifferentiation and that of Differentiation. On this second plane He moves out into creative activity. And thus He is both knowable and unknowable: knowable in so far as He passes outwards into such activity, unknowable in that His Being passes inwards into Undifferentiation. Thus He is known in His acts but not in His ultimate Nature.

[2] He is the Super-Essence of all things, wherein all things possess their true being *outside of themselves* [as our perceptions are outside of ourselves in the things we perceive. (*Vide* Bergson, *Matière et Mémoire.*)].

[3] This is experience and not mere theory.

draw this knowledge of Wisdom from all things; for wisdom it is (as saith the Scripture)[1] that hath made all things and ever ordereth them all, and is the Cause of the indissoluble harmony and order of all things, perpetually fitting the end of one part unto the beginning of the second, and thus producing the one fair agreement and concord of the whole.

4. And God is called "Word" or "Reason"[2] by the Holy Scriptures, not only because He is the Bestower of Reason and Mind and Wisdom, but also because He contains beforehand in His own Unity the causes of all things, and because He penetrates all things, "reaching" (as the Scripture saith) "unto the end of all things,"[3] and more especially because the Divine Reason is more simple than all simplicity, and, in the transcendence of Its Super-Essential Being, is independent of all things.[4] This Reason is the simple and verily existent Truth: that pure and infallible Omniscience round which divinely inspired Faith revolves. It is the permanent Ground of the faithful, which builds them in the Truth and builds the Truth in them by an unwavering firmness, through which they possess a simple knowledge of the Truth of those things which they believe.[5] For if Knowledge unites the knower and the objects of knowledge,

---

[1] Prov. viii.
[2] The reference is, of course, to the opening verses of St. John's Gospel. The present passage shows that by the term "God" D. means not one Differentiation of the Godhead singly (*i. e.* not God the Father), but all Three Differentiations together; the undivided (though differentiated) Trinity.
[3] Wisdom viii. 1.
[4] God is called Reason: (1) because He is the Giver of reason; (2) because reason causes unity (*e. g.* it unifies our thoughts, making them coherent), and God in His creative activity causes unity and in His ultimate Godhead *is* Unity.
[5] The Divine Omniscience is: (1) the Object of our faith because we trust in it; (2) the Ground of our faith because the development of our faith comes from it. Faith is a faint image of Divine Knowledge, and is gradually perfected by being changed into knowledge.

L

and if ignorance is always a cause of change and of self-discrepancy in the ignorant, naught (as saith Holy Scripture) shall separate him that believeth in the Truth from the Foundation of true faith on which he shall possess the permanence of immovable and unchanging firmness. For surely knoweth he who is united to the Truth that it is well with him, even though the multitude reprove him as one out of his mind. Naturally they perceive not that he is but come out of an erring mind unto the Truth through right faith. But he verily knows that instead of being, as they say, distraught, he hath been relieved from the unstable ever-changing movements which tossed him hither and thither in the mazes of error, and hath been set at liberty through the simple immutable and unchanging Truth. Thus is it that the Teachers from whom we have learnt our knowledge of Divine Wisdom die daily for the Truth, bearing their natural witness in every word and deed to the single Knowledge of the Truth which Christians possess : yea, showing that It is more simple and divine than all other kinds of knowledge, or rather that it is the only true, one, simple Knowledge of God.

CHAPTER VIII

Concerning " Power," " Righteousness," " Salvation,"
" Redemption " ; and also concerning " Inequality."

1. NOW since the Sacred Writers speak of the Divine Truthfulness and Supra-Sapient Wisdom as Power, and as Righteousnes, and call It Salvation and Redemption, let us endeavour to unravel these Divine Names also. Now I do not think that any one nurtured in Holy Scripture can fail to know

that the Godhead transcends and exceeds every mode of Power however conceived. For often Scripture attributes the Dominion to the Godhead and thus distinguishes It even from the Celestial Powers.[1] In what sense, then, do the Sacred Writers speak of It also as Power when It transcends all Power? Or in what sense can we take the title Power when applied to the Godhead?

2. We answer thus: God is Power because in His own Self He contains all power beforehand and exceeds it, and because He is the Cause of all power and produces all things by a power which may not be thwarted nor circumscribed, and because He is the Cause wherefrom Power exists whether in the whole system of the world or in any particular part.[2] Yea, He is Infinitely Powerful not only in that all Power comes from Him, but also because He is above all power and is Very Power, and possesses that excess of Power which produces in infinite ways an infinite number of other existent powers; and because the infinitude of powers which is continually being multiplied to infinity can never blunt that transcendently infinite [3] activity of His Power whence all power comes; and because of the unutterable, unknowable, inconceivable greatness of His all-transcendent Power which, through its excess of potency, gives strength to that which is weak and maintains and governs the lowest of its created copies, even as, in those things whose power strikes our senses, very brilliant

---

[1] The highest power our minds can conceive is that of the angels. But God has the dominion over them, and hence His power is of a yet higher kind such as we cannot conceive.

[2] Since the ultimate Godhead is undifferentiated God's power is conceived of as an undifferentiated or *potential* energy.

[3] The inexhaustible multiplication of things in this world, though it should go on for ever, is a series made up of separate units. God's inexhaustible energy is beyond this series because it is *one* indivisible act. The Undifferentiated transcends infinite divisibility. Cf. IX. 2.

illuminations can reach to eyes that are dim and as loud sounds can enter ears dull of hearing. (Of course that which is *utterly* incapable of hearing is not an ear, and that which cannot see *at all* is not an eye.[1])

3. Thus this distribution of God's Infinite Power permeates all things, and there is nothing in the world utterly bereft of all power. Some power it must have, be it in the form of Intuition, Reason, Perception, Life, or Being. And indeed, if one may so express it, the very fact that power exists [2] is derived from the Super-Essential Power.

4. From this Source come the Godlike Powers of the Angelic Orders ; from this Source they immutably possess their being and all the ceaseless and immortal motions of their spiritual life ; and their very stability and unfailing desire for the Good they have received from that infinitely good Power which Itself infuses into them this power and this existence, and makes them ceaselessly to desire existence, and gives them the very power to desire that ceaseless power which they possess.

5. The effects of this Inexhaustible Power enter into men and animals and plants and the entire Nature of the Universe, and fill all the unified organizations with a force attracting them to mutual harmony and concord, and drawing separate individuals into being, according to the natural laws and qualities of each, without confusion or merging of their properties. And the laws by which this Universe is ordered It preserves to fulfil their proper functions, and keeps the immortal lives of the individual angels inviolate ; and the luminous stars of

---

[1] This is meant to meet the objection that if God's power is infinite there should be no decay or death. Things, says D., are sometimes incapable of responding, as a blind eye cannot respond to the light.

[2] *i. e* Power in the abstract.

heaven It keeps in all their ranks unchanged, and gives
unto Eternity the power to be; and the temporal
orbits It differentiates when they begin their circuits
and brings together again when they return once
more; and It makes the power of fire unquenchable,
and the liquid nature of water It makes perpetual;
and gives the atmosphere its fluidity, and founds the
earth upon the Void and keeps its pregnant travail
without ceasing. And It preserves the mutual
harmony of the interpenetrating elements distinct
and yet inseparable, and knits together the bond
uniting soul and body, and stirs the powers by which
the plants have nourishment and growth, and governs
the faculties whereby each kind of creature maintains
its being and makes firm the indissoluble permanence
of the world, and bestows Deification [1] itself by giving
a faculty for it unto those that are deified. And, in
short, there is nothing in the world which is without
the Almighty Power of God to support and to surround it. For that which hath no power at all hath
no existence, no individuality, and no place whatever
in the world.

6. But Elymas [2] the sorcerer raises this objection:
"If God is Omnipotent" (quoth he) "what meaneth
your Sacred Writer by saying that there are some
things He cannot do?" And so he blames Paul the
Divine for saying that God cannot deny Himself.[3]
Now, having stated his objection, I greatly fear that
I shall be laughed at for my folly, in going about to
pull down tottering houses built upon the sand by
idle children, and in striving to aim my arrow at an
inaccessible target when I endeavour to deal with this

[1] See Intr., p. 43.
[2] The name is introduced to support the fiction of authorship, and
an objection, current no doubt in the writer's day (as in every age), is
put into the mouth of one who belonged to the same time as St. Paul's
Athenian convert.
[3] 2 Tim. ii. 13.

question of Divinity.[1]   But thus I answer him :   The
denial of the true Self is a declension from Truth.   And
Truth hath Being ; and therefore a declension from
the Truth is a declension from Being.   Now whereas
Truth hath Being and denial of Truth is a declension
from Being, God cannot fall from Being.   We might say
that He *is not* lacking in Being, that He *cannot* lack
Power, that He *knows not* how to lack Knowledge.
The wise Elymas, forsooth, did not perceive this ; and
so is like an unskilled athlete, who (as often happens),
thinking his adversary to be weak, through judging
by his own estimation, misses him each time and
manfully strikes at his shadow, and bravely beating
the air with vain blows, fancies he hath gotten him a
victory and boasts of his prowess through ignorance
of the other's power.[2]   But we striving to shoot our
guard home to our teacher's mark celebrate the
Supra-Potent God as Omnipotent, as Blessed and the
only Potentate, as ruling by His might over Eternity,
as indwelling every part of the universe, or rather
as transcending and anticipating all things in His
Super-Essential Power, as the One Who hath bestowed
upon all things their capacity to exist, and their existence through the rich outpouring of His transcendent
and abundant Power.

7. Again, God is called " Righteousness " because
He gives to all things what is right, defining Proportion, Beauty, Order, Arrangement, and all Dispositions of Place and Rank for each, in accordance
with that place which is most truly right ; and
because He causeth each to possess its independent
activity.   For the Divine Righteousness ordains all
things, and sets their bounds and keeps all things

---

[1] He seems to mean two distinct things : (1) The objection is
childish and needs no answering ; (2) The whole question is beyond
the reach of our understanding.

[2] This unskilled athlete is not very convincing. Presumably D.
could not box !

unconfused and distinct from one another, and gives
to all things that which is suited to each according to
the worth which each possesses.[1]   And if this is true,
then all those who blame the Divine Righteousness
stand (unwittingly) self-condemned of flagrant un-
righteousness ; for they say that immortality should
belong to mortal things and perfection to the imperfect, and necessary or mechanical motion to those
which possess free spiritual motion, and immutability
to those which change, and the power of accomplishment to the weak, and that temporal things should be
eternal, and that things which naturally move should be
unchangeable, and that pleasures which are but for a
season should last for ever ; and, in short, they would
interchange the properties of all things.   But they
should know that the Divine Righteousness is found
in this to be true Righteousness, that it gives to all
the qualities which befit them, according to the worth
of each, and that it preserves the nature of each in its
proper order and power.[2]

8. But some one may say : "It is not right to
leave holy men unaided to be oppressed by the
wicked."   We must reply, that if those whom you
call holy love the earthly things which are the objects
of material ambition, they have utterly fallen from
the Desire for God.   And I know not how they can
be called holy where they do this wrong to the things
which are truly Lovely and Divine, wickedly rejecting
them for things unworthy of their ambition and their
love.   But if they long for the things that are real,
then they who desire aught should rejoice when the

---

[1] *Vide supra* on Exemplars.
[2] D. is least satisfactory when he becomes an apologist, and when
(like other apologists) he tries to explain away the obvious fact of evil
and imperfection.   Within certain limits what he says will hold.   A
rose fulfils its true function by being a rose, and not by trying to be
an elephant.   But to hold that whatever is, is best, is quietism.   The
variety of the world is good, but not its imperfections.

object of their desire is obtained. Now are they not nearer to the angelic virtues when they strive, in their desire for Divine Things, to abandon their affection towards material things, and manfully to train themselves unto this object in their struggles for the Beautiful? Thus, 'tis true to say that it is more in accordance with Divine Righteousness not to lull into its destruction the manliness of the noblest characters through bestowing material goods upon them, nor to leave them without the aid of Divine corrections if any one attempt so to corrupt them. It is true Justice to strengthen them in their noble and loyal stability, and to bestow on them the things which befit their high condition.[1]

9. This Divine Righteousness is also called the Salvation or Preservation of the world, because It preserves and keeps the particular being and place of each thing inviolate from the rest, and is the inviolate Cause of all the particular activity in the world. And if any one speaks of Salvation as the saving Power which plucks the world out of the influence of evil, we will also certainly accept this account of Salvation since Salvation hath so many forms. We shall only ask him to add, that the primary Salvation of the world is that which preserves all things in their proper places without change, conflict, or deterioration, and keeps them all severally without strife or struggle obeying their proper laws, and banishes all inequality and interference from the world, and establishes the due capacities of each so that they fall not into their opposites nor suffer any transferences.[2] Indeed, it would be quite in keeping with

[1] True again within certain limits. The Saints are made perfect through suffering. But what of the innocent child victims of war atrocities?

[2] Salvation is that which, when persons or things are in a right state, keeps them therein; when they are in a wrong state, transfers them thence. The first meaning is positive and essential, the second negative

the teaching of the Divine Science to say that this
Salvation, working in that beneficence which preserves the world, redeems all things (according as
each can receive this saving power) so that they fall
not from their natural virtues. Hence the Sacred
Writers call It Redemption, both because It allows
not the things which truly exist [1] " to fall away into
nothingness," [2] and also because, should anything
stumble into error or disorder and suffer a diminution of the perfection of its proper virtues, It redeems
even this thing from the weakness and the loss it
suffers : filling up that which it lacks and supporting
its feebleness with Fatherly Love ; raising it from its
evil state, or rather setting it firmly in its right state ;
completing once more the virtue it had lost, and
ordering and arraying its disorder and disarray ;
making it perfect and releasing it from all its defects.
So much for this matter and for the Righteousness
whereby the equality or proportion of all things is
measured and given its bounds, and all inequality or
disproportion (which arises from the loss of proportion
in the individual things) is kept far away. For if one
considers the inequality shown in the mutual differences of all things in the world, this also is preserved
by Righteousness which will not permit a complete
mutual confusion and disturbance of all things, but
keeps all things within the several forms naturally
belonging to each.[3]

---

and incidental. The Scriptural view includes both sides, with the
emphasis on the first. Protestantism (being in this as in other matters
of a negative tendency) ignores the positive side to the great detriment
of Religion.   [1] *i. e.* All good things.

[2] Nothingness includes (1) mere non-entity ; (2) evil. (Perhaps
both meanings are intended.) Salvation maintains all good things
both in their being and in their excellence. If they fell away towards
nothingness the result is first corruption and then destruction.

[3] The word *ἰσότης* implies that a thing is identical in size, etc. (1) with
other things ; (2) with its own true nature. It thus = (1) "equality" ;
(2) "rightness." D. maintains that all things possess the latter
though not the former.

CHAPTER IX

*Concerning " Great," " Small," " Same," " Different," " Like,"
" Unlike," " Standing," "Motion," " Equality."*

1. NOW, since Greatness and Smallness are
ascribed to the Universal Cause, and Sameness and
Difference, and Similarity and Dissimilarity, and
Rest and Motion, let us also consider these Titles of
the Divine Glory so far as our minds can grasp them.
Now Greatness is attributed in the Scriptures unto
God, both in the great firmament and also in the thin
air whose subtlety reveals the Divine Smallness.[1]
And Sameness is ascribed to Him when the Scripture
saith, " Thou art the same," and Difference when He
is depicted by the same Scriptures as having many
forms and qualities.   And He is spoken of as Similar
to the creatures, in so far as He is the Creator of
things similar to Himself and of their similarity ; and
as Dissimilar from them in so far as there is not His
like.   And He is spoken of as Standing and Immovable and as Seated for ever, and yet as Moving and
going forth into all things.[2]   These and many similar
Titles are given by the Scriptures unto God.

2. Now God is called Great in His peculiar Greatness which giveth of Itself to all things that are great
and is poured upon all Magnitude from outside and
stretches far beyond it ; embracing all Space, exceeding all Number, penetrating beyond all Infinity[3] both

---

[1] Boundless space cannot contain God, yet He is wholly contained
in a single point of that apparent nothingness which we call air.   Cf.
Section 3.

[2] Cf. St. Augustine, *Confessions*, I, Section I.
The great paradox is that God combines perfect Rest and perfect
Motion.   Idealism has seized the first aspect, Pragmatism and Vitalism
the second.   A sense of both is present in the highest Mystical experience and in the restful activity or strenuous repose of Love.

[3] Cf. 155, n. 3.

in Its exceeding fullness and creative magnificence,
and also in the bounties that well forth from It, inasmuch as these, being shared by all in that lavish
outpouring, yet are totally undiminished and possess
the same exceeding Fullness, nor are they lessened
through their distribution, but rather overflow the
more. This Greatness is Infinite, without Quantity
and without Number.[1]   And the excess of Greatness
reaches to this pitch through the Absolute Transcendent outpouring of the Incomprehensible Grandeur.

3. And Smallness, or Rarity, is ascribed to God's
Nature because He is outside all solidity and distance
and penetrates all things without let or hindrance.
Indeed, Smallness is the elementary Cause of all
things ; for you will never find any part of the world
but participates in that quality of Smallness. This,
then, is the sense in which we must apply this quality
to God. It is that which penetrates unhindered unto
all things and through all things, energizing in them
and reaching to the dividing of soul and spirit, and of
joints and marrow ; and being a Discerner of the
desires and the thoughts of the heart, or rather of all
things, for there is no creature hid before God.[2]   This
Smallness is without Quantity or Quality;[3] It is
Irrepressible, Infinite, Unlimited, and, while com-
prehending all things, is Itself Incomprehensible.

[1] It is a Quality, not a quantity. Vulgarity consists in mistaking
quantity for quality.   This has been the mistake of the modern world.
[2] Heb. iv. 12.   We can conceive of the mind's search for God in
two ways : as a journey, (1) outwards, to seek Him beyond the sky, (2)
inwards, to seek Him in the heart. Psalm xix. combines both ways.
So does the *Paradiso.* Dante passes outwards through the concentric
spheres of space to the Empyrean which is beyond space and encloses
it.   There he sees the Empyrean as a point and his whole journey from
sphere to sphere as a journey inwards instead of outwards. (Canto
xxviii. 16.) The Mystics often speak of " seeing God in a Point."
God is in all things as the source of their existence and natural life ;
and in us as the Source of our existence and spiritual life.
[3] The Potentiality of all quality is without *particular* quality. Cf.
p. 155, n. 2.

4. And Sameness is attributed to God as a super-essentially Eternal and Unchangeable Quality, resting in Itself, always existing in the same condition, present to all things alike, firmly and inviolably fixed on Its own basis in the fair limits of the Super-Essential Sameness; not subject to change, declension, deterioration or variation, but remaining Unalloyed, Immaterial, utterly Simple, Self-Sufficing, Incapable of growth or diminition, and without Birth, not in the sense of being as yet unborn or imperfect, nor in the sense of not having received birth from this source or that, nor yet in the sense of utter non-existence; but in the sense of being wholly or utterly Birthless and Eternal and Perfect in Itself and always the Same, being self-defined in Its Singleness and Sameness, and causing a similar quality of Identity to shine forth from Itself upon all things that are capable of participating therein and yoking different things in harmony together.[1] For It is the boundless Richness and Cause of Identity, and contains beforehand in Itself all opposites under the form of Identity in that one unique Causation which transcends all identity.[2]

5. And Difference is ascribed to God because He is, in His providence, present to all things and becomes all things in all for the preservation of them all,[3] while yet remaining in Himself nor ever going forth from His own proper Identity in that one ceaseless act wherein His life consists; and thus with undeviating power He gives Himself for the Deifica-

---

[1] It causes each thing (1) to be a thing, (2) to co-exist harmoniously with other things.

[2] It contains the potential existence of all things, however different from each other, as the air contains the potential life of all the various plants and animals.

[3] Since He is the Super-Essence of all things, their life is *ultimately* His Life—*i. e.* He is, in every case, the underlying Reality of their individual existence.

tion of those that turn to Him.[1]   And the difference
of God's various appearances from each other in the
manifold visions of Him must be held to signify
something other than that which was outwardly
shown.   For just as, supposing we were in thought
to represent the soul itself in bodily shape, and
represent this indivisible substance as surrounded by
bodily parts, we should, in such a case, give the
surrounding parts a different meaning suited to the
indivisible nature of the soul, and should interpret
the head to mean the Intellect, the neck Opinion (as
being betwixt reason and irrationality), the breast to
mean Passion, the belly Animal Desire, and the legs
and feet to mean the Vital Nature: thus using the
names of bodily parts as symbols of immaterial
faculties; even so (and with much greater reason)
must we, when speaking of Him that is beyond all
things, purge from false elements by sacred heavenly
and mystical explanations the Difference of the
Forms and Shapes ascribed to God.   And, if thou
wilt attribute unto the intangible and unimaged God,
the imagery of our threefold bodily dimensions, the
Divine Breadth is God's exceeding wide Emanation
over all things, His Length is His Power exceeding
the Universe, His Depth the Unknown Mystery
which no creature can comprehend.   Only we must
have a care lest, in expounding these different forms
and figures we unwittingly confound the incorporeal
meaning of the Divine Names with the terms of the
sensible symbols.[2]   This matter I have dealt with in
my *Symbolical Divinity:* the point I now wish to

[1] Because He is the underlying Reality of our separate personalities,
which have their true being outside themselves in Him, therefore in
finding our true selves we find and possess His Being. Cf. St. Bernard:
Ubi se mihi dedit me mihi reddidit.
[2] *i. e.* We must not take metaphorical titles literally (much bad philosophy and much sentimentality and also brutality in Religion has come
from taking anthropomorphic titles of God literally).

make clear is this : we must not suppose that Difference in God means any variation of His utterly unchanging Sameness. It means, instead, a multiplicity of acts wherein His unity is undisturbed, and His all-creative fertility while passing into Emanations retains its uniformity in them.

6. And if God be called Similar (even as He is called "Same," to signify that He is wholly and altogether like unto Himself in an indivisible Permanence) this appellation of "Similar" we must not repudiate. But the Sacred Writers tell us that the All-Transcendent God is in Himself unlike any being, but that He nevertheless bestows a Divine Similitude upon those that turn to Him and strive to imitate those qualities which are beyond all definition and understanding. And 'tis the power of the Divine Similitude that turneth all created things towards their Cause. These things, then, must be considered similar to God by virtue of the Divine Image and Process of Similitude working in them ; and yet we must not say that God resembles them any more than we should say a man resembles his own portrait. For things which are co-ordinate may resemble one another, and the term "similarity" may be applied indifferently to either member of the pair ; they can both be similar to one another through a superior principle of Similarity which is common to them both. But in the case of the Cause and Its effects we cannot admit this interchange. For It doth not bestow the state of similarity only on these objects and on those ; but God is the Cause of this condition unto all that have the quality of Similarity,[1] and is the Fount of Very Similarity ;[2] and all the Similarity in the world

---

[1] If anything derived this quality from some other source than God, that thing, instead of standing towards God in the relation of effect to Cause, would be co-ordinate with Him. But as it is, *all* things stand towards God in the relation of effect to Cause.

[2] *Vide supra* on Very Existence, Very Life, Very Wisdom, etc.

possesses its quality through having a trace of the
Divine Similarity and thus accomplishes the Unification of the creatures.

7. But what need is there to labour this point ?
Scripture itself declares [1] that God is Dissimilar to
the world, and not to be compared therewith. It
says that He is different from all things, and (what is
yet more strange) that there is nothing even similar
to Him. And yet such language contradicts not the
Similitude of things to Him. For the same things
are both like unto God and unlike Him : like Him in
so far as they can imitate Him that is beyond
imitation, unlike Him in so far as the effects fall short
of the Cause and are infinitely and incomparably
inferior.

8. Now what say we concerning the Divine attributes of " Standing " and " Sitting " ? Merely this—
that God remains What He is in Himself and is
firmly fixed in an immovable Sameness wherein His
transcendent Being is fast rooted, and that He acts
under the same modes and around the same Centre
without changing ; and that He is wholly Self-Subsistent in His Stability, possessing Very Immutability
and an entire Immobility, and that He is all this in
a Super-Essential manner.[2] For He is the Cause of
the stability and rest of all things : He who is beyond
all Rest and Standing. And in Him all things have
their consistency and are preserved, so as not to be
shaken from the stability of their proper virtues.

9. And what is meant, on the other hand, when
the Sacred Writers say that the Immovable God
moves and goes forth unto all things ? Must we not
understand this also in a manner befitting God ?
Reverence bids us regard His motion to imply no
change of place, variation, alteration, turning or

---

[1] Cf. *e. g.* Ps. lxxxvi. 8.
[2] *i. e.* This stability is due to Undifferentiation.

locomotion, whether straightforward, circular, or com-
pounded of both ; or whether belonging to mind, soul,
or natural powers ; but to mean that God brings all
things into being and sustains them,[1] and exerts all
manner of Providence over them, and is present to
them all, holding them in His incomprehensible
embrace, and exercising over them all His providential Emanations and Activities. Nevertheless our
reason must agree to attribute movements to the
Immutable God in such a sense as befits Him.
Straightness we must understand to mean Directness
of aim and the unswerving Emanation of His
energies, and the outbirth of all things from Him.
His Spiral Movement must be taken to mean the
combination of a persistent Emanation and a productive Stillness. And His Circular Movement must
be taken to mean His Sameness, wherein He holds
together the intermediate orders and those at either
extremity, so as to embrace each other, and the act
whereby the things that have gone forth from Him
return to Him again.

10. And if any one takes the Scriptural Title of
" Same," or that of " Righteousness," as implying
Equality, we must call God " Equal," not only because
He is without parts and doth not swerve from His
purpose, but also because He penetrates equally to
all things and through all, and is the Fount of Very
Equality, whereby He worketh equally the uniform
interpenetration of all things and the participation
thereof possessed by things which (each according to
its capacity) have an equal share therein, and the
equal [2] power bestowed upon all according to their
worth ; and because all Equality (perceived or exercised by the intellect, or possessed in the sphere of

---

[1] St. Augustine frequently explains God's activity to consist in His
causing His creatures to act, while Himself resting.
[2] *i. e.* " Due," " right," cf. p. 161, n. 3.

reason, sensation, essence, nature, or will) is transcendently contained beforehand as an Unity in Him
through that Power, exceeding all things, which
brings all Equality into existence.

CHAPTER X

*Concerning " Omnipotent," " Ancient of Days "; and also
concerning " Eternity " and " Time."*

1. NOW 'tis time that our Discourse should
celebrate God (Whose Names are many) as "Omnipotent" and "Ancient of Days." The former title is
given Him because He is that All-Powerful Foundation of all things which maintains and embraces the
Universe, founding and establishing and compacting
it; knitting the whole together in Himself without a
rift, producing the Universe out of Himself as out of
an all-powerful Root, and attracting all things back
into Himself as unto an all-powerful Receptacle,
holding them all together as their Omnipotent
Foundation, and securing them all in this condition
with an all-transcendent bond suffering them not to
fall away from Himself, nor (by being removed from
out of that perfect Resting Place) to come utterly to
destruction. Moreover, the Supreme Godhead is
called "Omnipotent" because It is potent over all
things, and rules with unalloyed sovranty over the
world It governs; and because It is the Object of
desire and yearning for all, and casts on all Its
voluntary yoke and sweet travail of Divine all-
powerful and indestructible Desire for Its Goodness.
2. And "Ancient of Days" is a title given to God
because He is the Eternity[1] of all things and their

---

[1] In the Super-Essence each thing has its ultimate and timeless
being.

M

Time,[1] and is anterior [2] to Days and anterior to Eternity and Time. And the titles " Time," " Day," " Season," and " Eternity " must be applied to Him in a Divine sense, to mean One Who is utterly incapable of all change and movement and, in His eternal motion, remains at rest; [3] and Who is the Cause whence Eternity, Time, and Days are derived. Wherefore in the Sacred Theophanies revealed in mystic Visions He is described as Ancient and yet as Young : the former title signifying that He is the Primal Being, existent from the beginning, and the latter that He grows not old. Or both titles together teach that He goes forth from the Beginning through the entire process of the world unto the End. Or, as the Divine Initiator [4] tells us, either term implies the Primal Being of God : the term " Ancient " signifying that He is First in point of Time, and the term " Young " that He possesses the Primacy in point of Number, since Unity and the properties of Unity have a primacy over the more advanced numbers.[5]

3. Need is there, methinks, that we understand the sense in which Scripture speaketh of Time and Eternity. For where Scripture speaks of things as "eternal " it doth not always mean things that are absolutely Uncreated or verily Everlasting, Incor-

---

[1] In the Super-Essence each thing has the limits of its duration predetermined. Or else D. means that in the Super-Essence the movement of Time has the impulse which generates it.

[2] Temporal precedence is metaphorically used to express metaphysical precedence. God cannot in the literal sense of the words, *temporally* precede *time*.

[3] He transcends both Rest and Motion.

[4] Presumably Hierotheus.

[5] He is the Source of all extension both in Time and in Space, Unity *underlies* all counting (for 2, 3, 4, etc. =twice 1, three times 1, four times 1, etc.). Hence it is the Origin, as it were, of all number. And, being at the beginning of the arithmetical series (as youth is at the beginning of life) it is symbolized (according to D.) by youthfulness.

ruptible, Immortal, Invariable, and Immutable
(*e.g.* "Be ye lift up, ye eternal doors,"[1] and such-
like passages). Often it gives the name of "Eternal"
to anything very ancient ; and sometimes, again, it
applies the term "Eternity" to the whole course
of earthly Time, inasmuch as it is the property
of Eternity to be ancient and invariable and to
measure the whole of Being. The name "Time" it
gives to that changing process which is shown in
birth, death, and variation. And hence we who are
here circumscribed by Time are, saith the Scripture,
destined to share in Eternity when we reach that
incorruptible Eternity which changes not. And
sometimes the Scripture declares the glories of a
Temporal Eternity and an Eternal Time, although
we understand that in stricter exactness it describes
and reveals Eternity as the home of things that are
in Being, and Time as the home of things that are in
Birth.[2] We must not, therefore, think of the things
which are called Eternal as being simply co-ordinate
with the Everlasting God Who exists before Eternity ;[3]

---

[1] Ps. xxiv. 7.

[2] We cannot help thinking of Eternity as an Endless Time, as we
think of infinite number as an endless numerical process. But this is
wrong. Eternity is timeless as infinite number is superior to all
numerical process. According to Plato, Time is "incomplete life"
and Eternity is "complete life." Thus Eternity fulfils Time and yet
contradicts it, as infinite number fulfils and contradicts the properties of
finite numbers. If Time be thought of as an infinite series of finite
numbers Eternity is the sum of that series and not its process. But the
name may be applied loosely to the process, though this is generally to
be avoided. According to St. Thomas, Eternity measures Rest, and
Time measures Motion : Eternity is a *totum simul* and Time is *succes-
sivum*. The difference between them is *not*, he says, that Time has a
beginning and an end whereas Eternity has neither, though he admits
that each of the particular objects existing in Time began and will end.
(*Summa*, Pars I. Q. x. Art. iv.) But this is, he says, not essential to
the nature of time : it is only *per accidens* (*ibid.* Art. v.). Cf. Aristotle's
distinction between "unlimited Time" and limited Time.

[3] He alludes to Angels and the perfected souls of men and to their
celestial abode.

but, strictly following the venerable Scriptures, we had better interpret the words " Eternal" and " Temporal" in their proper senses, and regard those things which to some extent participate in Eternity and to some extent in Time as standing midway between things in Being and things in Birth.[1] And God we must celebrate as both Eternity and Time,[2] as the Cause of all Time and Eternity and as the Ancient of Days ; as before Time and above Time and producing all the variety of times and seasons ; and again, as existing before Eternal Ages, in that

---

[1] St. Thomas speaks of *aevum* as standing between Eternity and Time and participating in both. Time, he says, consists in succession, *Aevum* does not but is capable of it, Eternity does not and is incapable of it (*Summa*, Pars I. Q. x. Art. v.). Thus the heavenly bodies, he says, are changeless in essence, but capable of motion from place to place ; and the angels are changeless in nature, but capable of choice and so of spiritual movement. Maximus's note on the present passage explains this to be D.'s meaning.

There is in each one of us a timeless self. It is spoken of by all the Christian Mystics as the root of our being, or as the spark, or the *Synteresis*, etc. Our perfection consists in this ultimate reality, which is each man's self, shining through his whole being and transforming it. Hence man is at last lifted on to the eternal plane from that of time. The movements of his spirit will then be so intense that they will attain a *totum simul*. We get a foretaste of this when, in the experience of deep spiritual joy, the successive parts of Time so coalesce (as it were) that an hour seems like a moment. Eternity is Rest and Time is Motion. Accelerate the motion in the individual soul, through the intensification of that soul's bliss to infinity. There is now in the soul an infinite motion. But Infinite Motion is above succession, and therefore is itself a form of repose. Thus Motion has been changed into Rest, Time into Eternity. Mechanical Time, or *dead* Time (of which Aristotle speaks as mere movement or succession) is the Time measured by the clock ; developing or *living* Time (which is Plato's "incomplete life") is real Time, and this is *Aevum*, which partakes both of mechanical Time and of Eternity. The best treatment of the subject is probably to be found in Bergson's theory of *durée*. (Cf. Von Hügel's *Eternal Life*.)

The words "eternal," "everlasting," etc., being loosely employed, may refer to three different things : (1) endless *mechanical* Time, *i. e.* mere endless succession ; (2) *Aevum*, or developing and finally perfected *living* Time ; (3) True Timeless Eternity.

[2] *Vide* pp. 169 n. 1, 170 n. 1.

He is before [1] Eternity and above Eternity and His
Kingdom is the Kingdom of all the Eternal Ages.
Amen.

CHAPTER XI

*Concerning " Peace " and what is meant by " Very Being " Itself,
" Very Life," "Very Power," and similar phrases.*

1. NOW let us praise with reverent hymns of peace
the Divine Peace which is the Source of all mutual
attraction.   For this Quality it is that unites all
things together and begets and produces the harmonies and agreements of all things.   And hence it
is that all things long for It, and that It draws their
manifold separate parts into the unity of the whole
and unites the battling elements of the world into
concordant fellowship.   So it is that, through participation in the Divine Peace, the higher of the mutually
Attractive Powers [2] are united in themselves and to
each other and to the one Supreme Peace of the
whole world ; and so the ranks beneath them are by
them united both in themselves and to one another
and unto that one perfect Principle and Cause of
Universal Peace,[3] which broods in undivided Unity
upon the world, and (as it were with bolts which
fasten the sundered parts together) giveth to all
things their laws, their limits, and their cohesion ; nor

---

[1] *Vide* p. 170, n. 2.
[2] *i. e.* The Seraphim.
[3] The Divine Energy and Light streams through the medium of the
higher orders to the lower.   This is worked out in the *Celestial
Hierarchy* of the same writer.   We get the same thought in Dante's
Paradiso, where the *Primum Mobile*, deriving its motion from an
immediate contact with the Empyrean, passes them on to the next
sphere and so to all the rest in turn, the movement being received
and conveyed by the succeeding angelic orders presiding severally, in
descending scale of dignity, over the concentric spheres.—See *Convito*,
II. 6.

suffers them to be torn apart and dispersed into the boundless chaos without order or foundation, so as to lose God's Presence and depart from their own unity, and to mingle together in a universal confusion. Now as to that quality of the Divine Peace and Silence, to which the holy Justus [1] gives the name of "Dumbness" and "Immobility" (*sc.* so far as concerns all emanation which our knowledge can grasp),[2] and as to the manner in which It is still and silent and keeps in Itself and within Itself and is wholly and entirely one transcendent Unity in Itself, and while entering into Itself and multiplying Itself,[3] doth not leave Its own Unity, but, even in the act of going forth to all things, remains entirely within Itself through the excess of that all-transcendent Unity: concerning these things 'tis neither right nor possible for any creature to frame any language or conception. Let us, then, describe that Peace (inasmuch as It transcends all things) as "Unutterable," yea and "Unknowable"; and, so far as 'tis possible for men and for ourselves who are inferior to many

---

[1] *Vide* Acts i. 23; xviii. 7; or Col. iv. 11.

[2] Victorinus calls God the Father *Cessatio, Silentium*, or *Quies*, and also *Motus*, as distinguished from Motio (the name he gives God the Son), the former kind of movement being the quiescent generator of the latter, since Victorinus was an older contemporary of St. Augustine (see *Conf.* viii. 2–5) his speculations may have been known to D. The peace of God attracts by its mysterious influence. This influence is, in a sense, an emanation or outgoing activity (or it could not affect us), but it is a thing felt and not understood.

[3] It multiplies Itself by entering into the creatures and seeking to be reproduced in each of them. This whole passage throws light on the problem of Personality. If our personalities are ultimately contained in the Absolute, the Absolute is not a Person but a Society of Persons. D. would reply that the Absolute is Supra-Personal, and that in It our personalities have their ultimate existence, outside of themselves, as an undifferentiated Unity, though that ultimate plane needs also and implies the existence of the relative plane on which our personalities exist as differentiated individuals. The Holy Spirit enters into the various individuals, but still possesses One Supra-Personal Godhead. Plotinus says the Godhead is indivisibly divided.

good men, let us examine those cases where It is amenable to our intuitions and language through being manifested in created things.

2. Now, the first thing to say is this : that God is the Fount of Very Peace and of all Peace, both in general and in particular, and that He joins all things together in an unity without confusion whereby they are inseparably united without any interval between them, and at the same time stand unmixed each in its own form, not losing their purity through being mingled with their opposites nor in any way blunting the edge of their clear and distinct individuality. Let us, then, consider that one and simple nature of the Peaceful Unity which unites all things to Itself to themselves and to each other, and preserves all things, distinct and yet interpenetrating in an universal cohesion without confusion. Thus it is that the Divine Intelligences derive that Unity whereby they are united to the activities and the objects of their intuition ;[1] and rise up still further to a contact, beyond knowledge, with truths which transcend the mind. Thus it is that souls, unifying their manifold reasoning powers and concentrating them in one pure spiritual act, advance by their own ordered path through an immaterial and indivisible act of spiritual intuition. Thus it is that the one and indissoluble connection of all things exists by reason of its Divine harmony, and is fitted together with perfect concord, agreement and congruity, being drawn into one without confusion and inseparably held together. For the entirety of that perfect Peace penetrates to all things through the simple, unalloyed presence of Its unifying power, uniting all things and binding the extremities together through the intermediate parts,

[1] Contemplation, Act of Contemplation, and Object Contemplated are all united together, and so imply a fundamental Unity which exists ultimately in God.

all things being thus conjoined by one homogenous attraction. And It bestows even upon the utmost limits of the universe the enjoyment of Its Presence, and makes all things akin to one another by the unities, the identities, the communions and the mutual attractions which It gives them; for the Divine Peace remains indivisible and shows forth all Its power in a single act, and permeates the whole world without departing from Its own Identity. For It goes forth to all things and gives to all things of Itself (according to their kinds), and overflows with the abundance of Its peaceful fecundity, and yet through the transcendence of Its unification It remains wholly and entirely in a state of Absolute Self-Unity.[1]

3. "But," some one perchance will say, "in what sense do all things desire peace? Many things rejoice in opposition and difference and distinction, and would never choose willingly to be at rest." Now if the opposition and difference here intended is the individuality of each thing, and the fact that naught (while it remains itself) wishes to lose this quality, then neither can we deny this statement; but, however, we shall show that this itself is due to a desire for Peace. For all things love to have peace and unity in themselves and to remain without moving or falling from their own existence or properties. And the perfect Peace guards each several individuality unalloyed by Its providential gift of peace, keeping all things without internal or mutual discord or confusion, and establishing all things, in the power of unswerving stability, so as to possess their own peace and rest.[2]

---

[1] Cf. p. 174, n. 3.

[2] D.'s paradox is the paradox of sanity. We must hold at the same time two apparent contradictions. On one side all things are, in a sense, merged, in the other side they are not. Their Super-Essence is identical and is *one and the same Super-Essence* for all. Yet

4. And if all things which move be found desiring not to be at rest but always to perform their proper movements, this also is a desire for that Divine Peace of the Universe which keeps all things in their proper places so that they fall not, and preserves the individual and the motive life of all moving things from removal or declension. And this it doth by reason that the things which move perform their proper functions through being in a constant state of inward peace.[1]

5. But if, in affirming that Peace is not desired by all, the objector is thinking of the opposition caused by a falling away from Peace, in the first place there is nothing in the world which hath utterly fallen away from all Unity; for that which is utterly unstable, boundless, baseless, and indefinite hath neither Being nor any inherence in the things that have Being. And if he says that hatred towards Peace and the blessings of Peace is shown by them that rejoice in strife and anger and in conditions of variations and instability, I answer that these also are governed by dim shadows of the desire for Peace; for, being oppressed by the various movements of their passions, they desire (without understanding) to set these at rest, and suppose that the surfeit of fleeting pleasures will give them Peace because they feel themselves

---

each one *severally and individually* possesses It. The paradox is due to the fact that the question is one of ultimate Reality.

All life and individuality start in the individual's opposition to the rest of the world, for by distinguishing myself from the world I, in a sense, oppose myself to it. This is the basis of selfishness and so of moral evil. But being transmuted by Love, it becomes the basis of all harmony and moral good, and so leads to Peace. And the same principles of opposition and harmony are at work in the whole creation, animate and inanimate alike. (Cf. Dante, *Paradiso*, I. 103 to end.)

[1] *Vide supra* [Movet Deus sicut Desideratum]: True peace is restful energy, both elements of which are incomplete in the present world but complete in the Godhead.

disturbed by the unsatisfied cravings which have mastered them.[1] There is no need to tell how the loving-kindness of Christ cometh bathed in Peace, wherefrom we must learn to cease from strife, whether against ourselves or against one another, or against the angels, and instead to labour together even with the angels for the accomplishment of God's Will, in accordance with the Providential Purpose of Jesus Who worketh all things in all and maketh Peace, unutterable and foreordained from Eternity, and reconcileth us to Himself, and, in Himself, to the Father. Concerning these supernatural gifts enough hath been said in the *Outlines of Divinity* with confirmation drawn from the holy testimony of the Scriptures.

6. Now, since thou hast, on a previous occasion, sent me an epistle asking what I mean by Very Being Itself, Very Life Itself, Very Wisdom Itself: and since thou saidst thou couldst not understand why sometimes I call God "Life" and sometimes the "Fount of Life": I have thought it necessary, holy man of God, to solve for thee this question also which hath arisen between us. In the first place, to repeat again what hath often been said before, there is no contradiction between calling God "Life" or "Power" and "Fount of Life, Peace, or Power."[2] The former titles are derived from forms of existence, and especially from the primary forms,[3] and are applied to Him because all existences come forth from Him; the latter titles are given Him because in a super-essential manner He transcends all things, even the

---

[1] Cf. Dante, *Paradiso.* "E se altra cosa vostra amor seduce Non è se non di quella alcun vestigio," etc.

[2] Absolute Existence or Life, etc., is in God super-essentially, and timelessly emanates from Him. It is in Him as a Super-Essence and projected from Him as an Essence.

[3] *i. e.* The angels, who, being the highest creatures, possess Existence, Life, Peace, Power, etc., in the greatest degree.

primary existences.[1] " But," thou wilt say, "what mean we at all by Very Being and Very Life and those things to which we ascribe an Ultimate Existence derived primarily from God ? " We reply as follows: " This matter is not crooked, but straightforward, and the explanation thereof is easy. The Very Existence underlying the existence of all things is not some Divine or Angelic Being (for only That Which is Super-Essential can be the Principle, the Being and the Cause of all Existences and of Very Existence Itself)[2] nor is It any life-producing Deity other than the Supra-Divine Life which is the Cause of all living things and of Very Life,[3] nor, in short, is It identical with any such originative and creative Essences and Substances of things as men in their rash folly call "gods" and "creators" of the world, though neither had these men themselves any true and proper knowledge of such beings nor had their fathers. In fact, such beings did not exist.[4] Our meaning is different: " Very Being," " Very Life," " Very Godhead " are titles which in an Originating Divine and Causal sense we apply to the One Transcendent Origin and Cause of all things, but we also apply the terms in a derivative sense to the Providential Manifestations of Power derived from the Unparticipated God, *i. e.* to the Infusion of Very Being, Very Life, and Very Godhead, which so transmutes the creatures where each, according to its nature, participates therein, that these obtain the

---

[1] The titles "Absolute Life," etc., correspond to the *Via Affirmativa*, and the titles " Cause of Absolute Life," etc., to the *Via Negativa*.

[2] The Godhead causes: (1) the particular existent thing, (2) the ultimate fact of Existence, *i. e.* Absolute Existence. The Exemplars are in the Godhead and not in the emanating Absolute Existence.

[3] See last note.

[4] Perhaps under the pretence of attacking Paganism D. is really aiming his shafts against Manicheism or some Gnostic heresy current in his day.

qualities and names : " Existent," " Living," " Divinely Possessed," etc.[1]   Hence the Good God is called the Fount, first, of the Very Primaries : then, of those creatures which share completely therein ; then, of those which share partially therein.[2]   But it needs not to say more concerning this matter, since some of our Divine Teachers have already treated thereof. They give the title " Fount of Very Goodness and Deity " to Him that exceeds both Goodness and Deity; and they give the name of " Very Goodness and Deity " to the Gift which, coming forth from God, bestows both Goodness and Deity upon the creatures ; and they give the name of " Very Beauty " to the outpouring of Very Beauty ; and in the same manner they speak of " complete Beauty " and " partial Beauty," and of things completely beautiful and things beautiful in part.[3]   And they deal in the same way with all other qualities which are, or can be, similarly employed to signify Providential Manifestations and Virtues derived from the Transcendent God through that abundant outpouring, where such qualities proceed and overflow from Him. So is the Creator of all things literally beyond them all, and His Super-Essential and Supernatural Being altogether transcends the creatures, whatever their essence and nature.

[1] (1) God possesses and *is* Absolute Being, Absolute Life, etc.
   (2) He pours forth Absolute Being that the creatures may share it and so exist and be ennobled.
[2] Migne's text here is corrupt, I have emended it.
   (1) The First Things = Absolute Existence, etc.
   (2) Those that share completely therein = the angels and perfected human souls.
   (3) Those that share partially therein = the lower orders of creation which possess existence without life, or life without consciousness, or consciousness without spirituality (stones, plants, animals).
[3] The beauty of a human being is more complete than that of a horse, and spiritual beauty is more complete than mere physical beauty.

CHAPTER XII

Concerning " Holy of holies," " King of kings," " Lord of lords," " God of gods."

1. FORASMUCH as the things which needed to be said concerning this matter have been brought, I think, to a proper ending, we must praise God (whose Names are infinite) as " Holy of holies" and "King of kings," reigning through Eternity and unto the end of Eternity and beyond it, and as " Lord of lords" and " God of gods." And we must begin by saying what we understand by "Very Holiness," what by " Royalty," " Dominion," and " Deity," and what the Scripture means by the reduplication of the titles.

2. Now Holiness is that which we conceive as a freedom from all defilement and a complete and utterly untainted purity. And Royalty is the power to assign all limit, order, law, and rank. And Dominion is not only the superiority to inferiors, but is also the entirely complete and universal possession of fair and good things and is a true and steadfast firmness ; wherefore the name is derived from a word meaning " validity" and words meaning severally "that which possesseth validity " and "which exerciseth " it.[1] And Deity is the Providence which contemplates all things and which, in perfect Goodness,

[1] D. holds that God's dominion is an absolute quality in Himself apart from all reference to the creation. The Greek word, as he truly says, supports his view.

The Latin *Dominus*, on the other hand, implies the notion of governing, and so has a necessary reference to the creation. Hence St. Augustine says that God could not actually be spoken of as " Lord" before the world or the angels were made. Eckhart says that before the creation God was not God, " Er war was Er war." D. holds that the title " God" is relative to us. But then he holds— and here explains—that the roots of this relationship exist *timelessly* in the undifferentiated Godhead.

goes round about all things and holds them together and fills them with Itself and transcends all
things that enjoy the blessings of Its providential
care.

3. These titles, then, must be given in an absolute
sense to the All-Transcendent Cause, and we must
add that It is a Transcendent Holiness and Dominion,
that It is a Supreme Royalty and an altogether
Simple Deity.[1] For out of It there hath, in one
single act, come forth collectively and been distributed
throughout the world all the unmixed Perfection of
all untainted Purity; all that Law and Order of the
world, which expels all disharmony, inequality and
disproportion, and breaks forth into a smiling aspect
of ordered Consistency [2] and Rightness, bringing into
their proper place all things which are held worthy
to participate in It; all the perfect Possession of all
fair qualities; and all that good Providence which
contemplates and maintains in being the objects of
Its own activity, bounteously bestowing Itself for the
Deification of those creatures which are converted
unto It.

4. And since the Creator of all things is brim-full
with them all in one transcendent excess thereof, He
is called "Holy of Holies," etc., by virtue of His
overflowing Causality and excess of Transcendence.[3]
Which meaneth that just as things that have no
substantial Being [4] are transcended by things that
have such Being, together with Sanctity, Divinity,
Dominion, or Royalty; and just as the things that

---

[1] "Transcendent," "Supreme," "Simple," all express the same
fact—that, being Super-Essential, it is above the multiplicity of the
creatures.
[2] Cf. Shelley, *Adonais*: "That Light whose smile kindles the
universe."
[3] "Holiness" especially contains the notion of Transcendence.
[4] *i e.* The material things (cf. *Myst. Theol.* I.). This is the ordinary
meaning of the phrase in D.

participate in these Qualities are transcended by the Very Qualities themselves—even so all things that have Being are surpassed by Him that is beyond them all, and all the Participants and all the Very Qualities are surpassed by the Unparticipated [1] Creator. And Holy Ones and Kings and Lords and Gods, in the language of Scripture, are the higher Ranks in each Kind [2] through which the secondary Ranks receiving of their gifts from God, show forth the abundance of that Unity thus distributed among them in their own manifold qualities—which various qualities the First Ranks in their providential, godlike activity draw together into the Unity of their own being. [3]

[1] Material things are surpassed by angels and perfected human souls, and these by the Divine Grace which they all share ; and this, together with the whole creation on which it is bestowed, is surpassed by God from Whom it emanates. For while this emanation can be communicated the Godhead cannot. (Cf. *Via Negativa*. See esp. *Myst. Theol.* I.).

[2] *i. e.* The higher ranks whether among angels or among human souls. (Cf. "I have said, ' Ye are gods,' " "hath made us kings and priests," etc.)

[3] The highest ranks (*i. e.* the Seraphim and the Contemplative Saints) have a direct version of God, Whom they behold by an act of complete spiritual contemplation.

Others, learning from them, behold God truly but less directly—by knowing rather than by Unknowing, by discursive Meditation rather than by intuitive Contemplation—or are called to serve Him chiefly in practical works. Contemplation is a complete activity of the concentrated spirit, unifying it within itself and uniting it to all kindred spirits (for true Mysticism is the same in every age and place). Meditation and practical works are partial activities which imply a succession of different images in the same mind and a shifting variety of different mental types and interests in the same Community.

CHAPTER XIII

Concerning "Perfect" and "One."

1. So much for these titles. Now let us, if thou art willing, proceed to the most important Title of all. For the Divine Science attributes all qualities to the Creator of all things and attributes them all together, and speaks of Him as One.[1] Now such a Being is Perfect : not only in the sense that It is Absolute Perfection and possesseth in Itself and from Itself distinctive Uniformity of Its existence,[2] and that It is wholly perfect in Its whole Essence, but also in the sense that, in Its transcendence It is *beyond* Perfection ; and that, while giving definite form or limit to all that is indefinite, It is yet in Its simple Unity raised above all limitation, and is not contained or comprehended by anything, but penetrates to all things at once and beyond them in Its unfailing bounties and never-ending activities.[3] Moreover, the

---

[1] Religion, in its highest forms, and Philosophy and Natural Science postulate and seek some Unity behind the world. Hence Unity is regarded as the *ultimate* attribute. Thus Plotinus calls the Absolute "The One." God possesses all Attributes not separately but indivisibly, as pure light contains all colours.

[2] Though the Godhead is the Super-Essence of the creatures, yet on the other hand It is distinct from them because It transcends them. (See next note.) This aspect of distinctness is manifested in the fact that the Emanation of Absolute Life, etc., is distinct from the Persons of the Trinity, the aspect of identity is manifested in the fact that They possess Absolute Life antecedently to the act of Emanation.

[3] The Godhead is Perfect : (1) *absolutely*, and not by participation in some other essence ; (2) *transcendently*, and not in such a manner as to be differentiated from other essences (for on the super-essential plane of the Undifferentiated Godhead there is no other essence than It). The Emanation of Absolute Life, etc., is perfect absolutely, because, being a direct overflow from the Godhead, it does not participate in any other Essence ; but not transcendently, because it is differentiated from the particular things which share it. That is why it does not contain Exemplars. The creatures possess their true and undifferentiated being not in the Emanation but in the ultimate Godhead. The Emanation

Title " Perfect " means that It cannot be increased (being *always* Perfect) and cannot be diminished, and that It contains all things beforehand in Itself and overflows in one ceaseless, identical,[1] abundant and inexhaustible supply, whereby It perfects all perfect [2] things and fills them with Its own Perfection.

2. And the title " One " implies that It is all things under the form of Unity through the Transcendence of Its single Oneness,[3] and is the Cause of all things without departing from that Unity. For there is nothing in the world without a share in the One; and, just as all number participates in unity (and we speak of *one* couple, *one* dozen, *one* half, *one* third, or *one* tenth) even so everything and each part of everything participates in the One, and on the existence of the One all other existences are based, and the One Cause of all things is not one of the many things in the world,[4] but is before all Unity and Multiplicity and gives to all Unity and Multiplicity their definite bounds.[5] For no multiplicity can exist except by

---

is, we may say, *transcendental*, or timeless, but not *transcendent*, or undifferentiated. D., by saying that "in Its transcendence . . . It penetrates to all things at once and beyond them," teaches incidentally that the Godhead's Transcendence and Immanence are ultimately the same fact. They are two ways of looking at the one truth of Its Undifferentiation. Since It is undifferentiated the Godhead is beyond our individual being; but since It is undifferentiated It is not ultimately other than ourselves. It is *beyond* our essence and *is* our Super-Essence. The theory of mere Transcendence is Deism, that of mere Immanence is Pantheism. True religion demands both in one fact and as one fact. So God is both near and far (see the Bible *passim*). He is far because He is *nearer to us than our own souls are*. " Thou wast within, I was outside" (St. Augustine). Hence true Introversion is an act of self-transcendence. We must lose ourselves to find ourselves.

[1] Identical because *timeless*.

[2] " Perfect," a term taken from the Mysteries expressing the final state of the initiated.

[3] See p. 184, n. 3.   [4] Cf. X., 2.

[5] The Godhead is not one individual, or essence, among others, but is the Super-Essence of them all. The numbers 1, 2, 3, 4, etc. = 1 × 1, 1 × 2, 1 × 3, 1 × 4, etc. Thus in the form " 1 × 1 " the first figure

N

some participation in the One : [1] that which is many in its parts is one in its entirety ; that which is many in its accidental qualities is one in its substance ; [2] that which is many in number or faculties is one in species ; [3] that which is many in its emanating activities is one in its originating essence.[4] There is naught in the world without some participation in the One, the Which in Its all-embracing Unity contains beforehand all things, and all things conjointly, combining even opposites under the form of oneness. And without the One there can be no Multiplicity ; yet contrariwise the One can exist without the Multiplicity just as the Unit exists before all multiplied Number.[5] And if all things be conceived as being ultimately unified with each other, then all things taken as a whole are One.[6]

3. Moreover, we must bear this in mind : that when we attribute a common unity to things we do so in

---

represents the unity underlying all numbers, the second figure represents unity as a particular number among other numbers. The first figure may thus be taken as a symbol of the Godhead, the second figure as a symbol of all created unity.

[1] Though created unity differs (see last note) from Uncreated Unity, yet it is, so to speak, a reflection thereof, as essence is a reflection of Super-Essence. So each number, because based on an underlying Unity, is itself a unit, and the underlying Unity of the Godhead shines through the world in all the harmonies and systems of things.

[2] A tree is one tree though (1) made up of root, trunk, branches, leaves, etc., (2) green in the leaves and brown in the trunk, etc.

[3] There are many oaks with different capacities of growth and productiveness, yet all belong to the same "oak species"; and there are many species or kinds of trees (oaks, chestnuts, firs, etc.) yet all belong to the genus "tree."

[4] A man's thoughts, desires and acts of will all spring from his one personality.

[5] Just as in the series 1 × 2, 1 × 3, 1 × 4, etc., if you destroy the 2, 3, 4, etc., the 1 remains, so if the universe disappeared the Godhead would still remain. (Cf. Emily Brontë : "Every existence would exist in Thee.")

[6] All things possess the same Super-Essence, and that is why they are connected together in this world.

accordance with the preconceived law of their kind
belonging to each one, and that the One is thus the
elementary basis of all things.[1] And if you take
away the One there will remain neither whole nor
part nor anything else in the world; for all things
are contained beforehand and embraced by the One
as an Unity in Itself. Thus Scripture speaks of the
whole Supreme Godhead as the Cause of all things
by employing the title of "One"; and there is One
God Who is the Father and One Lord Jesus Christ
and One unchanging Spirit, through the transcendent
indivisibility of the entire Divine Unity, wherein all
things are knit together in one and possess a supernal
Unity and super-essentially pre-exist. Hence all
things are rightly referred and attributed unto It,
since by It and in It and unto It all things possess
their existence, co-ordination, permanence, cohesion,
fulfilment, and innate tendency. And you will not
find anything in the world but derives from the One
(which, in a super-essential sense, is the name of the
whole Godhead) both its individual existence and the
process that perfects and preserves it.[2] And we also
must, in the power of the Divine Unity, turn from
the Many to the One and declare the Unity of the
whole single Godhead, which is the One Cause of all
things; before all distinctions of One and Many,
Part and Whole, Definiteness and Indefiniteness,[3]

[1] Cf. p. 186, n. 3.

[2] *i.e.* Both its unity in space and its unity in time.

[3] A thing is definite when we can say of it: "This is not that,"
indefinite when it is doubtful whether this is, or is not, that. The Godhead not being a particular thing, belongs to a region where there is no
"this" or "that." So we cannot say, on that ultimate plane either:
"This is not that," or, "It is doubtful whether this is that." Hence
the mystical act of Unknowing. Knowledge distinguishes things, Unknowing passes beyond this act yet without confusion. In Unknowing
the distinction between Thinker and Object of Thought is (from one
point of view) gone; and yet the psychical state is a luminously
clear one. Our personalities in their Super-Essence are merged yet
unconfused.

Finitude and Infinitude ; [1] giving definite shape to all things that have Being, and to Being itself; the Cause of everything and of all together—a Cause both co-existent and pre-existent and transcendent, and all these things at once ; yea, beyond *existent* Unity itself, and giving definite shape to existent Unity itself. For Unity, as found in the creatures, is numerical ; and number participates in Essence : but the Super-Essential Unity gives definite shape to existent unity and to every number, and is Itself the Beginning, the Cause, the Numerical Principle and the Law of Unity, number and every creature. And hence, when we speak of the All-Transcendent Godhead as an Unity and a Trinity, It is not an Unity or a Trinity such as can be known by us or any other creature, though to express the truth of Its utter Self-Union and Its Divine Fecundity we apply the titles of " Trinity " and " Unity " to That Which is beyond all titles, expressing under the form of Being That Which is beyond Being.[2] But no Unity or Trinity or Number or Oneness or Fecundity or any other thing that either is a creature or can be known to any creature, is able to utter the mystery, beyond all mind and reason, of that Transcendent Godhead which super-essentially surpasses all things. It hath no name, nor can It be grasped by the reason ; It dwells in a region beyond us, where our feet cannot tread. Even the title of " Goodness " we do not ascribe to It because we think such a name suitable ; but desiring to frame some conception and language about this Its ineffable Nature, we consecrate as primarily belonging to It the Name we most revere. And in this too we shall be in agreement with the Sacred Writers ; nevertheless the actual

---

[1] See p. 162 on "Greatness" and "Smallness."

[2] Numerical unity is a number among other numbers and so implies differentiation. The Godhead is undifferentiated.

truth must still be far beyond us. Hence we have given our preference to the Negative method, because this lifts the soul above all things cognate with its finite nature, and, guiding it onward through all the conceptions of God's Being which are transcended by that Being exceeding all Name, Reason, and Knowledge, reaches beyond the farthest limits of the world and there joins us unto God Himself, in so far as the power of union with Him is possessed even by us men.

4. These Intelligible Names we have collected and endeavoured to expound, though falling short not only of the actual meaning thereof (for such a failure even angels would be forced to confess), nor yet merely of such utterance as angels would have given concerning them (for the greatest of those among us who touch these themes are far inferior to the lowest of the angels); nor yet do we merely fall behind the teaching of the Sacred Writers thereon or of the Ascetics, their fellow-labourers, but we fall utterly and miserably behind our own compeers. And hence if our words are true and we have really, so far as in us lies, attained some intellectual grasp of the right way to explain the Names of God, the thanks are due to Him Who is the Creator of all things; granting first the faculty of speech and then the power to use it well. And if any Synonym hath been passed over we must supply and interpret that also by the same methods. And if this treatment is wrong or imperfect, and we have erred from the Truth either wholly or in part, I beg thy loving-kindness to correct my unwilling ignorance, to satisfy with argument my desire for knowledge, to help my insufficient strength and heal my involuntary feebleness; and that, obtaining thy stores partly from thyself and partly from others and wholly from the Good, thou wilt also pass them on to us. And I pray thee be not weary

in this kindness to a friend, for thou seest that we have not kept to ourselves any of the Hierarchic Utterances which have been handed down to us but have imparted them without adulteration both to yourselves and to other holy men, and will continue so to do as long as we have the power to speak and you to hear. So will we do no despite unto the tradition, unless strength fail us for the perception or the utterance of these Truths. But be these matters as God wills[1] that we should do or speak.

And be this now the end of our treatise concerning the Intelligible Names of God. Now will I proceed, God helping me, to the Symbolical Divinity.

---

[1] This anthropomorphic phrase is not inconsistent with the conceptions D. has been expounding; because he regards the limits of individual human capacities, etc., as timelessly existent in the Super-Essence. By a natural, though inadequate, metaphor, the limits of the resulting activities are spoken of as due to God's Will.

THE MYSTICAL THEOLOGY

CHAPTER I

What is the Divine Gloom.

TRINITY, which exceedeth all Being, Deity, and Goodness![1] Thou that instructeth Christians in Thy heavenly wisdom! Guide us to that topmost height of mystic lore [2] which exceedeth light and more than exceedeth knowledge, where the simple, absolute, and unchangeable mysteries of heavenly Truth lie hidden in the dazzling obscurity of the secret Silence, outshining all brilliance with the intensity of their darkness, and surcharging our blinded intellects with the utterly impalpable and invisible fairness of glories which exceed all beauty! Such be my prayer; and thee, dear Timothy, I counsel that, in the earnest exercise of mystic contemplation, thou leave the senses and the activities of the intellect and all things that the senses or the intellect can perceive, and all things in this world of nothingness, or in that world of being, and that, thine understanding being laid to rest,[3] thou strain (so far as thou mayest) towards an union with Him whom neither being nor understanding can contain. For, by the unceasing and absolute renunciation

[1] Lit. "Super-Essential, Supra-Divine, Super-Excellent."
[2] Lit. "Oracles"; *i. e.* to the most exalted and mystical teaching of Holy Scripture.
[3] Gk. ἀγνώστως here refers to a transcendent or spiritual Unknowing (as distinguished from mere ignorance).

of thyself and all things, thou shalt in pureness cast
all things aside, and be released from all, and so shalt
be led upwards to the Ray of that divine Darkness
which exceedeth all existence.[1]

These things thou must not disclose to any of the
uninitiated, by whom I mean those who cling to the
objects of human thought, and imagine there is no
super-essential reality beyond, and fancy that they
know by human understanding Him that has made
Darkness His secret place.[2]   And, if the Divine
Initiation is beyond such men as these, what can be
said of others yet more incapable thereof, who describe
the Transcendent Cause of all things by qualities
drawn from the lowest order of being, while they deny
that it is in any way superior to the various ungodly
delusions which they fondly invent in ignorance of
this truth?[3]   That while it possesses all the positive
attributes of the universe (being the universal Cause),
yet in a stricter sense It does not possess them, since

---

[1] "The Super-Essential Ray of Divine Darkness."
[2] *i. e.* Philosophers and unmystical theologians.
[3] *i. e.* Those who accept "popular theology."   The first stage of
theistic Religion is anthropomorphic, and God is thought of (like
Jehovah) as a magnified man of changing moods.   Popular religion
seldom rises above this level, and even gifted theologians often sink
to it.   But it is, D. tells us, the lowest stage.   Then comes a metaphysical stage.   God is now thought of as a timeless Being and therefore
changeless, but the conception of a magnified man has been refined
rather than abolished.   The ultimate truth about God and our relation
to Him is held to be that He is a "Person" and that He has "made"
the world.   (This attitude is seen at its worst in Unitarian theology.
Bradley's criticisms on Lotze show how this fails on the intellectual
side.   The Doctrine of the Trinity, by insisting on an unsolved Mystery
in God, prevents Orthodox theology from resting permanently in this
morass, though it often has one foot there.)   And non-Christian
thinkers, in opposition to this conception, regard the ultimate Reality
as impersonal, which is a worse error still.   We must get beyond our
partial conceptions of "personality," "impersonality," etc.   They are
useful and necessary up to a point, but the Truth lies beyond them and
is to be apprehended in a supernatural manner by what later writers
call "infused" contemplation.   The sum of the whole matter is that
God is *incomprehensible.*

It transcends them all, wherefore there is no contradiction between affirming and denying that It has them inasmuch as It precedes and surpasses all deprivation, being beyond all positive and negative distinctions?[1]

Such at least is the teaching of the blessed Bartholomew.[2] For he says that the subject-matter of the Divine Science is vast and yet minute, and that the Gospel combines in itself both width and straitness. Methinks he has shown by these his words how marvellously he has understood that the Good Cause of all things is eloquent yet speaks few words, or rather none; possessing neither speech nor understanding because it exceedeth all things in a super-essential manner, and is revealed in Its naked truth to those alone who pass right through the opposition of fair and foul,[3] and pass beyond the topmost altitudes of the holy ascent and leave behind them all divine enlightenment and voices and heavenly utterances and plunge into the Darkness where truly dwells, as saith the Scripture, that One Which is beyond all things. For not without reason[4] is the blessed Moses bidden first to undergo purification himself and then to separate himself from those who have not undergone it; and after all purification hears the many-voiced trumpets and sees many lights flash forth with pure and diverse-streaming rays, and then stands separate from the multitudes and with the chosen priests presses forward to the topmost pinnacle of the Divine Ascent. Nevertheless he meets not with God Himself,

[1] On *Via Affirmativa* and *Via Negativa*, *vide* Intr., p. 26 f.

[2] No writings of St. Bartholomew are extant. Possibly D. is inventing, though not necessarily.

[3] *Vide* Intr., p. 21. "Beyond Good and Evil" (though not in Nietzsche's sense). When evil disappears Good ceases to be an opposition to it, and so Good attains a new condition.

[4] In the following passage we get the three stages tabulated by later Mystical Theology: (1) Purgation, (2) Illumination, (3) Union.

yet he beholds—not Him indeed (for He is invisible)
—but the place wherein He dwells.   And this I take
to signify that the divinest and the highest of the
things perceived by the eyes of the body or the mind
are but the symbolic language of things subordinate
to Him who Himself transcendeth them all.   Through
these things His incomprehensible presence is shown
walking upon those heights of His holy places which
are perceived by the mind ; and then It breaks forth,
even from the things that are beheld and from those
that behold them, and plunges the true initiate unto
the Darkness of Unknowing wherein he renounces
all the apprehensions of his understanding and is
enwrapped in that which is wholly intangible and invisible, belonging wholly to Him that is beyond all
things and to none else (whether himself or another),
and being through the passive stillness of all his
reasoning powers united by his highest faculty to Him
that is wholly Unknowable, of whom thus by a rejection of all knowledge he possesses a knowledge that
exceeds his understanding.

CHAPTER II

How it is necessary to be united with and render praise to Him
Who is the cause of all and above all.

Unto this Darkness which is beyond Light we pray
that we may come, and may attain unto vision
through the loss of sight and knowledge, and that in
ceasing thus to see or to know we may learn to know
that which is beyond all perception and understanding
(for this emptying of our faculties is true sight and
knowledge),[1] and that we may offer Him that tran-

[1] See Intr., p. 27, on the ecstasy.   D.'s terminology is always exact
though exuberant—or rather exuberant *because* exact.   And, since if
the mind, in thinking of any particular thing, gives itself to that thing

scends all things the praises of a transcendent hymnody, which we shall do by denying or removing all things that are—like as men who, carving a statue out of marble, remove all the impediments that hinder the clear perceptive of the latent image and by this mere removal display the hidden statue itself in its hidden beauty.[1] Now we must wholly distinguish this negative method from that of positive statements. For when we were making positive statements[2] we began with the most universal statements, and then through intermediate terms we came at last to particular titles,[3] but now ascending upwards from

---

and so belongs to it, in utterly ceasing to belong to itself it ceases to have any self-consciousness and possesses a God-consciousness instead. This would be a mere merging of the personality, but that the Godhead, according to D., is of such a paradoxical nature as to contain all the creatures fused and yet distinct (Intr., p. 28) so the self is merged on one side of its being and distinct on the other. If I lose myself in God, still it will always be " I " that shall lose myself There.

[1] This simile shows that the *Via Negativa* is, in the truest sense, positive. Our "matter-moulded forms" of thought are the really negative things. (Cf. Bergson.) A sculptor would not accept a block of ice in place of a block of marble (for ice will not carve into a statue) ; and yet the block of marble is not, as such, a statue. So, too, the Christian will not accept an impersonal God instead of a personal God (for an impersonal Being cannot be loved), and yet a "personal" God is not, as such, the Object of the Mystical quest. The conception of Personality enshrines, but is not, the Ultimate Reality. If D. were open to the charge of pure negativity so often brought against him, he would have wanted to destroy his block of marble instead of carving it.

[2] Namely, in the *Divine Names* and in the *Outlines ;* see Chap. III.

[3] In the *Divine Names* D. begins with the notion of Goodness (which he holds to be possessed by all things) and proceeds thence to Existence (which is not possessed by things that are either destroyed or yet unmade), and thence to Wisdom (which is not possessed either by unconscious or irrational forms of Life), and thence to qualities (such as Righteousness, Salvation, Omnipotence) or combinations of opposite qualities (such as Greatness and Smallness) which are not, in the full sense, applicable to any creature as such. Thus by adding quality to quality ("Existence" to "Goodness," "Life" to "Existence," "Wisdom" to "Life," "Salvation," etc., to "Wisdom") he reaches the conception of God. But he constantly reminds us in the *Divine Names* that these qualities apply adequately only to the manifested Godhead which, in Its ultimate Nature, transcends them.

particular to universal conceptions we strip off all qualities [1] in order that we may attain a naked knowledge of that Unknowing which in all existent things is enwrapped by all objects of knowledge, [2] and that we may begin to see that super-essential Darkness which is hidden by all the light that is in existent things.

CHAPTER III

What are the affirmative expressions respecting God, and what are the negative.

Now I have in my *Outlines of Divinity* set forth those conceptions which are most proper to the affirmative method, and have shown in what sense God's holy nature is called single and in what sense trinal, what is the nature of the Fatherhood and Sonship which we attribute unto It; what is meant by the articles of faith concerning the Spirit; how from the immaterial and indivisible Good the interior rays of Its goodness have their being and remain immovably in that state of rest which both within their Origin and within themselves is co-eternal with the act by which they spring from It; [3] in what manner

---

[1] The process from the universal to the particular is the process of actual development (existence before life, and life before rationality, etc.); the converse is the natural process of thought, which seeks to refer things to their universal laws of species, etc. (*Divine Names*, V. 3). But this latter process is not in itself the *Via Negativa*, but only the ground plan of it, differing from it as a ground plan of a mountain path differs from a journey up the actual path itself. The process of developing life complicates, but enriches, the world; that of thought simplifies, but eviscerates it. Contemplation, being an act of the human spirit, is a process of developing life, and yet follows the direction of thought. Hence it enriches and simplifies at the same time.

[2] Cf. p. 194, n. 1.

[3] The Good = (1) the Undifferentiated Godhead, and hence, in Manifestion, (2) God the Father as the Fount of Godhead to the other

Jesus being above all essence[1] has stooped to an essential state in which all the truths of human nature meet ; and all the other revelations of Scripture whereof my *Outlines of Divinity* treat. And in the book of the *Divine Names* I have considered the meaning as concerning God of the titles Good, Existent, Life, Wisdom, Power and of the other titles which the understanding frames, and in my Symbolic Divinity I have considered what are the metaphorical titles drawn from the world of sense and applied to the nature of God ; what are the mental or material images we form of God or the functions and instruments of activity we attribute to Him ; what are the places where He dwells and the robes He is adorned with ; what is meant by God's anger, grief, and indignation, or the divine inebriation and wrath ; what is meant by God's oath and His malediction, by His slumber and awaking, and all the other inspired imagery of allegoric symbolism. And I doubt not that you have also observed how far more copious are the last terms than the first for the doctrines of God's Nature and the exposition of His Names could not but be briefer than the Symbolic Divinity.[2] For

Persons. The Rays = God the Son and God the Holy Ghost, Who, as manifested Differentiations, eternally proceed from the Father.

The separate being of the Three Persons exists on the plane of Manifestation (cf. St. Augustine, who says : "They exist *secundum relativum* and not *secundum essentiam*"). [Augustine says *non secundum substantiam*. The translator quotes it correctly in his introduction, p. 10.—ED.] But this plane is eternal. They wholly interpenetrate, and the state of rest is co-eternal with the Act of Their Procession, because They possess eternal repose and eternal motion.

[1] This is a case of *communicatio idiomatum* (cf. the title "Mother of God" applied to the Blessed Virgin Mary). The Godhead of our Lord is Super-Essential, not His Manhood.

[2] The *Symbolical Divinity* was an attempt to spiritualize "popular" theology, the *Divine Names* sought to spiritualize philosophical theology, the present treatise is a direct essay in Spiritual Theology.

the more that we soar upwards the more our language becomes restricted to the compass of purely intellectual conceptions, even as in the present instance plunging into the Darkness which is above the intellect we shall find ourselves reduced not merely to brevity of speech but even to absolute dumbness both of speech and thought. Now in the former treatises the course of the argument, as it came down from the highest to the lowest categories, embraced an ever-widening number of conceptions which increased at each stage of the descent, but in the present treatise it mounts upwards from below towards the category of transcendence, and in proportion to its ascent it contracts its terminology, and when the whole ascent is passed it will be totally dumb, being at last wholly united with Him Whom words cannot describe.[1]   But why is it, you will ask, that after beginning from the highest category when one method was affirmative we begin from the lowest category where it is negative?[2]   Because, when affirming the existence of that which transcends all affirmation, we were obliged to start from that which is most akin to It, and then to make the affirmation on which the rest depended ; but when pursuing the negative method, to reach that which is beyond all negation, we must start by applying our negations to those qualities which differ most from the ultimate goal. Surely it is truer to affirm that God is life and goodness than that He is air or stone, and truer to deny that drunkenness or fury can be attributed to Him

---

[1]   At the last stage but one the mind beholds an Object to Which all terms of thought are inadequate.   Then, at the last stage, even the distinction between Subject and Object disappears, and the mind itself *is* That Which it contemplates.   Thought itself is transcended, and the whole Object-realm vanishes.   One Subject now knows itself as the part and knows itself as the Whole.

[2]   In the *Divine Names* the order of procedure was : Goodness, Existence, Life, etc.   Now it passes from sense-perception to thought.

than to deny that we may apply to Him the categories of human thought.[1]

CHAPTER IV

That He Who is the Pre-eminent Cause of everything sensibly perceived is not Himself any one of the things sensibly perceived.

WE therefore maintain [2] that the universal Cause transcending all things is neither impersonal nor lifeless, nor irrational nor without understanding : in short, that It is not a material body, and therefore does not possess outward shape or intelligible form, or quality, or quantity, or solid weight ; nor has It any local existence which can be perceived by sight or touch ; nor has It the power of perceiving or being perceived ; nor does It suffer any vexation or disorder through the disturbance of earthly passions, or any feebleness through the tyranny of material chances, or any want of light ; nor any change, or decay, or division, or deprivation, or ebb and flow, or anything else which the senses can perceive.   None of these things can be either identified with it or attributed unto It.

[1] This shows that the *Via Negativa* is not purely negative.

[2] Being about to explain, in these two last chapters, that no material or mental qualities are *present* in the Godhead, D. safeguards the position against pure negativity by explaining that they are not *absent* either. The rest of this chapter deals with the qualities (1) of inanimate matter ; (2) of material life.

CHAPTER V

That He Who is the Pre-eminent Cause of everything intelligibly perceived is not Himself any one of the things intelligibly perceived.

ONCE more, ascending yet higher we maintain[1] that It is not soul, or mind, or endowed with the faculty of imagination, conjecture, reason, or understanding; nor is It any act of reason or understanding; nor can It be described by the reason or perceived by the understanding, since It is not number, or order, or greatness, or littleness, or equality, or inequality, and since It is not immovable nor in motion, or at rest, and has no power, and is not power or light, and does not live, and is not life; nor is It personal essence, or eternity, or time; nor can It be grasped by the understanding, since It is not knowledge or truth; nor is It kingship or wisdom; nor is It one, nor is It unity, nor is It Godhead[2] or Goodness; nor is It a Spirit, as we understand the term, since It is not Sonship or Fatherhood; nor is It any other thing such as we or any other being can have knowledge of; nor does It belong to the category of non-existence or to that of existence; nor do existent beings know It as it actually is, nor does It know them as they actually are;[3] nor can the reason attain to It to name It or to know It; nor is it darkness, nor is It light, or error, or truth;[4]

It is not (1) a Thinking Subject; nor (2) an Act or Faculty of Thought; nor (3) an Object of Thought.

[2] *Divine Names*, II. 7. Godhead is regarded as the property of Deified men, and so belongs to relativity.

[3] It knows only Itself, and there knows all things in their Super-Essence—*sub specie aeternitatis.*

[4] Truth is an Object of Thought. Therefore, being beyond objectivity, the ultimate Reality is not Truth. But still less is It Error.

nor can any affirmation or negation[1] apply to it; for while applying affirmations or negations to those orders of being that come next to It, we apply not unto It either affirmation or negation, inasmuch as It transcends all affirmation by being the perfect and unique Cause of all things, and transcends all negation by the pre-eminence of Its simple and absolute nature—free from every limitation and beyond them all.[2]

[1] Cf. p. 199, n. 2.
[2] It is (1) *richer* than all concrete forms of positive existence; (2) more *simple* than the barest abstraction. (Cf. p. 196, n. 1.)

THE INFLUENCE OF DIONYSIUS
IN RELIGIOUS HISTORY

By W. J. Sparrow-Simpson

THE significance of the teaching of Dionysius cannot be appreciated aright without tracing to some extent his influence on subsequent religious thought.

Four works of the Areopagite survive. They are: Concerning the Heavenly Hierarchy; Concerning the Ecclesiastical Hierarchy; Concerning the Divine Names; and, Concerning Mystical Theology.

Commentaries upon them began to be written at an early date. The first great propagator of Dionysian theories was the very able monk and confessor Maximus. Maximus, who died in the year 662, wrote notes on all four treatises. These still survive, and may be found in the collected edition of the works of the Areopagite. Maximus is remarkably clear and acute, and contributed not a little to extend his Master's reputation. He was gifted with a simplicity of style which the Areopagite by no means shared, and expounded with great clearness the difficult passages of Dionysius. And certainly the reader will not deny that those passages are by no means few.

Already, before Maximus's labours, the teaching of the Areopagite was known in the West, and was appealed to by Pope Martin the First in the Lateran

Council of 649. Martin complained that the doctrine of the Areopagite was being misrepresented. Dionysius was being credited with ascribing to Christ one divino-human activity (*una operatio deivirilis*), whereas what Dionysius had written was a new divino-human activity (καινὴ θεανδρικὴ ἐνέργεια, *nova operatio deivirilis*).[1] Apart from the theological controversy implied in the respective phrases, it is remarkable to find what authority is already ascribed to its teaching.

But it is really quite impossible to appreciate the historic place of Dionysius without a study of John Scotus Erigena. It was Erigena who in reality popularized Dionysius for Latin Christendom. The Greek writings of the Areopagite had been sent to the Gallican Church by Pope Paul in 757, and remained for nearly a century unread in the Abbey of St. Denis. Then Erigena, at the request of Charles the Bald, undertook to translate them into Latin. This he accomplished for all the four principal works.

But Erigena did vastly more than merely act as translator. He incorporated the principles of the Areopagité in his celebrated treatise *De Divisione Naturæ*, in which his own speculative system is contained, and which may be said to be as representative of his mind as the *De Principiis* is for Origen or the *Summa* for St. Thomas.

Erigena bases his whole conception of Deity on the teaching of Dionysius. The treatise is thrown into the form of a discussion between the Master and a Disciple. It is an attempt to reconcile Theology with Philosophy. After the Master has insisted on the ineffable and incomprehensible nature of the Divine essence, the Disciple inquires how this proposition is to be reconciled with the teaching of the

---

[1] See Hefele, *Conciliengeschichte*, Bd. III. 196.

Theologians on the Unity and Trinity of God. The incomprehensibility of the First Cause appears self-evident. And if Deity is incomprehensible, definition is impossible. For that which cannot be understood certainly cannot be defined. We can only say that God *is;* but *what* He is we are unable to affirm. But if this is so, why have the Theologians ventured to predicate Unity and Trinity as characteristics of the ultimate reality?

To the Disciple's criticism the Master replies by appealing to the teaching of the Areopagite. Did not the Areopagite affirm that no words, no names, no expression whatever, can express the supreme and causal essence of all things? That authority is quoted as decisive.

Neither the Unity nor the Trinity in God is such that the clearest human intellect is able to conceive it. Why, then, have the Theologians taught these doctrines?

Erigena's answer is : In order to provide religious people with some definite object for contemplation and instruction.

For this purpose the faithful are bidden to believe in their heart and confess with their lips that God is good, and that He exists in one Divine essence and three persons.

And this teaching of the Theologians is, in the Master's opinion, not without philosophical justification.

For contemplating the ineffable cause of all things, the Theologians speak of the Unity.

Then again, contemplating this Divine Unity as extended into multiplicity, they affirm the Trinity. And the Trinity is the unbegotten, the begotten, and the proceeding.

The Master goes on to explain the distinction between affirmative and negative theology. Negative theology denies that certain things can be predicated of Deity. Affirmative theology asserts propositions which can be predicated. This again is altogether based on the teaching of Dionysius.

Here the Disciple desires to be informed why it is that the Areopagite considers such predicates as goodness, truth, justice, wisdom, which appear to be not only Divine but the divinest of attributes, as merely figuratively transferred from man to Deity.

The Master replies that no characteristics applicable to the finite and limited can be strictly applicable to the infinite and eternal.

Thus, according to Erigena, following closely on the principles of the Areopagite, although goodness is predicated of Deity, yet strictly speaking He is not goodness, but *plus quam bonitas* or *super bonus*. Similarly, Deity is not Truth, but *plus quam Veritas*, and *super eternitas*, and *plus quam Sapiens*.

Hence affirmation and negation are alike permissible in reference to Deity.

If you affirm that Deity is super-essential, what is it precisely that is meant by the use of "super"? You do not in reality affirm what God is, but simply that He is more than those things which exist. But where the difference consists you do not define.

But the reason why Erigena asserts the strict inapplicability of the term essential to Deity is, that he interprets the term in a way which involves spacial relations. Essence in all things that exist is local and temporal. But Deity is neither.

Deity as Erigena contemplates it is simply the Infinite and the Absolute; and of that, nothing whatever can be strictly predicated beyond the fact that it is. The Cause of all things can only be known to exist, but by no inference from the creature can we understand what it is.

Since, then, Erigena has postulated the philosophic

Absolute, the immutable, impassible First Cause, as
the Deity, he is compelled to go on to deny that
Deity can be subject to affection or capable of
love.

This conclusion the Disciple confesses to be profoundly startling. It appears to contradict the whole
authority both of the Scriptures and of the Fathers.
At the same time it is all logical enough, granting
the First Cause to be incapable of action or passion,
which seems to involve the Immutable in change: a
contradiction of the very idea of Deity. It is all
logical enough. But what about the Scriptures,
which teach the contrary? And what of the simple
believers, who will be horrified if they hear such
propositions?

The Master assures the Disciple that there is no
need to be alarmed. For he is now employing the
method of speculative reason, not the method of
authority. He agrees with Dionysius, for Dionysius
had said as much, that the authority of the Scripture
is in all things to be submitted to. But Scripture
does not give us terms adequate to the representation
of Deity. It furnishes us with certain symbols and
signs, by condescension to our infirmities. Dionysius
is again appealed to in confirmation of this.

It is curious to notice how, while professedly en-
gaged in the method of speculative inquiry, Erigena
falls back on the authority of Dionysius: a very
significant proof of the value which he ascribed to
the Areopagite.

So, then, at last the conclusion is reached that,
strictly speaking, nothing whatever can be predicated
concerning Deity, seeing that He surpasses all understanding, and is more truly known by our nescience,
ignorance concerning Him being the truest wisdom,
and our negations more correct than our affirmations.
For whatever you deny concerning Him you deny

correctly, whereas the same cannot be said of what you may affirm.

Nevertheless, subject to this premise of acknowledged inadequacy, qualities may be rightly ascribed to Deity by way of symbolical representation.

Hence, it is correct to maintain that true authority does not contradict right reason, nor right reason true authority. Both spring from one source, and that one source is Divine.

Thus by a metaphor God may be described as Love, although, as a matter of fact, He transcends it.

It has been a matter of frequent dispute whether the system of Erigena is fundamentally Christian or Pantheistic. In the careful study of Erigena by Theodor Christlieb it is maintained that, while sentences may be quoted on either side, and the author vacillates, now towards Theism, now in a Pantheistic direction, his attempted reconciliation of Theology with Philosophy ends in the supremacy of the latter, and in the abolition of the essential characteristics of the Christian Revelation.

That the Deity cannot be comprehended by human intelligence is a commonplace of all the great early theologians of the Church. It can be richly illustrated from the theological orations of St. Gregory Nazianzen, or the writings of St. Augustine and St. Hilary upon the Holy Trinity. But then these theologians also maintained with equal conviction that God could be apprehended by man. For this balancing consideration Erigena finds no place. God is for Erigena that of which no distinctive quality can be predicated. God is in effect the Absolute.

But then what becomes of God's self-consciousness? In Christlieb's opinion Erigena's conception of the Deity precludes any firm hold on the Divine self-consciousness. Self-consciousness involves a whole content of ideas, a world of thought, which contradicts the absolute self-identity ascribed by Erigena to the Deity.

In his anxiety to explain the transcendent excellence of Deity, the superlative exaltation above the contingent and the mutable, Erigena seems in the opinion of his critics to have over-reached the truth and reduced the Deity to an abstraction in which perfection and nothingness are identified.

Erigena's conclusion raises in reality the all important problem so constantly debated in modern thought, whether the Absolute is the proper conception of Deity, and whether the God of religion and of fact is not rather spirit, self-consciousness, and perfect personality.   The teaching of Dionysius in the exposition of Erigena became scarcely distinguishable from Pantheism.

Christlieb finds a similar unsatisfactoriness in Erigena's theory of the Trinity.

It will be remembered that, after maintaining as his fundamental position that Deity cannot be defined because it cannot be comprehended, and that nothing whatever can be affirmed concerning it beyond the fact of its being, Erigena went on to justify the theologians of the Church in affirming the Unity and the Trinity.   But the grounds on which Erigena justified the authorities of the Church are significant. He did not justify the doctrine on the ground that it was a truth revealed, or because it was an inference demanded of the fact and claim of Christ.   It is remarkable how obscure a place Christ occupies in Erigena's conception of Deity.   The ground on which Erigena would justify the doctrine is that Unity and Multiplicity may fairly be ascribed to the First Cause of all things, because Deity can be regarded in its simplicity as one and then regarded as extended into multiplicity.

But it is impossible to avoid the criticism that this

ascription of Unity and Multiplicity to Deity is not
the same thing as the doctrine of the Trinity. Nor
is it obvious why Trinity should be substituted for
Multiplicity. Moreover, this Multiplicity exists sub-
jectively in the human mind rather than in the being
of Deity: since it is expressly forbidden by the
author's fundamental principle to say anything whatever concerning Deity beyond the fact that it exists.
And further still, on the author's principles neither
Unity nor Multiplicity can be strictly ascribed to
Deity. Both must be merged in something else
which is neither the one nor yet the other, and which
escapes all possible definition.

It is scarcely wonderful, therefore, that Christlieb
should conclude that on Erigena's principles the
doctrine of the Trinity is not really tenable. Erigena
certainly endeavours to approximate to the Church's
Tradition, and to give it an intellectual justification.
But in spite of these endeavours he is unable to
maintain any real distinctions in his Trinity. They
have no actual substantial existence whatever. They
are mere names and not realities. There may be
appearances. But in its essential being, according to
Erigena, Deity is neither unity nor trinity, but an
incomprehensible somewhat which transcends them
both. For Erigena both the Unitarian and the
Trinitarian representations of God are alike products
of subjective human reflection. They are neither of
them objective realities. If you rest on either of them
you are according, to Erigena, mistaken. For God is
more than Unity and more than Trinity.

Looking back on the whole course of Erigena's
exposition of Dionysian principles, we see that the
Areopagite had identified God with the Absolute.
Dean Inge says that "Dionysius the Areopagite
describes God the Father as 'superessential indeter-
mination,' 'the unity which unifies every unity,' 'the

absolute no-thing which is above all reality.' 'No moral or trial,' he exclaims in a queer ebullition of jargon, 'can express the all-transcending hiddenness of the all-transcending superessentially superexisting super-Deity.'"[1] And Erigena did not hesitate to deny Being to Deity. Being, in his opinion, is a defect. The things that are not, are far better than the things that are. God, therefore, in virtue of His excellence, is not undeservedly described as Nihil—nothingness.

Two conceptions of Deity emerge in this exposition. One is, that the Deity is identical with the Absolute. It is beyond personality, beyond goodness, beyond consciousness, beyond existence itself. Nothing whatever can be predicated concerning it. Being is identical with nothingness. It is above the category of relation. This is the philosophic conception.

The other conception is that Deity possesses the attributes of self-conscious personality. This is the religious conception.

In the exposition of Erigena the philosophic conception is affirmed to be the true, while the religious conception is regarded as the creation of the theologians for the purpose of explanation and of faith.

From this distinction certain things seem clear. It seems clear that the philosophic conception of Deity as identical with the Absolute, cannot satisfy the requirements of religion, and that Deity cannot become an object of adoration unless it is invested with the attributes of personality. That of which nothing can be predicated cannot become the object of our worship.

But at the same time if the religious conception of Deity as self-conscious and personal is offered to our contemplation with the express proviso that it does not represent what God really is, the proviso paralyses

[1] Cf. Inge, *The Philosophy of Plotinus*, II. 112.

the wings of our aspiration and renders Deity impossible as an object of prayer.[1]

Erigena was by no means a *persona grata* to the Church of his age. He was a metaphysician, without the mystical tendencies of Dionysius, and while he expounded the Areopagite's ideas roused suspicion and resentment by the boldness of his conclusions. At the same time his translations of Dionysius made the Greek Master's principles familiar to the Latin world.

In the Eastern Church the Areopagite's influence is clearly present in the great Greek Theologian, St. John of Damascus. When speaking of the inadequacy of human expressions to represent the reality of God John Damascene appeals to Dionysius.[2] And the whole of his teaching on the Divine incomprehensibility is clearly due to the influence of the Areopagite. When we read that an inferior nature cannot comprehend its superior, or when we find the distinction drawn between negative theology and affirmative, between that which declares what God is not and that which declares what He is ; and that the former presents the Divine superiority to all created things ; when further still we read of the super-essential essence, and the super-divine Deity: we see in a moment the influence of Dionysian conceptions. Nevertheless St. John Damascene is anything rather than a blind adherent of Areopagite teaching. On the contrary it is profoundly true, as Vacherot[3] has said, that he follows Dionysius with discrimination : or rather, perhaps, that he supplements the Doctrine of the Divine incomprehensibility by very definite teaching on the reality of the distinctions within the

---

[1] Cf. Inge, *The Philosophy of Plotinus*, II. 115.
[2] *De Fide Orthodoxa*, Bk. I. ch. xii.
[3] Vacherot's *Histoire Critique de l'École d'Alexandrie*, III. 40, 1851.

Deity and on the reality of the personal Incarnation of the eternal Son of God in Mary's Son. That is to say, that while the Philosopher appears in the Areopagite to eclipse the Theologian, the Theologian in St. John Damascene controls the Philosopher. The careful, discriminate use of Dionysius by the great Greek Schoolman is most remarkable. He assimilated the true elements while rejecting the questionable or exaggerated.

Returning once more to the Church of the West, the influence of Dionysius is seen extending, through Erigena's translations, into the Monastic studies. The theologian Hugh, of the Abbey of St. Victor at Paris, wrote in ten books a Commentary on the Heavenly Hierarchy of the Areopagite, full of enthusiastic appreciation of the great mystic's teaching.

Far more important than this is the influence exerted by Dionysius over the mind of St. Thomas. It is not only that St. Thomas wrote a *Commentary on the Divine Names*,[1] but in the works of Aquinas his ideas are constantly reappearing. He is one of St. Thomas's favourite authorities. As one becomes increasingly more familiar with the greatest of all the scholastic theologians this ascendancy of the Greek mystic becomes more and more impressive. But it is almost needless to say that Aquinas treats the Areopagite critically. St. Thomas is profoundly averse from everything which resembles a Pantheistic tendency. His teaching alike on the Trinity and on the Incarnation belongs to another realm of thought from that of the neo-Platonist.

At a later period misgivings arose in the Church whether the theology of the Areopagite was, in fact, altogether above suspicion. So long as his traditional identification with the disciple of St. Paul was main-

[1] See Parma edition of *St. Thomas*, Tom. XV. Opusculum vii. pp. 259-405.

tained, and he was credited with being, by apostolic appointment, first Bishop of Athens, these distinctions made suspicion of his orthodoxy seem irreverent and incredible. But when the identification was questioned by the historical critics of the seventeenth century, and the tradition completely dispelled, then the term Pseudo-Dionysius began to be heard and to prevail, and criticism upon its orthodoxy arose in the learned schools in France.

Le Quien, in a dissertation prefixed to the works of St. John Damascene, propounds the formidable inquiry : Num Pseudo-Dionysius hæreticus fuerit.[1] Le Quien is convinced that Dionysius employs language which confuses the Divine and the Human in our Lord; fails to distinguish accurately between person and nature ; and betrays unquestionable monophysite tendencies.

On the other hand, Bernard de Rubeis, in his *Dissertation*,[2] says that Le Quien fails to do justice to the author's meaning ; and that Aquinas understood the author better, and thought him orthodox.

The University of Paris defended the Areopagite. The University of Louvain agreed. The Jesuits eagerly advocated his orthodoxy. Lessius, the celebrated author of the *Treatise on the Divine Perfections*, corresponding with another Jesuit, Father Lanssel, declared that he had read the Areopagite frequently, and had carefully studied all his writings. For thirty-six years Dionysius had been his chosen patron, always remembered by him in the Sacrifice of the Mass, with a prayer to be permitted to share the Areopagite's wisdom and spirit.[3] What disturbed Lessius was that the Areopagite had not been better

---

[1] Migne, *Patrol. Græc.*, Tom. XCIV. i. 281.
[2] See also the Parma edition of *St. Thomas*, Tom. XV. 430 ff., where this Dissertation is printed.
[3] Migne, *Patrol. Græq.*, Tom. IV. 1002.

translated. Inadequate terms had been put in the Latin rendering which might easily lead the reader into error. For many instances of this might be produced. Father Lanssel, however, is compelled to admit quite frankly that the Areopagite's writings contain difficulties which cannot be laid to the charge of his translators. St. Thomas himself had said as much.

That Master of the Schoolmen, that *theologiæ apex*, who solved the hardest problems in theology more easily than Alexander cut the Gordian knot, did not hesitate to say that Dionysius habitually suffered from obscurity of style. This obscurity was not due to lack of skill, but to the deliberate design of concealing truth from the ridicule of the profane. It was also due to his use of platonic expressions which are unfamiliar to the modern mind. Sometimes the Areopagite is, in the opinion of St. Thomas, too concise, wrapping too much meaning into a solitary word. Sometimes, again, he errs the opposite way, by the over-profuseness of his utterances. Nevertheless, this profuseness is not really superfluous, for those who completely scrutinize it become aware of its solidity and its depth. The fact is, adds Father Lanssel, as Isaac Casaubon asserted, the Areopagite invents new words, and unusual unheard-of and startling expressions. The Confessor Maximus admitted that his Master obscures the meaning of the superabundance of his phraseology.

When we come to the nineteenth century we find the Treatises of the Areopagite criticized, not only, or chiefly, for their form and style, but also for their fundamental principles.

The System of the Areopagite was subjected to a very searching critical analysis by Ferdinand Christian Baur. (*Christliche Lehre von der Dreieinigkeit und Menschwerdung Gottes*, 1842; Bd. II. 207–251.)

According to Dionysius, as understood by Baur, God is the absolute Unity which stands contrasted with the Many. The Many denotes the world of concrete reality. Doubtless there is a process from Unity to Multiplicity, affirmation and negation, but this process takes place solely in the subjective consciousness.

How, then, asks Baur, can this Areopagite conception of Deity be reconciled with the Christian conception, with which it appears to be in obvious contradiction ?

The Areopagite speaks often of a Triad, and dwells on the Church's Doctrine of the Trinity. But the terms which in his system represent the Godhead are such as the super-good, the super-divine, the super-essential. These terms represent an abstraction. If any distinction exists, that distinction in no case exists within the Deity, but only in the activities which proceed from God as the super-essential Cause. Distinctions exist in our subjective consciousness. But they have no objective reality. If we call the Divine Mystery God, or Life, or Essence, or Light, or Word, we only mean thereby the influences which emanate from that Mystery.

In Baur's opinion, therefore, the Trinitarian conception, as held in the Tradition of the Church, is in the system of Dionysius reduced to little more than names.

Baur's criticism on the Areopagite's notion of Incarnation is not less severe.

The System of Dionysius allows no distinctive and peculiar Incarnation at all. It allows no special and new relationships, but only a continual becoming. The Incarnation is, in the Areopagite's view, nothing more than the process from Unity to Multiplicity ; which is essential to Its conception of Deity. If Dionysius speaks of the God-man as an individual, that is either a mere concession to Tradition, or a lack of clearness in its own conception. The union of God with an individual such as the Christian Tradition postulates cannot, in Baur's opinion, be reconciled with the system of the Areopagite.

A second modern opinion on the theological teaching of Dionysius is given by that singularly clear and sceptical Frenchman, Vacherot, in his *Histoire de l'École d'Alexandrie*, 1851, Tome III. pp. 23 ff.

Vacherot considers the group of treatises ascribed to Dionysius to be the most curious monument of neo-Platonist influence over Christian theology. Philosophy affirms that negations concerning Deity are true on condition that they express nothing definite. In the author's opinion Theology cannot really give any positive instruction. Dionysius is understood by Vacherot to teach that mystical theology is the suppression of definite thought. To know God we must cease to think of Him. The devout is lost in a mystical obscurity of ignorance. Nothing definite can in reality be said of Deity.

In Vacherot's opinion the orthodoxy of the Areopagite is more than doubtful.

The Christian conception presents the living personal self-conscious God, Creator and Father of the world, in eternal inseparable relation with His Son and His Spirit, a Trinity inaccessible in itself, but manifested directly in Incarnation.

But in the conception of this neo-Platonist thinker Deity is removed to an infinite distance from the human soul, and the Trinity is reduced to a mere abstraction. We are here far removed from the genuine Christian theology.

Dionysius is to Vacherot a neo-Platonist philosopher in disguise, who while going over to Christianity retained his philosophic ideas which he adroitly combined with the principles of his new belief.

A third modern critic of Dionysius is the Lutheran theologian, Dorner.   Dorner was concerned only with the bearing of the Areopagite principles on the doctrine of the Person of Christ.[1]

In Dorner's opinion the mystical Christology of the Areopagite "forms an important link of connection between Monophysitism and the doctrine of the Church."   "Not that we mean to affirm that the Areopagite was a declared Monophysite; certainly, however, that his entire mode of viewing the world and God belong to this family."

With regard to the doctrine of the Trinity, Dorner holds that on the principles of Dionysius "seeing that God is the One Who is at once in all and above all—yea, outweighs the negation of the many by the Divine Unity—all idea of distinct hypostasis in God ought consistently to be renounced; in the Super-Essential God everything sinks down into unity without distinctions.   Much is said, indeed, of the Many, along with the One; but the Trinity in God retains merely a completely precarious position."

Dorner adds: "The result as far as Christology is concerned is very plain; after laying down such premises, it was impossible for the Areopagite to justify, either anthropologically or theologically, a specific incarnation in one individual.   If he taught it at all, it was because he had adopted it from the Creeds of the Church, and he was quite unable to put himself into a sincere and true relation towards it."

To these criticisms may be added the remarks of a fourth modern writer, this time from the standpoint of the Roman Church.   Bach, in his very able *History of Dogma in the Middle Ages*, says that, in the works of the Areopagite, Christ is frequently treated in so idealistic a fashion that the concrete

---

[1] Dorner, *Doctrine of the Person of Christ*, Div. II. i. 157 ff.

P

personality of the God-man is driven into the shade. The mysticism of Dionysius is not founded on the historical person of Christ, nor on the work of Redemption as a fact once actualized in time.

Here may be added a criticism on Dionysius from a Bishop of the English Church. Bishop Westcott wrote—

"Many, perhaps, will be surprised that such a scheme of Christianity as Dionysius has sketched should even be reckoned Christian at all."[1] Dr. Westcott went on to say of the Areopagite's principles: "It must be frankly admitted that they bear the impress not only of a particular age and school, but also of a particular man, which is not wholly of a Christian type." And again elsewhere "very much of the system was faulty and defective."

In closing this short survey of the place of Dionysius in the history of religious thought it is evident enough that we are confronted with an exceptional figure of unusual ascendancy. He is not made less perplexing by the variety of estimates formed upon his theology by men of different schools and of marked ability. The student must be left to draw his own conclusions. But if those conclusions are to be correctly drawn he must have before his mind, at least in outlines, the fact of the Areopagite's historic influence.

The general impression left upon the mind by the Areopagite's critics is that the author's strength consisted in his combination of philosophy with mysticism; but that he was far more strong as a philosophic thinker than he was as a Christian theologian; and that in his efforts to reconcile Christianity with neo-Platonism it is the philosophy which prevails, not without serious results to the theology of the Church. His greatest admirers appear to have employed him with

[1] Westcott, *Religious Thought in the West*, p. 188.

discretion ; to have balanced his statements with more proportion, and to have read him in the light of strong Catholic presuppositions which to some extent neutralized his over-emphasis, and supplemented his omissions. It is an interesting speculation for the theological student what the position of these writings would have been if their author had never been identified with the disciple of St. Paul.

INDEX TO TEXT

Affirmative Theology, 196

Bartholomew, 193

Clement, 141

Differentiations in Deity, 67 ff.
Divine Names, 51–190
Elements of Divinity, 76, 83
Elymas, 157–158
Emanations, 79–80
Evil (Nature of), 86 ff., 111–130

Fatherhood, 56

GOD as Goodness, 86 ff.
,, Light, 91–94
,, Beauty, 95 ff.
,, Love, 104
,, Being, 131 ff.
,, Life, 144
,, Wisdom, 146
,, Reason, 148–153
,, Power, 154
,, Righteousness, 158, 160
,, Great and Small, 162
,, Omnipotent, 169
,, Peace, 173–178
,, Holiness, 181
,, Perfection, 184
,, Unity, 185–190

Hierotheus, 76–83, 86–107
Hymns of Yearning, 107, 108, 109

Ignatius, 104
Illumination, 55, 58
Incarnation, 76

James, St., 84

Negative Theology, 196

Outlines of Divinity, 51, 196, 197

Paul, St., 83
Peter, St., 84

Scriptures, 52, 53
Simplicity, 55
Super-essential, 52, 53, 54, 56, 59, 71, 139, 191
Super-excellent, 191
Super-intellectual, 52
Supra-Divine, 191
Symbolical Revelation, 56 ff.

Timothy, 191
Trinity, 56, 65, 66, 79, 191

Undifferenced Names of GOD, 65, 68

INDEX TO NOTES AND INTRODUCTION

Aquinas, 3, 81, 107, 143, 151, 171, 172, 212
Aristotle, 81, 92, 101, 171
Augustine, 9, 10, 41, 42–65, 77, 103, 134, 136, 141, 143, 162, 168, 181, 185, 197

Bach, 217
Baur, 214–216
Bergson, 143, 152, 195
Bernard de Rubeis, 213
Bernard, St., 165
Blake, 140
Bradley, 114, 192
Brontë, E., 186

Contemplation, 25, 30, 33

Damascenus, 211
Dante, 88, 107, 140, 173, 177, 178
Dionysius, influence, 202–219; writings, 47
Dorner, 217

Eckhart, 122, 181
Erigena, 3, 203–211
Evil, problem of, 20–25

Fox, George, 87

GOD as Unity, 65–80
  ,,   Goodness, 86–130
  ,,   Being, 131–143
  ,,   Life, 144–146
  ,,   Wisdom, 146–154
      Power, 154–161

GOD as Great, 162–169
  ,,   Almighty, 169–173
  ,,   Peace, 173–180
  ,,   Holy, 181–183
  ,,   Perfection, 184, 190
Godhead, 4–6, 6–19

Hierotheus, 107
Hugh of St. Victor, 212

Ignatius, St., 104
Inge, 29, 210, 211

John of the Cross, 103
Julian of Norwich, 102, 143

Lanssel, 213
Lateran, C. (649), 213
Le Bon, 109
Le Quien, 213
Lotze, 192

Martin (i. Pope), 202
Maximus, 3, 202

Nietzsche, 90, 193

Pachymeres, 3
Pascal, 118
Personality, 4
Philosophy (Modern), D.'s relation to, 30
Plato, 107
Plotinus, 2, 109, 138
Proclus, 1
Psychology, 33–40

Ruysbroeck, 122

Scripture, D.'s relation to, 40
Severus, 3
Shelley, 182
Spencer, 107
Super-essential, 15, 16, 17, 45, 51, 52, 53, 191
Super-excellent, 191
Supra-Divine, 191

Tauler, 122
Trinity, 9, 10, 42, 44, 45

Vacherot, 211, 216
Via Negativa, 195, 196
Victorinus, 174
Von Hügel, 172

Westcott, 218
Wordsworth, 95, 99